A SAVING REMNANT

A
SAVING
REMNANT

The Radical Lives of Barbara Deming
and David McReynolds

Martin Duberman

THE NEW PRESS

NEW YORK
LONDON

Epigraph on page vii from the poem "Natural Resources," from
The Dream of a Common Language by Adrienne Rich (courtesy of W.W. Norton, 1980)

Requests for permission to reproduce selections from this book should be mailed to:
Permissions Department, The New Press, 38 Greene Street, New York, NY 10013.

First published in the United States by The New Press, New York, 2011
This paperback edition published by The New Press, 2012
Distributed by Perseus Distribution

LIBRARY OF CONGRESS CATALOGING-IN-PUBLICATION DATA

Duberman, Martin B.
A saving remnant : the radical lives of Barbara Deming and David McReynolds /
Martin Duberman.
p. cm. Includes bibliographical references and index.
ISBN 978-1-59558-323-9 (hc.)
ISBN 978-1-59558-776-3 (pbk.)
1. Deming, Barbara, 1917–1984. 2. McReynolds, David. 3. Political activists—
United States—Biography. 4. Radicals—United States—Biography.
5. Women authors, American—Biography. 6. Feminists—United States—
Biography. 7. Lesbians—United States—Biography. 8. Gay men—
United States—Biography. 9. Social justice—United States—History—
20th century. 10. Peace movements—United States—History—20th century.
I. Title.
PS3554.E475D83 2010
322.42092'273—dc22
[B] 2010045060

The New Press was established in 1990 as a not-for-profit alternative to the large,
commercial publishing houses currently dominating the book publishing industry.
The New Press operatesin the public interest rather than for private gain, and is
committed to publishing, in innovative ways, works of educational, cultural,
and community value that are often deemed insufficiently profitable.

www.thenewpress.com

Composition by Westchester Book Composition
This book was set in Janson Text

Printed in the United States of America

2 4 6 8 10 9 7 5 3 1

For Marcia Gallo
loving friend

My heart is moved by all I cannot save:
so much has been destroyed

I have to cast my lot with those
who age after age, perversely,

with no extraordinary power,
reconstitute the world.

—ADRIENNE RICH, from "Natural Resources"

Contents

CONTENTS

Author's Note

The phrase "a saving remnant" has historically referred to that small number of people neither indoctrinated nor frightened into accepting oppressive social conditions. Unlike the general populace, they openly challenge the reigning powers-that-be and speak out early and passionately against injustice of various kinds. They attempt, with uneven degrees of success, to awaken and mobilize others to join in the struggle for a more benevolent, egalitarian society.

One of my intentions in writing this book is to demonstrate that in the mid-to-late twentieth century in the United States, the "saving remnant" included, in some cases prominently, a number of gay people. I'd initially expected to write about some half dozen of them but ultimately found myself concentrating on only two: Barbara Deming and David McReynolds. Several factors went into that decision. Both were left-wing *radicals*, not mere liberals, and on most critical issues of their day—including nuclear disarmament, the black civil rights struggle, nonviolence, and the war in Vietnam—they were ardently engaged, calling early on, for example, for the United States' *immediate* withdrawal from Vietnam.

On those issues, Deming's and McReynolds's views coincided, and they often worked together politically. But regarding several other issues—in particular feminism and the rise of a gay rights movement—they came to sharply disagree. In this they mirrored the congruence and discord that often existed side by side on the Left in general. On the two matters of feminism and gay rights, Barbara would prove more radical than David—though she never became the lesbian separatist he would accuse her of being. (I realize that referring to my two subjects on a first-name basis—as I do throughout the book—may antagonize some, and I should explain a bit further. I've known David, casually, for many years, and though I never met Barbara, she's come to feel like an intimate friend—making the use of last names seem artificially formal.)

Radicals were not as uncommon in national gay organizations themselves forty years ago as they are today. Currently, the large LGBT (lesbian, gay, bisexual, and transgender) organizations reflect the outlook of a significant majority of gay people in general, whose politics remain mostly focused on their own issues. This is less true—a lot less true, I feel, when in an optimistic mood—of the younger generation, especially those involved in political work on the local level. But the two issues that are currently at the top of the agenda for most gay people—legalizing gay marriage and abolishing "don't ask, don't tell"—radicals scorn as "centrist" and "assimilationist." The radical goal is to *abolish* the right of the state to define the terms and procedures that legitimize certain kinds of relationships and not others, and they want to rid the world of armies and war—of the killing machine known as the military. Radical gay people engaged with a wide variety of issues *besides* "gay liberation" (like the continuing struggle against racial discrimination) do still exist in the gay community, but they lack the influence they once wielded in the half-dozen years following Stonewall.

Another reason that Barbara and David came to seem like ample subjects is that each has large, and (particularly for Barbara) largely unused, archives, which in David's case include his extraordinary personal correspondence with his parents. (Barbara's papers are housed at the Schlesinger Library, Harvard, and David's mostly at the Swarthmore Peace Center.) Their archives are so rich in left-wing history that the further I went in my research, the more obvious it became that to do justice to their lives, and to the movements they were involved with, I'd have to forgo—short of attempting a multivolume work—my original plan to include other figures as well.

But my intention has never been to portray Barbara and David simply as political creatures. That would be an absurd disservice to their rich, highly individualized lives. Both *were* deeply committed to the social justice issues of their time, but both also had a complex range of personal interests, relationships, loyalties, doubts, and afflictions. Although their political commitments sometimes invaded and complicated their intimate lives, they never wholly consumed them. To even suggest as much, to ignore or minimize their private histories, would be to risk reducing them to cardboard polemicists—which they were not.

I'm certain that my empathy, both political and personal, for Barbara and David had a lot to do with my being drawn to write about them in the first place and may well have affected how I chose to narrate their lives. Although unsympathetic critics—especially those with a centrist or right-wing political bias—will perhaps accuse me of whitewashing my subjects, I've nevertheless done my best to recognize and record their foibles and shortcomings.

Empathy, in fact, often expands understanding, just as hostility can restrict it. Most historians (and even some scientists) have come to recognize that a degree of subjectivity (the influence of one's own experiences and values) will—no matter how conscientiously one tries to adhere to the known evidence—inevitably invade and distort their understanding of events. Besides, historians deal only with that portion of the evidence which happens to survive. Past events can never be fully reproduced as they actually happened. Objectivity remains the goal, but it can only be approached, never entirely achieved. Not even those historians with the most clear-eyed awareness can ever produce a complete or value-free account—which is one reason why history is continuously rewritten.

To acknowledge my identification with Barbara and David is simply to say that somewhat different accounts of their lives could be drawn—but not necessarily more complete or more accurate ones. The best analogy would be a roomful of artists painting the same sitter; although their portraits would vary considerably, each would nonetheless convey, and often valuably, different aspects of the same subject.

A SAVING REMNANT

Preface

The friendship between Barbara Deming and David McReynolds, along with their shared political activism, went back some fifteen years. But in 1976, and then sporadically for another half-dozen years, they became intensely tangled in disagreement. It began when Barbara asked David to sign a petition calling for censorship of the notorious film *Snuff*, which purportedly (though it was never proven) captured on camera the mutilation and murder of one of the actresses in the movie.[1]

David refused—heatedly. Though he hadn't seen the film, he strenuously objected to what he presumed was Barbara's underlying assumption that most men on the Left (as he wrote her) were "deserting women—or have always seen them as less than human." Besides, he himself, on principle, opposed "*any* censorship." Where would Barbara draw the line? He told her to walk through a porn shop one day and she'd see depictions of scenes they'd both deplore—young boys being violated by older men, bound and gagged women being raped, whip-wielding women beating men *and* women. He claimed to fully understand the outrage at *Snuff*, but "for women to protest *this* movie implied that they accept the brutalizing" of all the other ones. He insisted the broad issue was not that women's lives were held cheap but that most lives were.

In saying as much, David strenuously denied that he was anti-feminist: "the women's movement interests me much more than the gay liberation movement which, at least in the 'men's division,' I find more concerned with arranging dances than overturning a structure." He felt, moreover, that "there is a certain natural contour of nature which puts both of us, as homosexuals, at its edge and places the heterosexual much closer to the center." He'd decided that he was basically an "integrationist" and did not want to live within the context of a "gay community."

About feminism, he wanted Barbara to know that his support was not unconditional: "when women tell me they know all about men or that men are such and such, I know they speak *part* of the truth." He reminded her that for some time now she'd talked of "waiting, of silence, of hoping men would change and see patriarchy as the enemy." Yet in his view, "the attack on the patriarchy is possible only because it is, in a sense, already over." He felt that Barbara's pain was "a human condition, not a female one" and believed she was edging away "from the overarching humanity which is at the core of nonviolence," to which both of them had long been committed: "we need one another, our common humanity being more urgent in this short life than our blackness, whiteness, or elseness. That is a truth you once knew and I sense you have lost or are losing it somewhere along the way."

Barbara was deeply hurt at David's vehemence and his painful misunderstanding of her position. Yet characteristically—"we must *listen* to the Other" was central to her being—she began her reply by thanking him "for taking such care in writing me. I take it as an act of brotherliness." She asked him to take equal care in reading her response. And in the various exchanges by phone and mail that followed, she (and David as well) often reiterated their love and respect for one another—though that didn't prevent them from forcefully speaking their minds.

Barbara accused David of making assumptions about her that were "inaccurate." She was *not* a "correct-liner: I just try to act out the truth I feel as best I can." She did *not* believe that "men and women are different in essential nature." She did *not* want to turn the clock back and reinstall the Matriarchy, though she did believe that eons ago women were either co-partners in power or fully ruled. She was *not* a separatist: "I have never given myself that name"; it was true that, for a time, she felt that women, in consciousness-raising groups, "must talk above all among ourselves, act above all together" so that later—"may it be soon—we can come into each other's presence as distinct persons." Nor, as a corollary, did she to any degree repudiate her past. She remained proud of having worked side by side with David and other radical men—with "kindred spirits"—in the pacifist War Resisters League and in the many actions they'd taken together in the 1960s against racism, the arms buildup, civil defense, and the war in Vietnam.

When, in the early 1970s, she'd begun to read and encounter radical feminists, she'd been convinced that her brothers "would welcome feminism and would come to see feminism and nonviolence as 'inextricable'—would be quick to acknowledge that women have been oppressed by men." But only a few "have moved in this direction" and most had not. *Why* they had not deeply puzzled and upset her, though she continued to regard her male comrades as "brothers." But how could they not understand that "under Patriarchy *all* our natures are distorted. If Patriarchy were dissolved, I think we would all of us," among much else, "be not heterosexual or homosexual but simply sexual." She was shocked at David's belief that the power of the Patriarchy was "already over . . . you leave me wordless. Please do try to persuade me that it is so. And I'm not being sarcastic."

Barbara had become unhappily convinced, she told David, that the vast majority of men, including those on the Left, had no real feel for the profound power that (white) men continued to exert over all others. She now felt that "our lives, women's lives, are not real to you (and to men generally)—except in so far as they support the lives of men." Yet she felt strongly that those who called themselves "anti-imperialists" (as both she and David long had) needed to recognize "that *women* are treated as a colonized people—here and everywhere."

Barbara urged him to read—she knew only one man (David Dellinger) on the Left who had—at least some of the "extraordinary" books that feminists had written over the last few years, and specifically named the works of Shulamith Firestone, Kate Millett, Adrienne Rich, Mary Daly, and Andrea Dworkin. David would have none of it. He acknowledged his ignorance of the books Barbara cited—along with many other books he never seemed to have time enough to read. But he accused Barbara of "guilt-tripping" him and of setting "a bad example of communicating." Besides, he indignantly added, he refused to "read a book written by someone who won't attend planning meetings with men, someone who insists on separate demonstrations, separate book stores, separate bars" (none of which was true of most of the women Barbara had mentioned, including herself)—"they can bloody well have a separate audience for their writing."

They were at a stalemate, these longtime friends and political allies who shared so many values, as well as personally held each other in high regard ("for all my disagreements and angers," David wrote in one letter, "I love and respect you"—and Barbara felt the same way). Given the times, the divergence between them was hardly unique. The mid-1970s and early 1980s were marked by sharp divisions among activists on the Left—though this had always been true, it was more pronounced during some periods than others—as well as between self-identified gay men and lesbians. Antagonism between the New Left and the Old went back to the 1960s and hinged on the centrality of the class struggle. David had been one of the few older leftists—in 1970 he was forty-one—who strongly identified with the New Left, though not with its patronizing attitude toward women's liberation.

Both feminism and the gay movement had also, from their inception in the late 1960s, been marked by internal conflict, yet the mid to late 1970s marked a period of heightened infighting. Liberal feminists like Betty Friedan denounced the "lavender menace" specifically and radicals generally for putting the women's movement in a negative light and jeopardizing its growth. Radical feminists were themselves split into divergent ideological factions, some wanting to retain their ties to the male Left and to broad social reconstruction—even while opposing male supremacy—and others arguing for an autonomous women's movement focused on building alternative institutions and grounded in the conviction (which mistakenly discounted significant variations in class, race, and ethnicity) that all women shared a universal and biologically intrinsic identity different from that of men.[2]

Within the gay movement, the rise in influence of the National Gay Task Force (later renamed the National Lesbian and Gay Task Force), with its emphasis on homosexuals being "just folks" and its reliance on mainstream political strategies like lobbying and voting, signaled a shift away from the radical days of the earlier Gay Liberation Front. The GLF had formed immediately after the 1969 Stonewall riots and had emphasized an androgynous ideal (men and women sharing characteristics that had previously been parceled out to one gender *or* the other), as well as the importance of allying with other oppressed groups. The rise of lesbian separatism, moreover, threatened to weaken the fledgling movement. Those women who championed the split (and consensus on separation was far from complete) blamed it, with considerable justification, on endemic gay male sexism and on the divergent lifestyles of gay women and men, such as "sexual adventuring" (the judgmental word "promiscuity" had become *verboten*) characteristic of a segment of the gay male community.

1

Barbara's Youth

Katherine Deming once confided to her adult daughter Barbara that she'd never loved her husband, Harold, Barbara's father, and that her own mother had persuaded her to marry him, assuring her that love would follow. It hadn't, and over time their marriage had become less and less satisfying. Katherine periodically considered divorce, and once, having fallen in love with another man, actually asked for one. The tradition-minded Harold refused on the grounds that the marriage vow should never be broken. When she persisted, he presented Katherine with two options: stay in the marriage and never see the other man again or join the other man and lose her children (three sons and one daughter).[1]

Katherine chose her children. Many years later, she confided to Barbara that she'd accepted Harold's ultimatum because she feared that there might be nothing else "out there besides it"; her belief that she lacked any other options in life filled Barbara with anguish and "planted the first seeds" of her later feminism. "How could her mother, how could any woman," she asked herself, "preserve the atmosphere of love without accepting slavery?"

The upper-middle-class Deming family into which Barbara was born in 1917 lived in Manhattan. Katherine had been known for her beauty and before marriage had begun a singing career. In general, Barbara seems to have been closer to her father, Harold ("I feel very much your daughter," she once wrote him. "And I feel you as a large source of whatever strength is in me"). Harold dabbled a bit in poetry and painting, and had a great love of nature, which he passed on to his daughter; when a young man, he'd hoped to become a naturalist, but his father had vetoed that plan in favor of the law.

Reflecting later in life, Barbara felt there had been "too *little* yelling in our house . . . too much of the truth was not spoken." She once complained in a letter that the family talked together so infrequently that "we have established no common, familiar, vocabulary." Both Katherine and Harold Deming were in many ways traditional in their habits and opinions. Katherine abhorred the expression of strong feeling ("the slightest, most justifiable anger seems to her murderous"), but the strenuous effort it took never to raise her voice or "get excited about anything" was itself an enormous strain and she occasionally became "hysterical."

When in that state, Barbara would "hear her screaming at my father, uncontrolled"—and it would fill her "with helplessness and panic." She'd "always defend" her mother against her father, but the unnerving variance between Katherine's tight control over her feelings and her occasional outbursts encouraged Barbara to keep a safe distance. Later in life she concluded that her mother was essentially a narcissist: she "loves to be photographed with a baby in her arms, a look of infinite tenderness on her face. She is in love with the image of herself as a tender person. But actually cares very little, really, for anyone but herself." Barbara—preternaturally sensitive about people—perhaps wrote that passage in an angry, passing mood, for she knew full well that her mother, having given up both her career and her one true love, had understandably become an embittered woman who'd turned within—which could look like narcissistic self-absorption but may have been closer to self-protection.

Barbara felt less wary of her father and thought him overall a "very caring and principled man." But she did have her reservations about him, centering on his "too God-like eye upon me." Barbara came to the conclusion that if she "just did his bidding" she'd "never find life." His view of her destiny was confined to finding "a good man to marry," but Barbara came to feel that she'd be "lost, diminished," just as her mother had been, if she adhered to his notion of what a "full" life looked like for a woman.

The family had a country place in New City, Rockland County: something of an artists' colony, though Katherine had initially preferred to remain in New York. Harold, on the other hand, adored working outdoors. Many years later, when he was busy making a new garden plot, he had a heart attack and fell in the loose dirt. With help on the way—though all efforts at resuscitation would fail—Barbara half-lay on the ground next to him, her arms around his body. She realized "that was the first time in my life that I had felt able to really touch my father's body. I was holding to it hard—with my love—and with my grief . . . it's unbearable to me that the only time I would feel free to touch him without feeling threatened by his power over me was when he lay dead." Yet all the while she was aware "that his death would allow me to feel freer. I mourned that this had to be so."

At age sixteen, Barbara fell in love with her mother's best friend, Norma Millay, sister of Edna St. Vincent Millay, and a neighbor at the family's New City country home. Barbara boldly wrote in her journal: "I am a lesbian. I must face it." There wasn't at the time any "movement" or "community" to "come out" into, but when she became lovers with Norma Millay, she—surprisingly—confided in her mother: "I worship her—and mummy, she really likes me. I can never truly believe it . . . oh, I love her, I love her, I love her." Katherine wasn't judgmental with her daughter, perhaps in part because Norma had earlier proved a wise counselor to Katherine herself. She'd described to Norma her distaste for performing her "wifely duties" *every single night*—even after Harold had learned of her love for another man. Norma told her she shouldn't ever feel that she *had* to sleep with Harold if she didn't want to.

It was Norma who inspired one of Barbara's very first, emotionally exuberant, poems:

> I had leaned always to the wind and thought me lover
> of the stars
> but tonight
> there is no wind up and no stars
> and
> I am desiring oh so your breasts[2]

9

Not exactly up there with the great love poems, but it did succeed in conveying Barbara's passionate nature. Yet for quite a while longer she'd periodically tell herself—while continuing to fall in love only with women—that she'd "outgrow" her lesbianism and "manage to fall in love with a man and marry"—and *that* would be "finding my more mature self." Such moods would be brought on not out of fear of God but of public opinion. Barbara ceased being Christian when still fairly young, but (much like David McReynolds) "certain things that Jesus had said" continued to reverberate in her; she simply "altered the language a bit." Instead of "love the Lord thy God with all your heart, soul, mind," Barbara substituted "to love the spirit of life in everything that is. And: love your neighbor as your self."

The affair with Norma ended when Barbara left for Bennington College in Vermont in the fall of 1934. Since kindergarten, she'd attended a Quaker school, and her parents had hesitated (her father more than her mother) before giving their reluctant approval to Bennington, known in its day as a fairly freewheeling place. Still, Barbara was taught by the largely male faculty to stop reading poetry by women (whose work her mother had first put in her hands) and to start reading the "much greater" male poets—Donne, Yeats, T.S. Eliot. As a result, she wrote less poetry herself—"I was taught to be suspicious of my feelings"—and when she did, it was now usually in the third person. Yet Barbara was "very, very happy at Bennington—as a woman among women," and not having "to relate to each other relating to men."

By the time she arrived at college, Barbara had grown into a strikingly attractive woman, tall and willowy, with straight black hair and bangs, regular features unadorned with makeup, simply dressed—like many of the other undergraduates, she often wore pants—and with an unguarded, candid, vaguely aristocratic (but not haughty) manner. She was known, too, to be perceptive and serious-minded, and though modest, was an unintentionally emphatic presence.

Soon after arriving at Bennington to study English literature for two years and drama for another two, she became intermittently involved with an older student, Dorothy ("Casey") Case. Neither woman was monogamous; each experimented with other lovers, both women and men. Casey, who was actually bisexual, did more experimenting than Barbara. Once again, the relationship inspired a burst of poetry in Barbara:

my wings unfolded
from the rocking sweetness of you
alone now
i ride the waves. . . . [3]

When she graduated from Bennington in 1938, Barbara went to live on Morton Street in Greenwich Village, where she had a brief affair with the singer and actress Lotte Lenya, whom she'd originally met as a neighbor, along with Truman Capote, at her parents' country home in New City. For three months, Barbara worked at Orson Welles's famed Mercury Theatre, primarily with the company of *The Cradle Will Rock* (which she'd been involved with since her senior year at Bennington). During the winter of 1938–39, she also directed, unpaid, the Mercury Theatre's apprentice group.

She next got a job as assistant director for a new group that planned to produce Shelley's *The Cenci*; she worked with them for a month, but the group was never able to get financial backing. During the summers of both 1938 and 1939, Barbara returned to Bennington to serve as co-director of the stock company she'd helped to found, and then went back as a teaching fellow in the summers of 1940–41. It was there that she met a Bennington senior named Vida Ginsberg, and they subsequently became romantically and sexually involved. Vida would be one of the great loves of Barbara's life. Brilliant and well-read (Vida would become a professor at Bard College), some thought her too good a talker and not a good-enough listener. She and Barbara would be together for seven years.[4]

In New York, Barbara mostly "tramped the sidewalks from one producing office to the next and ended up very much discouraged"— not simply because she failed to find steady work in the theater but from the growing realization that she didn't *want* to find employment with any of the groups she'd seen. It seemed to her they weren't nearly as interested in hiring an apprentice as in finding someone who could sell themselves or a production without actually having much to offer.

Barbara spent the winter of 1939–40 in the family house at New City "trying to size things up" and to write. She thought, too, of teaching, for she felt it was unlikely she'd be able to support herself on writing alone. With that goal in mind, she got a scholarship from Western Reserve University (now Case Western) in Cleveland for a one year master's degree in drama, picking up some extra money on the side as a research assistant for the National Theatre Conference. But Western Reserve proved disappointing. As an undergraduate at Bennington, Barbara had never had to suffer through a survey course but had been taught to work patiently at texts and not, by one tag or another, glibly come to believe that she'd mastered them. At Western Reserve, the survey courses seemed designed to encourage a facile sense of "knowing" a subject, or even several centuries of history. But there was nothing superficial about Barbara, and she instinctively rejected the approach. She returned to New York City and, starting in 1942, took a job at the Museum of Modern Art as a film analyst for a Library of Congress project aimed at establishing a national film library. The Rockefellers had given a substantial grant for the project, but that money ran out in 1945, and Congress failed to come up with alternate funding, as had been hoped. The Library of Congress took over the project, using other funding sources. That put Barbara out of a job, and she gave up her apartment and moved back into her family's house in New City. But she did continue to study films on her own and in the mid-1940s got several articles on the subject published in the *Partisan Review*.

Her father didn't believe in "coddling" adult children and refused to provide further financial assistance after college. But in 1946 his resolution gave way, and at Christmas he surprised Barbara with "a generous check." That enabled her to move back to New York City, and she took an apartment at 130 East Nineteenth Street, where Vida often stayed (previously, the two had shared a house for a while when Vida began to teach drama at Bard).

Once Barbara fell in love, she committed herself passionately to that person. "Darling, darling, I do love you," she wrote Vida in one typical letter, "I want to occupy your days and nights, and every minute." Vida responded in kind ("I love you truly and as truly you own me"). But Vida's definition of "own" was elastic. Although their affair continued for years, they often lived apart, and Vida had periods (in her own words) of "occasional sulking or bitterness or blind blackness, a stubbornness" to not commit to any permanent arrangement between them.[5]

After she and Barbara had been together several years, Barbara's younger brother Quentin ("Chip") unexpectedly entered the picture. Chip was Barbara's favorite; she once described him as "like brown velvet. He is gentle, and though he is not sluggish he does not erupt." Vida began to realize that she felt attracted to brother and sister alike, though she initially kept her feelings for Chip to herself. There came a point when he—with Vida's encouragement and Barbara's knowledge—began actively to court Vida. Initially stunned at the development and at the growing seriousness of the relationship, Barbara made no effort to interfere.

In 1949 Vida and Chip would decide to marry and to move to the West Coast. Barbara would work hard to keep them both in her life (even, for a brief time, living with them in San Francisco). When Chip, a doctor, decided to set up a practice, he and Vida moved back to New York City, and whenever Barbara was in town, she'd almost always stay with them and their two daughters—who were like daughters to Barbara as well. And down the years, should Barbara ever find herself in one kind of trouble or another, Chip and Vida would be "always there for me." Barbara would later sum up the relationship as "we're very close, but also very far apart"—by which she meant that after she became politically radical, their opinions would widely diverge. Yet as late as 1969, Barbara would dedicate one of her books to "Quentin and Vida."

It would always be characteristic of Barbara that once she fell in love with a person, she never fully fell out of love, and even after their circumstances would change, wanted the person to remain in her life. She once wrote, "if love is really love, it cannot stop being what it is— though it can stop seeking. . . . Then it changes, certainly; but it does not expire. Even when one falls in love again."[6]

Barbara was fortunate in having a small income from a relative's bequest and knew that she would have still more in the future. Her mother had told her early on that she'd be leaving Barbara a house and "all her stocks and bonds" in her will. She also periodically sent Barbara small checks to supplement her income. All of which allowed her some flexibility while searching for the right job fit (though she had to supplement her income with at least part-time work). During her abortive attempts to make a life in the theater or as a teacher of drama, she did sense (she'd been writing poetry since her teens) that her true calling might be writing. She'd thought at one point of apprenticing herself to the prestigious (and racist) *Southern Review*, but after initial inquiries she backed off.

Her grandmother, Barbara's beloved "Amama," served as a role model of a woman with a wholly independent career. At a time when gender roles were even more rigidly adhered to, Amama had had a singing career, been a manager for other artists, and helped to found the American Conservatory in Chicago. But for a decade following her graduation from Bennington, Barbara was unable to duplicate Amama's unambiguous, imperative calling to a particular vocation. She still set her sights on becoming a writer, but most of the short stories, essays, and poetry she submitted before 1950 were rejected—with the exception of a few poems accepted for publication in the prestigious *Kenyon Review* and *Hudson Review*.[7]

Finally it dawned on her, after working for several years as a film analyst, that she'd seen a vast number of the country's contemporary films and had developed enough original ideas about what they revealed of our national sensibility to write a book. She finished it in 1950, gave it the title "A Long Way from Home" and, with considerable trepidation started the rounds of book publishers. None wanted it, but the magazine *City Lights* did begin to serialize it—until it ran out of funds and ceased to exist.[8]

Barbara sent a copy of the manuscript to Truman Capote, whom she'd gotten to know as a neighbor in New City, and he was full of praise: "What an achievement it is!" he wrote Barbara. "Of course it will have a publisher; such work is too rare. I've let [the playwright and actor] Emlyn Williams . . . read it . . . and he thinks it is brilliant" Even so, Barbara grew discouraged by the rejection slips and finally decided to put the manuscript away.[9]

Twenty years later she would take it out again, and when she did, she would be surprised to discover that "it was much more alive" than she'd remembered. She then decided to revise and retitle the book, to *Running Away from Myself: A Dream Portrait of America Drawn from the Films of the Forties*, and Grossman Publishers would finally bring it out in 1969. Though acutely intelligent and full of politely nightmarish insights into the American psyche, *Running* got almost no attention.

It wasn't until 1951, when Barbara was thirty-four, that she fell in love again, this time with a young woman, Annie Poor, with whom she'd grown up. Annie was a painter and the daughter of Bessie Breuer, a novelist and critic for whom Barbara worked off and on—at $8 a day—as an editorial assistant and with whom she became very close, though Bessie could be notoriously difficult. Her third husband, the well-known painter and architect Henry Varnum Poor, became Annie's stepfather when she was still quite young.[10]

Barbara wasn't shy in her pursuit of Annie. "I write to tell you that I love you," she began one letter—which she herself called "presumptuous"—and predicted to Annie that she was "going to marry me," because "I think you love me." Barbara may have been right. In another letter she wrote Annie, she recalled "that first night, your asking did I want to make love to you—and I moved toward you . . . my heart failing . . . [not wanting to] 'violate you.'" Barbara admitted that her stubborn persistence sometimes amounted to "battering"—to "hitting out without even taking aim."

But Annie proved a tough combatant. "You are hard," Barbara once wrote her, "which I love (although I suffer from it). You are not mild. And I love it that you are not. . . . You are hard because you respect yourself—and respect your work." Annie made it clear to Barbara that her "immense love and care and understanding" was something she was "grateful and happy for." She became *un*happy because "I can't give as much in return and that makes me strained and upset." Annie suggested they remain friends, so that she "won't be uneasy, worried about a whole complex of feelings I don't understand myself but I know aren't good." Realizing that she hadn't invented Annie's attraction to her, Barbara realized too that she could never win her over if Annie remained convinced that her feelings "aren't good." Though she loved Annie "most terribly," Barbara made it clear to Annie that she was glad to settle for friendship. She advised Annie to "never be sad about" the fact that "you cannot love me as much. . . . By the love you do give me—I live. Abundantly . . . what you give me is *full* return for my love. Believe this. It is true." Annie did remain a lifelong friend (and became a fairly well-known painter)—but she never married or, as far as is known, had a sexual or romantic partner.

Given this second disappointment in love, Barbara began to feel that she would "always be abandoned." Her mother implored her to accept a serious offer of marriage she'd recently received—"mother was in a frenzy: marriage was a necessary portion of the life she saw for me." Barbara herself was marginally tempted, but only because of her dejected state: "if he meant this—then I *was* flesh and blood, I did exist, and not in some loathsome shape—I could be loved!" But the slight temptation quickly passed. She knew perfectly well that women were the objects of her desire. Her sexuality, unlike that of some women, wasn't "fluid"; she was lesbian, not bisexual.[11]

Discouraged both emotionally and professionally, Barbara decided to travel. Her father's sister had left her a small legacy, and she thought that by living modestly ("actually I'm broke") she might manage a few months in Europe. Harold Deming refused his daughter's request to help her financially, feeling that as an adult she had to become entirely responsible for her own support. But her grandmother Amama felt otherwise: she gave Barbara enough money to plan a full year abroad. When Harold heard the news, he insisted that she put Amama's gift into savings and said that he would pay for the trip. She accepted the offer, though it surprised her. Just the year before, she'd appealed to her father for a small subsistence allowance until she could begin to earn a living as a writer. He'd refused, giving as his reason his fear that she'd become dependent on him. The refusal had made her feel ashamed. Why had he changed his mind in regard to Europe? Had he guessed—she certainly hadn't told him—that she still grieved for Vida, a rejection now amplified by Annie's withdrawal? Or was it more a matter of his hoping she might find a husband during her travels?[12]

Her mother surprised her still more. She saw Barbara off and left in her stateroom "a long box of flowers (mountain laurel she had picked)" and a note that made Barbara cry. She'd written that the two of them are "shy with one another," but she wanted Barbara to know how proud she was of her. "I can never talk to you about your poems," Katherine continued, for "to me they are so very personal it would seem a sort of intrusion. But my admiration is very deep." Some of the poems, of course, were about her love for Vida. Katherine—this "bitter and beautiful mother"—ended her note with a sudden burst: "Feel free!"

A few days after Barbara took ship for Europe, the war in Korea began. She was troubled that one of her brothers, who was in the marine reserves, might be deployed, but as someone still wholly apolitical, she was otherwise unconcerned. She decided that if the United Nations had concluded such a war was necessary, then it must be so. Barbara the political radical wouldn't emerge for some half dozen more years—though in 1952 she would hand out buttons for Adlai Stevenson, at that time her outermost limit of political engagement.

Italy was the first stop on her European trip. Barbara knew enough Italian to get around, and also a little French. She quickly met some congenial new friends, and one or two even became part-time traveling companions. In Turin, Barbara bought a small Lambretta bike to allow her the freedom "to head in any direction I wanted" and to see more than if confined by train or bus schedules. Some months after her arrival, when she was in Paris, a young man turned up at her door who'd been a college classmate of one of her brothers. She'd met Pete earlier, back in New York City, and had gone out with him several times.

They began to see each other quite a bit, until Barbara finally had to ask herself, "Could it be that [with] this young man—who seems either to love me or to want to learn to love me . . . I could learn to love *him*?" They did end up in bed together, but whereas Barbara caressed him amorously, Pete seemed single-mindedly intent only on "entering" her. She allowed him to but ended up feeling in no greater communication with him than before. Neither seemed to feel much regret when they decided to move ahead with separate travel plans.

They did meet again at the end of Barbara's trip, and she did go to bed with him again. But when, in the middle of intercourse, Pete spoke the words "I'm fucking you," Barbara's "whole self" flinched, "as if slapped by his words." No, she recognized with a jolt, "he never will know me and I never will know him. For this penis" has been taught to think itself "Lord and Master. And I am not the one to unteach it this inanity. . . . My spirit stands still—absolutely attentive at last. . . . I am this self that I am. I affirm it. Yes, I am. And I will not be robbed."

Barbara continued through Greece and Spain. She was a dedicated traveler, as eager to meet local people as to cover the certified masterworks—and did both, even if, at a few points, she risked her own safety. Along the way, she met a woman named Maria, a painter, and before long they found themselves tentatively in bed together. Barbara fell half in love with her, but Maria would disappoint no less than Pete had, though in different ways. Fully responsive to Barbara physically, Maria nonetheless told her firmly, "I shouldn't have. It can't happen again." They continued to see each other, but chastely—until the night before Maria's departure, when she again came into Barbara's bed and made love to her. When they hugged good-bye, Maria passionately whispered, "Such loving! Wonderful girl! Thank you! I'm happy that you came!" Then she was gone. The whole incident seemed like a mirage. "Meek and dispirited," Barbara wrote, "all my stubborn life spirits rebuked . . . in low spirits—still confusedly despising myself."

But her spirits gradually revived. Over potholed roads, she took buses that were "ancient noisy wrecks" that broke down several times a day in order to see spots like the ruins of the temple of Poseidon at Sounion. Almost everywhere she went men approached her, usually—but not always—politely. When she turned down their advances, she felt "ashamed," and managed to feel ashamed, too, that they had made them. To experience shame at one's refusal of "normal" sexuality—and on top of that, shame at one's actual desires—was an intrinsic part of being homosexual in those years, and to some significant degree, it still is. That was perhaps the very reason Barbara chose the subtitle "A Book of Travail" when, a year later, she wrote up her travels. Why "Travail"? she asked herself. The answer she came up with was that her journey had been "a labour of the spirit . . . the labour of accepting my sexual self; the labour of guarding it against scorn. My own scorn, of course, as well as that of others."

Returning to the States, Barbara wrote Vida, "I have a great hunger to begin to shape a life." During the early 1950s, she took significant steps in that direction both on professional and personal levels. She started with "A Book of Travail," based on her travel journals and written in the first person. But when she showed the first chapter to a few friends, "they all seemed embarrassed for me." Barbara thought "the writing must be poor; there must be something wrong with the book, its conception, its style." She told herself to set it aside. Only much later did she realize that the "friends" had been embarrassed because Barbara had spoken openly about being a lesbian. Not until 1971 would she reread the chapter and decide, after all, to continue with the book. The very next year, after minimal revision, she published the first chapter, "From a Book of Travail," in a collection of her short stories, *Wash Us and Comb Us*. But it took her many years to complete the rest of "Travail," and it wouldn't find a publisher until 1985.[13]

Her short stories were mostly drawn from her own life experience, yet she intentionally wrote them in the third person, still under the impression that when she wrote in the first person—in which, as she later understood, she did her best writing—it somehow "came out wrong, for some reason mysterious to me." She later realized that no mystery was involved; in the 1950s, writing openly about one's lesbianism was unacceptable. Shifting to the third person, her lesbianism now disguised, she began for the first time to find a few outlets for her stories and film reviews, including one in *Charm* and another in the *New Yorker*, which published "A Giro" in 1953. Mostly, though, she still got rejection slips, and almost all of the stories she wrote in the 1950s weren't published until the 1970s. In retrospect, Barbara thought that she "almost was killed as a writer in the '40s and '50s," and that it was her *best* work that got rejected. She again began to feel "demoralized, and very isolated." In 1953, she went traveling again, this time a brief trip to Mexico.[14]

The following year, during a visit to Bessie Breuer, Barbara was introduced to Mary Meigs, a painter friend of the family. Mary was exactly Barbara's age, and the two women took to each other immediately. Within just a few months they were exchanging passionate letters. "I think of you nine minutes out of ten," Mary wrote Barbara in a typical one. "I'm consumed by needless anguish and longing for you . . . I go on pretending to everybody that I'm still alone. Darling, darling, darling, darling."

Mary Meigs was an extraordinary person—keen-minded, well educated (at Bryn Mawr), self-exploratory, and splendidly candid. Physically she and Barbara were near duplicates: tall, thin, flat chested, unassuming yet charismatic. Unlike Barbara, Mary came from a wealthy, socially prominent (one ancestor had been a signer of the Constitution), and "proper" family; they lived in Washington, D.C., in a five-story redbrick house previously owned by Alice Roosevelt Longworth, complete with a live-in staff. The Meigses gave very grand dinner parties, with Crown Derby plates and Waterford wineglasses, and they tended to shun Jews, Roman Catholics, and black people, to say nothing of homosexuals.

Yet they had consciences, of a sort, believed in doing "good works," shunned ostentation (as opposed to fine living), and supported Roosevelt and the Democratic Party. As a child, Mary went to dances and receptions at the White House. But by age twenty she "turned against everything Victorian, despised all our family furniture and fell in love with colour." That, in turn, led her to choose painting as a career, though she made "infinitely slow progress" at it.

As for sex, Mary's morally strict governesses had taught her that it was a minor element in life, not to be spoken of in polite society. She had (in her own words) "no idea," at age twenty-four, that there were parts of her body that "could be 'aroused,' either by myself or by someone else. I had never touched or explored my body or, by accident, discovered the pleasure of masturbation." Finally, when twenty-five and in the WAVES during World War II, she was seduced by another WAVE and her sexual awakening began. But throughout her life, sex continued "to have relatively little importance" for her; as she once wrote, "the fact of my being a lesbian is not the center of my life and never has been."

That would eventually become a significant problem in her relationship with Barbara, though not in their early years together. In the beginning Mary was full of ardor, to the point where Barbara, who'd always enjoyed sex, confessed that she felt somewhat overwhelmed. But within a fairly short time, their roles reversed, with Mary becoming ever more reluctant to be amorous. Barbara was patience incarnate, and they would have long, earnest talks, during which Barbara would tenderly explain her body's need for physical love and Mary, by her own admission, would guiltily retreat into resentment and "sulkiness." Eventually they would decide that (in Mary's words) "the power of reason will not resolve the mysteries of body chemistry"—but that conclusion was far down the road.

In their first years together, they discovered the many ways in which they were alike, sharing the same habits and preferences. Both—despite Mary's luxurious upbringing—preferred to live rather austerely and close to nature. Barbara's reverence for the woods and her silence and stillness when wandering in them were such that one day a baby woodpecker comfortably landed on her head. Both women were artists, or incipient ones—Mary had had her first exhibition of paintings as early as 1950—and they tended to like the same books, music, paintings, and people. Both were politically liberal but not yet politically active.

The year before meeting Barbara, Mary had become friendly with the novelist Mary McCarthy (though she sometimes feared McCarthy's sharp tongue) and her then husband Bowden Broadwater, who Meigs sensed was basically homosexual. McCarthy was interested in settling on Cape Cod, in Wellfleet, something of an artists' colony and in the mid-1950s not yet overcrowded with tourists. On one of Mary's visits, the three went house hunting. They soon fell in love with two homes that were close to each other and surrounded by oak and pine trees. Mary and Bowden bought the larger one, which was painted red and stood higher on the hill, and Mary Meigs took the furnished yellow house.

McCarthy and her husband often gave elaborate dinner parties and usually invited Mary to them. She doubted that McCarthy had any real affection for her and felt the invitations resulted from a sense of obligation, so she accepted them infrequently. Later, when McCarthy published her Wellfleet novel, *A Charmed Life*, Mary's fears were confirmed. In the novel, the unappealing character Dolly Lamb was quite clearly based on her. Dolly comes across in the novel as a woman afraid of intimacy and sex, "a creature still more daunted and mild and primly scrupulous than the one the world saw," whose paintings were "cramped" and "crippled." The portrait hurt Mary deeply. She felt that McCarthy had quenched "my faith in myself . . . she activated the dormant seeds of doubt that made me so ready to hate myself and my work." For some time, Mary continued to see herself primarily through McCarthy's eyes.[15]

Though Mary had studied with Karl Knaths at the Phillips School in D.C., and later at the Skowhegan School, her confidence in her talent had never been secure. Its high-water mark was probably reached in 1957, when she had a show in Boston that was well received. She is "a major abstract-expressionist talent," the *Boston Sunday Herald*'s critic wrote, "who presents a glowing lyric view of nature with a wonderful economy of means and opulence of tone." Except for the little matter of Mary never having painted in the abstract style, she went about for a while "in a happy daze." But a follow-up show in a New York gallery soon brought her back to earth. The reviews were harsh. The *New York Times*, though it praised her drawings, characterized her paintings as "arch and efforted," and the other critics were no less negative.

It helped a little that the highly regarded painter Alex Katz dropped her a note to say that her work reminded him of Munch, and Barbara, as well, worked hard to dispel Mary's self-deprecations. But her galleries in both New York and Wellfleet soon dropped her, and she made the decision to stop painting for a while (though she continued to draw) until it might again become "a joyful experience" for her. She turned to making toys and small sculptures out of old shingles and beef marrow bones that she boiled and bleached.

By then Barbara had been living with Mary in her Wellfleet house for several years. Ironically, Vida Ginsberg (with whom Barbara had stayed in close touch) was a friend of Mary McCarthy's, the two having taught together at Bard in the early 1940s. Just as ironically, other nearby neighbors included McCarthy's ex-husband, the well-known critic Edmund Wilson, and his wife Elena; Mary and Barbara soon became friendly with both of them. Initially Barbara thought Edmund "rather haughty," but she soon recognized "how very far he could step forth from himself, put *off* that cloak of aloofness . . . he certainly knew (and let others know, bluntly) when something or somebody didn't move him; but so very many things and so many people did."

On his part, Edmund found Barbara impressive if shy, and particularly intelligent about literature. But he was less drawn to her than to Mary—perhaps because he and Barbara could both be stubborn in their convictions and in argument—though Barbara, unlike Edmund, was a careful listener and wasn't aggressively self-righteous about her views. But it was Mary who enchanted Edmund; he saw her frequently and wrote in his 1958 journal: "I began to feel a strange attraction exerted by Mary and a tendency, when sufficiently exhilarated, to kiss her." At one point he believed that what he felt for her "is love. I am not in love with her but what I feel for her is something unexpected. . . . It is rather queer, not, I think, like anything I have ever experienced before."

He once asked Mary directly if she was a lesbian, and Mary, startled—no one had ever asked her that before—hedged in her reply, answering with some equivalent of "sort of." It was, after all, the 1950s, when it was nearly universally assumed that homosexuality was pathological. Both Mary and Barbara still inhabited, as Mary once put it, "the shadowy world of denial and pretense," despite openly living together.[16]

It didn't help that Edmund, like most people of his generation, managed to convey his conviction that (in Mary's words) "homosexuality is in contravention of some immutable law" and that "lesbians are faintly ridiculous." At that point in her life, Mary sometimes had trouble admitting even to herself that she was a lesbian and could fall back on her earlier history of having had (unsatisfactory) sex with a few men to justify her ambiguous self-image. Similarly, Barbara's love poems invariably referred to "him" not "her"—though not, in her case, to deny her lesbianism but rather to make her third-person writings more publishable. This was a time, despite the existence of an incipient gay movement, when most homosexuals did their best to remain in hiding. "We lead double lives," Mary later wrote, "the most beautiful and loving experiences of our lives have to be kept secret; and the lies we live make us wary and cold."

Though Mary had grown up with a strong sense of entitlement and could have an unpredictably sharp tongue, she'd initially been afraid of Edmund: he "could be as irrational," Mary once wrote, "as a maddened water buffalo trampling everything in its path." Before long, though, she came to view him as "a marvelous companion, with his enthusiasm for everything under the sun." They would remain friends for many years, even though Mary never felt entirely comfortable with him when alone. Barbara, on the other hand, had no trouble engaging and arguing with him and wasn't put off, as Mary was, by his occasional testiness. She lacked Mary's self-consciousness and didn't much care what people thought of her.

At the end of the 1950s, perhaps because problems in their relationship had begun to surface, Barbara and Mary set off on a prolonged series of travels that they hoped would be healing. They started in Japan, included Israel (where Barbara somehow got to spend a whole evening alone with Martin Buber discussing the possibilities of nonviolence), and concluded in India, where Barbara read Gandhi much more deeply than before—which would have immediate, momentous consequences for her.

The following spring, Barbara vacationed with Annie Poor and her parents in Cuba soon after the overthrow of Batista. While out walking one day, Barbara by chance caught sight of Castro standing on the sidewalk outside the Sevilla Biltmore Hotel. She went boldly up to him and introduced herself as an American who felt distressed at the poor relations between the two countries (this was before the Bay of

Pigs). She understood, she said, that he had cause to feel bitterness; a munitions ship had just blown up in Havana Harbor, and she asked Castro if he had any evidence to back up the claim he'd made that the United States was responsible for the explosion. Remarkably, he acknowledged that he had no direct evidence, but he added that his angry words were directed "not to the United States [but] to the people of Cuba," trying to make them aware of the dangers and suffering that lay ahead. Barbara urged him to take "a less aggressive position." He touched her arm and asked her how *she* felt about the many "damaging acts" by the United States against his country. As she began to answer, two NBC reporters attempting to get a televised interview with Castro interrupted. Before moving off, Castro patted Barbara on the shoulder and announced to the gathering crowd that "she's a good girl. She advises me not to get angry."[17]

Far from feeling patronized, the encounter with Castro consolidated Barbara's view, which she'd heard from many Cubans, that the new regime was "absolutely honest"—in contrast to the widespread corruption and brutality that had marked Batista's rule—and that "for the first time we are full of hopes, we feel that life is possible." Cuba, Barbara was now convinced, having in effect been a colony of the United States, had under Castro finally "gained its independence from us," and that seemed to her "as it should be." But she would never think of Castro's Cuba as "an ideal society." It still relied "on violence of various kinds"—and she'd later add, after becoming a feminist, it remained a "patriarchal society" as well.

Barbara's exposure to Gandhi's nonviolent revolution and to Castro's violent one seems to have quite suddenly activated her earnest, searching, moral side, which the following year (1960) would lead her to become involved with the Committee for Non-Violent Action (CNVA) and, more generally, with the issues of race, civil defense, and nuclear disarmament. She would always remain staunchly committed to nonviolence but at the same time never rigidly dismissed *"for all people at all times and places* methods of violent and armed struggle"; they had, after all, been central to the success of the American, Cuban, and Chinese revolutions. Moreover, Barbara would add later that it was "crucial to establish women's *right* to violent self-defense" when under attack. (David McReynolds, too, would consider the Warsaw

Ghetto uprising an exception to his commitment to nonviolence, and also granted that violence sometimes worked, as in the revolt in Portugal that toppled the dictator Salazar.)

For several years, Mary would try to follow along with Barbara. She, too, became a pacifist and, for a time—driven by her own conscience, not merely trying to please Barbara—would join with her in attending a variety of demonstrations and meetings. But in direct contrast to Barbara, who became braver and more committed with each subsequent action, Mary became less so. Besides having "a mortal fear" of going to jail, she simply couldn't understand how anyone could really *like* attending meetings and demonstrations. She decided that her own true path was her art and "caring about the life around me . . . being attentive to my own rhythms, to the messages that I received when I kept very still." She added, "I'd rather be blown up than ever have to hand out another leaflet." She admired Barbara's deepening sense of mission ("she knew what she believed in," Mary would later write, "and would stick to it no matter what"). But their lives were clearly heading in different directions, even though, for a time, Barbara chose not to read the warning signs.

2

David's Early Activism, Bohemia, and Homosexuality

A dozen years younger than Barbara, David McReynolds became politically active more than a decade before her. While still in high school in Los Angeles, a teacher assigned him Lincoln Steffens's muckraking autobiography, and it had an enormous impact on him; for days he talked with his mother about little else. He soon became an avid reader of the *Nation* and the then-left-wing *New Republic*. During World War II and the years immediately following, he opposed, at the age of eighteen, the United States' active support of Chiang Kai-shek's attempt to stop the advance of Mao's troops and also denounced our conservative intervention in the Greek civil war.[1]

David was brought up as a devout Baptist. As a youngster he believed in the Gospels, in the concept of personal salvation, and in the saving grace of Jesus Christ. Yet even in high school he became something of a doubter—he was "horrified," for example, at the "extremely cruel" God of the Old Testament and felt there was "no basis whatever in the Gospels for the Pope and his cross-dressing cardinals." The older he got, the more completely David rejected the Christian religion, calling the Virgin Birth and the Resurrection entirely "mythical."[2]

He would continue to find Jesus "a significant figure," though as a historical person, "not a singular messiah." He'd increasingly discover "too much truth and power in the East" ever to return to Christianity and would ultimately call himself a "Buddhist atheist" (though when asked for his religious affiliation on various forms, he was often tempted to write "Bessie Smith"). As David became engrossed in social justice issues, he continued to be drawn to the historical figure of Jesus, interpreting him as putting special emphasis "on the obligation to build a new society."

David's first full foray into activism came when he joined the Prohibition Party, then a mere shadow of its considerable presence in the late nineteenth century and having shed its formerly progressive links to the labor movement. In 1948, he joined the Youth Council's Traveling Temperance Talking Team, winning all the medals for public speaking, which he quickly discovered he enjoyed and was good at. Unlike most of the other team members, he wrote his own speeches, and he also became editor of the party's youth paper. That same year, taking a break from his sophomore year at UCLA, he went to Finney County, Kansas, to work against the repeal of the state prohibition law, one of the few still on the books.

David hung a huge banner on his family's front lawn supporting the Prohibition Party's presidential candidate. His parents tolerated it while expressing dismay that their son wasn't concentrating more on his studies. Both of his parents, Charles and Elizabeth Anne McReynolds, regularly voted Republican and were conservative on most matters. Elizabeth was by far the more relaxed and tolerant of the two, but she tended to sit on her anger—for which Charles gave her abundant cause. She'd learned to repress feelings at an early age. Her own mother, who'd migrated from the northern part of Ireland in the late nineteenth century, gave birth to four girls but died when they were very young. Her father remarried—to a Native American—and they had two children of their own. But his new wife got along badly with the four girls, and life was difficult for them; they turned to each other for closeness.

Charles's own parents had been deeply religious, poor and not well matched, and he described himself as a "driven and difficult person by nature." His self-awareness about his temperament somewhat helped to modify what he called "the monkey on my back." At several points in his life, he suffered depression, sometimes severe: "I finally could not sleep, or work," Charles wrote during one crisis, "except by the most massive effort. I found myself frightened and disturbed almost beyond bearing and finally reached the point where I would wake up at night in a cold sweat of fear and clinging to one word 'Faith.'"

Throughout his life Charles rejected, on moral grounds, card playing, drinking, smoking, and dancing (his grandmother had been a fiery Pentecostal preacher). But he was also a smart, hardworking, honorable man who often worried that he'd passed on to his oldest child, David, his tense, controlling, stiff-necked ways. David was close to both of his two siblings, especially to his brother, Martin, who became a journalist and who shared most of David's left-wing views (during the 1965 uprising in the Dominican Republic, for example, he wrote articles from the perspective of the rebels and decried President Johnson's sending in of the marines to quell the uprising). David's sister, also named Elizabeth, chose to be a full-time mother. She could also be progressive on some issues, but her outside activities primarily related to her church.

Both parents tried to be attentive to their children's needs, though David felt much closer to his mother, an affectionate woman, strong without being a disciplinarian, who was much loved within the family. She'd worked as a nurse before marriage but thereafter became a traditional housewife. Toward his father, Charles, a more distant and often judgmental figure, David had conflicted feelings, sometimes bordering on dislike: "I wanted recognition from my father . . . who has never been a real father," David once wrote to a close friend. During World War II, Charles was stationed for four years in India, when David was going through adolescence. Even after he returned, he seemed to lack the gift of spontaneity, had trouble (unlike his wife) making friends, and devoted himself to church activities. He believed that "evil is within us and cannot be legislated out," that it was essential to "play by the rules," and that in raising children, mild corporal punishment was warranted.

In many ways, Charles was a deeply frustrated man. He'd been able to support himself for two years as an undergraduate at UCLA but had had to drop out of school for lack of money, and he would never become prosperous. Though intelligent, well informed, and even gifted (after retirement he became a genuinely creative potter), in order to provide for his family, he'd had to work most of his life at McGraw-Hill selling advertising, a job he loathed. Years later, when David saw

Arthur Miller's play *Death of a Salesman*, he realized that his own father closely resembled the main character, Willy Loman, and it made him feel overwhelmingly sad: "From that moment on . . . I had been freed from my father and from the need for rebellion because I understood him." In retrospect, he came to believe that overall he'd been raised in "a good family" and that his parents, on the whole, had done "a remarkable job in being supportive."

But as a young man, David would sometimes feel that his father resented him, especially his determination to spend his life working only at what he felt was enjoyable and important. Yet Charles would make it clear—perhaps too late—to the adult David that he thought of him as "a remarkably talented young man" who was in truth "quite a different person from me in many, many ways, and most of them admirable and, what is much more important, is quite lovable." When David was in his thirties, his father asked him to "engrave on your heart the conviction that my love for you has never faltered," which would have been difficult for the young David to believe, given the harshness his father sometimes directed at him.

That was especially true when he—unlike most gay people of that time—decided at age nineteen to tell his parents about his homosexuality. Both were predictably upset at the news, but unlike David's mother, his father would never be able to understand or accept it; he persistently referred to it as a "blind alley." Yet at the same time, Charles never rejected his son, and the two would argue about sex with a frankness remarkable for the 1950s.

David would never fully get over occasional bouts of guilt and regret about his homosexuality—a feeling that gay people of his generation more or less ingested with their Pablum—yet early on, he more or less came to terms with it and was publicly open about his sexuality long before Stonewall. But it wasn't easy. As he wrote a friend: "In our hatred of ourselves, in our fear of discovery, we can create a new façade which is the prototype of masculinity . . . we will live more easily if we stop trying to fit any pattern but our own, individual, intrinsic pattern. . . . To *be* homosexual is not to be effeminate. . . . To be gentle is not to be weak. To be firm is not to be harsh. . . . I think *very strongly* that the psychiatrists and Freudians are wrong when they say . . . that homosexuality is an infantile regression."[3]

David had begun to be sexually active while still in high school, though continuing to feel conflicted about it and hating the "frivolous" atmosphere of the local gay bars; he didn't want to live in "a ghetto which was created and imposed on us." Though he never lost the conviction that "nature wants you to have kids, wants you to pass on the genes . . . that's the norm," he later concluded that what the majority considered normal didn't mean that those with a homosexual orientation weren't "perfectly natural; they are."

David sometimes gave off an air of austere intensity, of being unapproachable, possibly because, at almost six four, he seemed an awkwardly imposing figure. Perhaps as a result, his own inner fears, shyness, and insecurity remained largely invisible: "my harsh side, shown the world, was a shell to make possible my survival." He rarely met men in gay bars, despite being a charismatic, unusually handsome young man—which he never believed: "it's . . . hard for me to accept the fact that I was in any way physically attractive." Typically exaggerating his negative qualities, he described himself at the time "as dry and cold as sand and ice." He decided that he preferred anonymous cruising for pickups in darkened alleys and streets.

Like so many of his generation, David continued to feel ambivalent about his "deviance": "My homosexuality weighs upon me terribly at times. . . . I feel degenerate and lost." But that did change dramatically after he met Alvin Ailey (not yet famous as a dancer and choreographer). Their initial encounter was in the notorious "queer" bathroom on the UCLA campus in 1949, where they had sex together. Alvin's guilt-free attitude toward his homosexuality became a model for David ("I came home walking on a cloud") and the two became good friends, though never lovers. David often visited Alvin's apartment in West Los Angeles and later in San Francisco, and he credits Alvin with greatly helping to reduce his self-hatred about being gay.[4]

A few years after meeting Alvin, David did fall in love, profoundly, with another young man, "Paul Royce," who was only eighteen but already a committed pacifist. Paul was trying to write a book at the time and looked up to David as an intellectual mentor; in turn, Paul taught him about New Orleans and jug-band jazz. At the time, Paul saw himself as basically straight, for he enjoyed having sex with women, and he didn't pretend to match David's passion. Much later, David realized that his own basic pattern was to commit to someone unwilling or unable fully to return his feelings; only then was he able to let himself go emotionally. As he once wrote Alvin, "I have such a terribly hard time ever expressing how I feel when I see you or any of my close friends . . . particularly when the friend is a man."[5]

The affair between David and Paul went on sporadically for several years, with Paul occasionally staying over at David's apartment. When Paul decided to end the relationship, David was in agony, filled with despair—"I feel so terribly lonely now." He continued for some time to write Paul love letters and to keep alive the hope that he'd change his mind. Paul never did, even after he became openly gay. But the two have remained friends down to the present day.

By 1951, when the country was heading into a conservative deep freeze, David went in the opposite direction politically. He gave up on the Prohibition Party (after the entire youth division had been expelled for being "Communist," which it wasn't) and began to explore socialism and pacifism. David also attended one meeting of the Mattachine Society, the recently formed pioneering homophile group that included Harry Hay and the designer Rudi Gernreich. But David felt it "wasn't my kind of group" and had no further contact with it. Instead David linked up with the comparatively moderate and religiously oriented Fellowship of Reconciliation, a long-standing organization he tried to "loosen up," but he ultimately had to admit failure: "You simply can't bohemianize these church people," he wrote a friend.

He began to concentrate his energy on socialism. While still an undergraduate, it had become clear to him that "consciousness is a reflection of the material reality; and therefore, you do change people by changing the society . . . you can't make people good, but you can create the conditions that make it easier for them to be decent." But David and his friends "were not good, disciplined Marxists." There was an "edge of Bohemia" to the L.A. local of the Socialist Party that predated the advent of the Beats. As David would put it much later, "we were still living with the memory of what the Party had been in the 1920s and '30s," when it had been at the heyday of its power. The L.A. Socialist Party was not part of the rigid Marxist Left, which had long been dominated by macho males and was firmly conformist on issues relating to social and sexual mores. It stood in contrast to some of the bold defenses of same-sex love (notably by Emma Goldman, Karl Kautsky, Edouard Bernstein, August Bebel, and Edward Carpenter) that had been a significant part of the nineteenth-century utopian socialist movement and, especially, the anarchist movement. David was openly gay with the socialist group he hung out with at UCLA and doesn't remember taking any flack for it. One of his friends *had* been expelled from the Socialist Youth League for being gay, and the Communist Party, as well as Trotskyist and Maoist groups, had a similarly dim view of homosexuality, labeling it a disease of capitalism.

Still enrolled at UCLA (and holding down menial nighttime jobs to pay the bills), David started to write letters to the campus paper, the *Daily Bruin*, about his emerging political beliefs. They were noticed by some of those in the so-called left wing of the local Socialist Party, a group of a dozen or so young people who hung out in Ocean Park, a very poor area of the city inhabited mostly by low-income Jews and "Okies." The left wing of the party in general opposed the Korean War, held up the early-twentieth-century socialist leaders Rosa Luxemburg and Eugene Debs as their heroes, and felt the party's current leader, Norman Thomas, was sometimes too conservative ("too moderate and pro-U.S.," David wrote to Thomas himself). Though nearly all heterosexual, the left-wingers tried to introduce a plank into the party's national platform that would have decriminalized homosexuality and that called for an end to discrimination against gay people—a remarkable effort, given the profound homophobia of the 1950s.[6]

The local left-wing socialists, only some dozen people, took David under their wing and began inviting him to their parties, which did something to ease the loneliness and isolation he'd long felt. He moved from his family's home to a $7-a-week beach shack closer to his new friends in Ocean Park. He enjoyed the irony that "those of us who were poorest had the nicest beach, while the posh crowd up in Santa Monica had their thin little strip of dirty sand, with their beach fences to keep out the riff raff."

The first time David went to one of the Ocean Beach parties, he nervously expected some version of a drunken sex orgy and for protection brought along a six-pack of Cokes. The door was opened by Maggie Phair, who became a lifelong mentor and friend. She quickly picked up on David's discomfort, told him that she'd put his Cokes in the refrigerator, and asked if he wouldn't mind standing at the door for a while, greeting new arrivals, since some of them were strangers to the group—thus ensuring that David would engage with people. Before long he felt at ease at their parties, joined in their many political demonstrations, and helped to put out the *Spark*, a weekly paper named after Lenin's *Iskra* which before the Revolution had been smuggled into Czarist Russia.

David soon made friends and became particularly close to Vern Davidson, who headed the socialist youth group on campus. Vern—who was also gay, though at the time closeted—became an important mentor to David, despite the fact that they were nearly the same age. Davidson would soon be imprisoned for a considerable length of time when he refused to be drafted during the Korean War. Occasionally David would go to the new gay bar, the Copper Mug, where dancing was permitted (though David wasn't loose enough to join in), but he disliked the place, finding it "swish and very depressing." Much more often he'd go, along with Vern, to the notorious Ocean Park bar the Tropic Village, frequented by gay people but also by a variety of bohemians, as well as prostitutes and drug addicts—and occasional celebrities like George Raft and Johnny Ray. The vice squad periodically cleared the place out, but the Village's tough-minded customers would quickly return and the bar would remain open.

David once did come close to being arrested—not in a gay bar but because he was taking pictures at night of the alleys of Ocean Park. He'd recently taken up photography, which would be a lifelong hobby, and had bought an ordinary Brownie box camera with time-exposure capability. The police stopped him, implied that he was cruising the alleys for pickups, and went back with him to his apartment. When they saw a poster on the wall of the "black agitator" Bayard Rustin (whom David would soon get to know well), the police threatened to arrest him. But after they called the station and made sure that there was no warrant out for him, they let him go with a warning. David sat on his anger during the interrogation, but after the police finally left, he exploded with fury over the incident.

By the time David graduated from UCLA in 1953, he'd become known as one of the most outspoken and magnetic student radicals on campus—"on the non-Communist side." Though considered an intellectual (he was a voracious, well-informed reader), David had never

done well in school—"my kind of intellect wasn't even in the running"—
and UCLA was no exception. He paid scant attention to his classes and
graduated with a course average of C.

Like his friend Vern Davidson, David refused to be inducted to
serve in the Korean War, rejecting a student deferment because "that
is a class rating—the workers get killed, the middle class goes to school."
He also refused "to testify to my religious beliefs on the ground that I
would be accepting discriminatory treatment not available to my agnostic friends like Vern." David pleaded with Norman Thomas to get
involved in Vern's case—"a socialist war resister who was denied due
process even before he was denied his C.O. exemption [because of] his
being an agnostic"—but Thomas didn't feel he could single out individuals for special pleading. Though David's own case dragged on and
he fully expected a prison sentence similar to Vern's, by some fluke the
FBI refused to release the files that served as the basis for denying
conscientious objector status, leaving the local draft board with no
choice but to grant him that status and assign him to two years of alternate service.

But he was fired from his job as "a political security risk" and, dead
broke, had to give up his Ocean Park beach shack and temporarily
move back home. By late 1955, he felt "burned out with mimeographing, letter-writing, speech making," and decided that he needed a change
of scene. He hadn't yet become sure that he had the courage "to continue . . . to end out life in cold flats with a handful of records, one
suit, etc. There is no way to solve this problem but to state it and face
it . . . to question my right to work in the radical movement unless I
am willing and able to give it my complete devotion."

During the early 1950s, David had twice been to New York City
for conferences, and he now felt that he'd surely be happier living
there, at least for a while, than in Los Angeles. On his 1953 trip to New
York, he'd been invited to participate in a special strategy conference
(which he thought "quite an honor") at the War Resisters League
(WRL). The leading figures in the pacifist movement at the time were
Bayard Rustin and A.J. Muste, both of whom would have a powerful
influence on David. The league had a long history in this country,
dating back to World War I, when Jessie Wallace Hughan, Tracy Mygatt (whom Barbara Deming knew well), and John Haynes Holmes

formed the Anti-Enlistment League to encourage war resisters. The league had progressively grown: it had thirteen thousand members in 1928, and its annual No More War parade in New York drew some fifteen thousand marchers.[7]

But the War Resisters League (as it was by then called) saw a sharp decline with the outbreak of World War II. The League's recommended policy of urging the Allies "to negotiate with the Germans for the release of all concentration camp prisoners" and to settle for less than their stated goal of unconditional surrender was a tough sell against Nazi barbarism and would have been even if the Germans had shown any interest in negotiations. In the late 1940s, with the rise of the Cold War, enthusiasm for pacifism had been further dampened. Yet despite its weakened ranks, the WRL participated in the first freedom ride in the South in 1947 and also played a leading role during the 1950s in challenging nuclear testing and civil defense drills.

David never fully embraced the WRL's policy during World War II. Much later in life, he wrote, "I 'condemn' all violence and put the quote marks around condemn only in that all things have a context. Do I condemn the violence of the Jews in the Warsaw Ghetto? Well, yes, but only barely and my heart isn't in it. In fact, in reality, I think violence in defense of justice is better than no action at all. Not as good as non-violence, but better than nothing." More generally, he once wrote a widely dispersed WRL memo in which he declared, "we are not talking about not hitting someone trying to mug you—or rape you—about that we couldn't care less. We *are* saying WRL does not, has not, and will not support the use of organized violence to achieve change, or to defend this country."

The year before David met him, Bayard Rustin had been arrested for homosexual activity, and David, though unacquainted at the time, had written to him sympathetically. During his 1953 visit to New York, he and Bayard had dinner together and had "a long talk" about homosexuality. Bayard reassured him that "unless we are going to limit sex to procreation, sex for enjoyment" with a man was no less "healthy" than with a woman, though he advised David to keep his orientation to himself. Their talk helped further to diminish David's residual guilt, and he also thought that he might be able to heed Bayard's advice to "overcome the need for 'revealing statements' "—especially because most people judge by behavioral stereotypes and "would never guess"

David's homosexuality from his outward appearance. After dinner, Bayard took him for a tour of the Greenwich Village bars, lingering at the famed White Horse Tavern, where the avant-garde, including the Young Socialists, noisily gathered.[8]

Once back again in Los Angeles, David decided to write both to Bayard and to A.J. Muste about job possibilities in New York. Neither could offer a paid position, but both said they'd welcome his participation, on a volunteer basis, in the pacifist and socialist movements. They thought he might find paid work, at least part-time, on the monthly publication *Liberation*, which had emerged as the voice of political radicalism.[9]

But it wasn't until early in 1956 that David moved to New York, and on arrival he felt that he'd made a bad mistake. He initially hated the city and missed L.A. (and Paul) far more than he'd expected; he felt "lonely, very lonely." Besides, he was constantly getting lost, couldn't believe how expensive everything was, and found the subways a nightmare ("What the NY citizens endure as a matter of course!"). Having no money, he stayed on the couch of friends, and during his first week in New York he "came near to starving."

As a chastened David wrote Norman Thomas, "When a young and inexperienced 'revolutionary democratic socialist' arrives in New York it takes a while to realize reality is always different from the abstract, and that there are few villains and perhaps no heroes in politics or in life. To whatever degree my earlier letters to you were tinged with a kind of dogmatic and automatic hostility I apologize." And well he might have: just the year before, he'd written Thomas that the "new thinking" the SP's leader had called for "by no means implies a more moderate course of action, even though I think this is generally how you have interpreted it."

Bayard and others he knew had him over for dinner, and Bayard suggested he check out the Brotherhood of Sleeping Car Porters for temporary work; they were looking for some extra hands to help out with a planned large-scale rally for civil rights at Madison Square Garden. David followed his advice and landed a secretarial job with the Brotherhood for several weeks, at $12 a day. He was the only white person in the Harlem office, and Bayard, who'd been working closely with Martin Luther King and the Montgomery bus boycott, filled him in on current developments in the accelerating black struggle.

David had long been an avid supporter of the movement ("there is a tide moving," he would write, "that no hand can stop or turn back . . . there is a light of freedom shining and streaming in and it will not be turned off").

Following his stint with the Brotherhood, David found another temporary job helping with the planning for the Prayer Pilgrimage to the nation's Capitol. He worked for a time under the well-known Ella Baker ("a tough, gutsy woman"). But he also knew that just below the surface "slumbers all the force of 100 years of absolute tyranny." After Bayard had told him that "arsenals of guns" were being hidden away in Montgomery, David, now a committed pacifist, worried whether the black movement would "go all out violently or non-violently." For that reason, he welcomed the moderating influence of the Southern church leadership, even though he shared Bayard's militancy about the struggle.

David also became involved with the Socialist Party. It had a long history of internal dissension; in earlier decades, there'd been particularly sharp struggles over U.S. participation in World Wars I and II. In contrast to Los Angeles, where David and his friends in the party's left wing had been in control, he found himself in the minority in the New York local, then dominated by right-wingers—defined in the socialist context as those periodically willing to support the Democratic Party's candidates or policies, and in particular Adlai Stevenson's bids for the presidency in 1952 and 1956. (Barbara Deming, not yet involved in radical politics, did become peripherally active in working for the Stevenson campaigns.) David found some of the right-wingers personally "delightful," but he met with "a generally cold and hostile reception" politically. In contrast, he'd been warmly welcomed and had functioned smoothly within the pacifist ranks of the War Resisters League and the Fellowship of Reconciliation, on whose national executive he served for a number of years, though uncomfortable with its religious orientation.

In the 1950s, the Socialist Party was a shadow—it had fewer than two thousand paid members—of the once-powerful party it had been at the turn of the century. The high point of its influence had come in the 1912 presidential election, when Eugene Debs had polled nearly a million votes, a full 6 percent of the electorate. In those years of bitter labor struggles—like the strikes of textile workers in Lawrence, Massachusetts, and coal miners in Colorado—the revolutionary IWW

(Industrial Workers of the World) was born, more than a million people read the socialist newspaper (*Appeal to Reason*), some one hundred socialists held public office, and the SP had a hundred thousand members.

Yet though a mere remnant of its former self, the party still managed to generate within its ranks a fair share of policy disagreements and bitter internal debates. The divisive issues, in relation to both domestic and foreign policy, were rarely trivial, though however decided, had a minuscule impact on the national agenda. In David's view, the Socialist Party was "not a social force any longer," and to again become one it needed to focus on broad unification with other marginal socialist groups, as well as recruiting *radical* pacifists from the ranks of the Fellowship of Reconciliation.

Despite the existing divisions within the SP, in David's view there was a tendency to avoid discussing some issues that he felt were of paramount importance and to rely instead "on the answers of ten or twenty years ago." Among those issues was the central question of whether or not the nationalization of the means of production and distribution, given its mixed accomplishments to date, should still be regarded as the chief instrument "to achieve all we had hoped for." Embedded in that issue, in turn, were still other questions: What should be the attitude and role the SP should adopt toward "a welfare state" and the growing centralism of state power acting primarily to protect the interests of the elite? Even further, David was concerned that ties between the peace movement and the SP, once historically strong, had disintegrated in recent years. Just as few socialists were any longer active in, say, the WRL or turned to it to inform their political analysis, the peace movement, in his view, was currently failing to pay "any serious attention to an economy intimately tied to the war machine."

Even when living in California, David had recognized that the positions he took on various issues placed him decisively in the ranks of the SP's left wing, though he did try his best—sometimes failing—to keep himself open to new information and arguments. The denial of civil liberties and the rise of McCarthyism dominated the national climate during most of the 1950s, and David never wavered in the view that "our liberty is being suppressed and democracy forced to retreat in the face of hysteria."[10]

He strongly disapproved of the various loyalty oaths then current, convinced that they "do not insure loyalty but serve to breed conformity." And he was a vocal opponent of "subversives" lists (first introduced by President Truman), of wiretapping and of unofficial censorship of the press, radio, and TV—all of which were being justified in the name of "containing communism." David himself had long been firmly opposed to Stalin's brand of totalitarian communism that had deformed the original legacy of the Bolshevik Revolution and been mistakenly equated in the West with "socialism"—thus leading the government to proscribe certain organizations, such as the Independent Socialist League (ISL), as subversive Communist groups.

David and others in the left wing of the Socialist Party advocated a socialist unity conference to create a new umbrella organization that embraced the ISL, the Jewish Labor Bund, ex-Trotskyists, "liberal" socialists currently inactive, members of the Fellowship of Reconciliation, and—after Khrushchev at the 1956 Twentieth Party Conference revealed for the first time the full extent of Stalin's crimes—the large number of those defecting in sorrow and revulsion from the Communist Party. As he wrote A.J. Muste, David could not "conceive of any occasion on which I would favor joint action with the Communist Party," but in regard to those who'd left the CP, he saw no reason why they "must be treated like lepers" or excluded from political intercourse and open debate. Or as David put it to Norman Thomas, it was important to let "individual members of the C.P. know the door is not closed on them if and when they make a fundamental break."

David knew full well that his hope for unification was utopian—the needed "social dynamic" to bring these fragmented groups together didn't exist—but he at least hoped the SP would initiate the process of discussion between them and would occasionally suggest joint action on a given issue. It was David's view, in opposition to the position taken by the right wing, that a socialist movement "which was honest about its position could not function effectively for more than a brief period" within a Democratic Party committed to capitalism. He reminded his California friend Vern Davidson, who was considering supporting Stevenson in 1956, that it was a Democratic attorney general who had first brought various Communist Party leaders to trial under the Smith Act. And Democratic as well as Republican Congresses had voted Senator McCarthy the funds for his investigations. Though the SP had long been an outspoken opponent of the Communist Party, David felt it important to defend its right to exist and for its members to enjoy "the inalienable rights" to free speech, free press, and free assembly.

Concerning foreign policy, David felt "a basic social crisis [existed] throughout the world due to the profound changes wrought by industrialism and technology." Most nations were divided into either the capitalist or the Soviet camp, but neither in his view could "democratically and peacefully resolve the revolutionary character of the period"—the "increasing power of the working class" and the struggle for independence from colonialist rule in Algeria, the rest of Africa, and Asia. Soviet totalitarianism, by masquerading as a revolutionary force, had deceived some elements involved in that anticolonial struggle. But fewer were fooled after the Soviets, late in 1956, had brutally suppressed rebellions against their rule in Poland and Hungary (David literally wept when he learned the news, then joined a hundred other demonstrators in picketing the Russian embassy). Not that David believed capitalism had anything more to offer in the struggle against colonialism—not after the United States revealed its reactionary colors by its ambiguous reaction to the British and French invasion of Egypt and seizure of the Suez Canal and by its support of Chiang Kai-shek in Taiwan and Emperor Bao Dai in Indochina.[11]

Only democratic socialism, he felt, truly had anything to contribute to the emerging Third World. That included its call for the social ownership of the means of production as a sound and concrete step toward economic egalitarianism, for universal disarmament and the destruction of existing nuclear weapons, for an end to colonialism and, through the United Nations, an "imaginative" policy of assistance to the industrially undeveloped nations of Asia, Africa, and Latin America.

David, and the SP's left wing in general, was as opposed to the Communist government in China as to the one in the Soviet Union (though they did advocate returning Taiwan to China), and also to the United States' persistent military and economic meddling in Latin American affairs. The left wing called for free elections, under UN supervision, as the basis for unification struggles in Germany, Korea, and Vietnam; fully supported the struggles for freedom throughout Africa; insisted that the French take immediate steps to grant Algeria independence; and condemned in the sharpest terms the racist government of South Africa.

David was able to attend the SP's June 1956 convention in Chicago, where he was delighted to see again the journalist Murray Kempton (they'd briefly met once before), whose political writing he admired. During the convention, the left wing (in David's words) "assumed a sharp new vitality," though not yet dominance, and he himself was elected to serve on one of the national committees, giving him a new prominence. But now and then his youthful verbal aggression during debate—probably in compensation for a self-image of being "too cautious and timid at times"—led some to regard him warily. "Pacifist though I am, I learned long ago you don't get anywhere with sweetness and light unless people know that you are prepared and able to deal firmly if they won't deal graciously."

In any case, David still lacked an effective power base, though that would soon change, and some of the propositions he advocated and cared most about were defeated. However, he had articulately and vigorously supported the convention's decision to run an independent ticket for the presidency rather than, as the right wing had argued for, support the Democratic Party slate. But that was about the only issue David considered critical for the SP's future that saw a favorable outcome.

The convention failed to pass the strong resolutions on disarmament and Algerian independence (though it did condemn the French prime minister, Guy Mollet, and affirm its solidarity with Algerian socialists), and called for civil liberties in the United States. David and others had worked especially hard on the latter, but the convention sent it back to committee for further study. In addition, the convention did vote to invite the Jewish Labor Bund to open discussions about joining the SP, but it rejected the idea of issuing a general call to other radical groups to discuss unification. In particular, the party declared itself unwilling to encourage unification with the ex-Trotskyist Max Shachtman's Independent Socialist League, despite the ISL's effective record of support for trade union struggles and despite its having attracted to its ranks many young intellectuals, including Irving Howe and Hal Draper (later author of the multivolume *Karl Marx: Theory of Revolution*).

The failure to call for a unification effort was the issue that most deeply troubled David; he despaired that the SP would ever champion unity, though he considered such an effort essential if socialism was to have any renewed impact on the larger society. But rather than give up on the idea—David had a stubborn and tenacious side—he resolved "to act effectively to bring new elements into the Party in order to help" the left wing expand and eventually succeed in taking control of at least the New York local. Initially, the one group he opposed affiliating with was the Social Democratic Front. The SDF had broken away from the Socialist Party in 1936 in order to back FDR; David considered the group "militaristic" and in support of some of the worst policies of the Democrats. But he later changed his mind about including the SDF and came to regard his earlier opinion as "one of the astounding blunders I have made"—a typical overstatement of his occasional misjudgments.[12]

On his return from the convention to New York, David got another typing job and then worked as a mimeographer and file clerk. But finally, in 1957, he found employment that fully engaged his interest and talent: the radical—and in left-wing circles, prestigious—monthly *Liberation* hired him at $60 a week as its executive secretary. At roughly the same time, David also found a new, small apartment that he liked and could afford in a Manhattan lower east side tenement, though he couldn't yet pay for a phone, refrigerator, or a decent bed. He decided that the city "depresses me less and less as I grow accustomed to it." He still missed California and still felt that at some point he wanted to return to the West Coast to live (though he never did)—especially after he learned how appreciated he was there: the Los Angeles local of the SP, unlike New York's, had voted unanimously to thank him for the work he'd done while in L.A. and to approve of the role he'd played at the recent convention. That further emboldened David to continue his "sharp attacks" on the more conservative New York local, even while feeling that its members "are really all good people."[13]

With his work and living situations less crisis ridden, David had more time for casual pickups on the street and occasional trips to gay bars (which he continued to dislike). He still hadn't fallen out of love with Paul; more than a year had passed since his arrival in New York, but (as he wrote Paul) "still I am in bondage. Damn you, bastard. . . . If you ever change your mind let me know and I'll either return as soon as I can do so, or wire you the money for a bus ticket to N.Y. . . . okay,

I'll lay off. . . ." David did take up with Tico, a Jamaican student, who lived with him for several years. But though he enjoyed the sex and company, David knew from the beginning that he could never fall in love with Tico—perhaps, he wisely acknowledged, because Tico had made it obvious that he was available. Tico also resented David's refusal to tell him much about himself; he'd accidentally come across one of David's letters to Paul and saw that he was quite capable of pouring out his soul. David's detachment and his inability to match Tico's interest finally led him angrily to move out.[14]

His mother and brother, David now belatedly learned, hadn't ever found him personally communicative either. His brother, Martin, reported a recent conversation he'd had with their parents, during which his mother said she'd been sure about David's homosexuality since his teens but that he wasn't "personal and she couldn't get through . . . your conversation was always general and impersonal." As for "Pop," he also insisted that he'd tried to tell David several times that they'd accepted "the worst" and only wanted him to be able to live with it— which was why they'd offered to pay for psychoanalysis. Martin, too, felt that David needed therapy.[15]

Pop would only admit to feeling guilty about the fact that, being a nervous person himself, he "couldn't stand to see nervous symptoms" in David, too, and had "tried to repress them." But Martin agreed with David that their father, unlike their mother, had been wholly unable to face David's homosexuality and was himself sexually repressed, even while he blamed his wife for being unwilling to match his sexual appetite. Both also agreed that even their mother, despite herself, continued to harbor some hope that David would ultimately marry and have a family.

David decided to write his parents a long letter spelling out, once and for all, the issue of his homosexuality. By this time Alfred Kinsey had published his pathbreaking books, in which (among much else) he revealed his finding that fully a third of adult American men had had sex with another man. The revelation had shocked the country and raised a storm of protest, but for David, Kinsey's findings confirmed his own general view that "*everyone* has homosexual tendencies . . . including you, Pop," but that "the price of adjusting to our society is the repression of this feeling and the tension resulting from this means that people often hate homosexuality."[16]

In his letter, David went on to tell his parents that no one had seduced or "corrupted" him, that his first homosexual experiences went all the way back to grammar school and junior high, that ever since he fell in love with Paul, he no longer had any guilt feelings (which wasn't exactly true, though he no longer hated himself, as he had when adolescent), that he did regret not having children, that he didn't *choose* his orientation, that no one should be *blamed* for it, that he wasn't asking for anybody's "forgiveness," that almost everyone (including the socialist and pacifist leadership) knew that he was homosexual and didn't seem to be bothered by it, and that most of the time "I live and enjoy living with a wonderful intensity."

Deciding that he needed more relaxation, David found a local pool and (for 25¢) went there nearly every day to swim and lie in the sun. He also picked up his friendship with Alvin Ailey again. He enjoyed the crowd of gifted young people who surrounded Alvin and only wished that he himself had the talent to become an artist. He did begin to explore New York's varied museums, art galleries, and theaters. He even—"with a kind of secret joy and sense of daring"—missed an SP meeting in order to accept Alvin's offer to go with him to the opening night of the Jackson Pollock show at the Museum of Modern Art. To David's surprise and delight, he very much liked Pollock's work: "he deserves his reputation in my opinion and is a fresh and really exciting artist."

This period of comparative relaxation gave way early in 1958 as the unification question once again began to heat up as the SP's June national convention approached. And David once again began turning out a series of proposition papers and contacting his long list of personal correspondents. His general argument (which both Bayard Rustin and Norman Thomas, the current head of the party, agreed with) was that the admission of Max Shachtman's ISL group, as David put it, would "symbolize our political vitality and willingness to become a broad socialist movement. Defeat . . . will mean we are determined to remain a sectarian organization." At which point, he felt, many of the younger party members would pull out, including him: "I will be damned if I'm going to go on pouring my energies into a sectarian cesspool." With the Communist Party USA in a state of collapse after Khrushchev's 1956 revelations about Stalin's crimes, this was the first opportune moment in many years to open the door to a broad movement.[17]

David had sensed for some time that the country had finally begun to move in a more progressive direction. There was mounting evidence to support his view. A number of powerful critiques of materialism and button-down conformity had become bestsellers, including David Riesman's *The Lonely Crowd*, William H. White's *The Organization Man*, and John Kenneth Galbraith's *The Affluent Society*. *Rebel Without a Cause* had propelled James Dean into superstardom. The birth control pill had passed successful trials in 1956 and would be approved for sale in 1960. Norman Mailer's essay "The White Negro" had drawn considerable attention; and the Beats, pre-eminently represented by Allen Ginsberg's poem *Howl* and Jack Kerouac's roman à clef *On the Road*, had captured the imagination of a significant segment of the young.

At the socialist convention, held in early June 1958, unity with the ISL not only won by a large majority (45–17), but marked a turnabout in David's personal standing in the party. Though the right-wing leadership had the year before removed him from the National Action Committee (a sub-body of the National Executive Committee), at the convention, David—who'd impressed enough people by that point—was invited to join a small group of influential party members, including Norman Thomas, to plan strategy. During the floor debates themselves, he was able personally to command fully one quarter of the delegates, was elected to the National Executive Committee, and emerged from the convention as the leader of the party's left wing. His success, he felt, was based not on his avoidance of errors—he accused himself at one point of making "enormous blunders"—but on his ability to learn from them.

Less than two months after the convention, David's new clout led to his being drafted to run on the SP ticket for Congress from the 19th District, the lower east side of Manhattan. He initially declined the nomination but was ultimately persuaded to accept, especially after it was pointed out that his candidacy marked the first time in more than twenty years that the party had entered a congressional race in the district (though during and just after World War I, voters in the 19th had twice sent Socialist Meyer London to Congress).[18]

One of David's first acts after being nominated was to join more than thirty other "Indians" in a "Brooklyn Tea Party" protesting a cargo of radioactive tea spread out on a pier awaiting inspection. Wearing a headdress of authentic eagle feathers, David told a reporter that "if the money spent on war were spent on welfare, we could create a paradise in this land . . . only democratic socialism offers a peaceful alternative to the military-minded policies of both the Soviet and the American blocs."

David drew some fifty campaign workers, most of them in their twenties, but to actually get on the ballot, three thousand valid petition signatures (which meant about six thousand in all) were required. That was a tall order in a still predominantly conservative national climate. It proved to be too tall an order. Despite a vigorous campaign and the personal appearance of Norman Thomas in the district to lend his support, David fell short of the requirement by a mere three hundred signatures. He himself felt ambivalent about the result ("there are things other than elections to concentrate on") but agreed to a write-in campaign on election day. The platform he drafted stressed disarmament (the Soviets had successfully launched Sputnik in 1957, leading to the creation of NASA), civil liberties, and an end to poverty. In the upshot David was unable to find out how many votes he'd gotten; the elections board told him "none," but that was an obvious lie since the SP's poll watchers saw at least hundreds of votes for him tabulated.

David was still only twenty-nine years old. Despite all of his successes (or perhaps because of them), he was seized in late October with a sudden and severe anxiety attack. It was not his first. Four times earlier in his life—just like his father, Charles—his "sense of reality" had started to slip; his body, sweaty and cramped, called out to him to leap through the window. It had been so long since his last attack that this one felt "unfamiliar and more shocking." Fortunately, after a terrifying few nights, he regained his equilibrium and was quick to find rational reasons to explain his descent—overwork, stress from the campaign, strain over the breakup with his Jamaican boyfriend, and a peyote trip in which he "saw God, and also realized there was no God."

But David knew perfectly well that deeper, unconscious factors had almost surely played the larger role, and when a more dilute version of anxiety soon returned, he resolved to see a psychiatrist as soon as possible and to "begin the process of analysis." But he let that resolution slide for some fifteen years.[19]

3

Joining the Black Struggle

David's and Barbara's first arrests, though at different times and places, were for the same cause: nonviolent demonstrations for peace. In the mid-1950s, New York State had passed a civil defense law mandating that when the CD alert sounded, the citizenry had to seek shelter during the drills; anyone who did not risked the penalty of a year in jail or a $500 fine. Initially, the brunt of protest against the law was borne by Dorothy Day and the radical Catholic Workers; from 1955 on, she and a handful of followers would sit in the park across from the New York City mayor's office to protest the statute and would invariably be jailed for ten to thirty days. In April 1959, David joined the group of about twenty people refusing to take shelter, impelled to do so out of the conviction that the city was "criminally insane" in jailing the group for sitting on a park bench.[1]

He argued that such drills, along with President Eisenhower's and the mainstream media's encouragement to build fallout shelters, falsely persuaded the populace that it could survive nuclear war. Jailed overnight in 1959 for refusing to take shelter, David's one regret was that throughout the protest he remained "a nervous young man who lacks [the] poise and spiritual depth . . . to be of any great help to other individuals." He did manage to admit that despite his anxiety ("being a physical coward is a terrible burden"), he'd at least gone ahead and joined the protest, having decided that "if a reluctance to act from a fear of prison holds a person back from a right action, then they are already imprisoned in a far more binding way than any jail."

The following year, he and Bayard Rustin decided that—given the government's vigorous determination to push the civil defense program—they might be able to mount a larger protest. The War Resisters League (WRL) in general played a pivotal role during this period in organizing protests against drills and shelters. When the day for the 1960 event arrived, David and Ralph DiGia—a leading figure in the WRL and an old-time jailbird dating back to his conscientious objector days during World War II—thought that with luck they might expect two or three hundred people. Over a thousand showed up, including such "notables" as Norman Mailer, Dwight Macdonald, and Murray Kempton. The police captain kept shouting over his megaphone that all those gathered would be subject to arrest. Eventually, only twenty-six people were briefly jailed.

Encouraged, David next began to speak on street corners on Sunday nights in Greenwich Village. Though he'd always felt at ease on a public platform, he initially felt real "dread" at the vulnerability of standing in the middle of a crowd, trying to get its attention. Yet he soon got a feel for it, and after a little practice turned out to be the only speaker able to silence hecklers and keep the attention of passersby. Impressed by David's activism and his earlier tax-refusal protest in 1957, the League elected him the following year to its Executive Committee. Then, after his participation (and second brief arrest) in the large 1960 demonstration in front of the Women's House of Detention in Greenwich Village, the WRL invited him to become its field secretary.

David accepted the position, which would entail a great deal of travel, even while remaining active in the Socialist Party and retaining his political association with *Liberation* magazine (though he did resign as editorial secretary)—to say nothing of doing more and more writing, mostly for the *Village Voice*. Several of his articles drew considerable attention and were reprinted in various college papers. He was also increasingly being offered speaking engagements and invited on a variety of radio programs, becoming a regular on the very popular late night *Long John Nebel Show*. "My star has momentarily risen," he exuberantly wrote his parents. He felt that the scary anxiety attack of the previous year was now solidly behind him and reported, "I am happy, and find in the intensity of life a very deep joy."[2]

Politically, too, he believed, somewhat presciently, that "things are alive everywhere—not in a decade have I seen students so active." The Socialist Party also seemed on the verge of resurgent popularity. By early 1960, hundreds of new members had joined the party, including such well-known figures as Murray Kempton and the prominent psychiatrist and author Erich Fromm; the number of active branches and locals had more than doubled; and the SP's financial situation, while not exactly secure, had significantly improved. Some of this growing strength, David believed, was due to the poor quality of leadership in both the major parties. He thought Barry Goldwater a man who seemed "to have only the vaguest idea which century he is living in," considered Richard Nixon "obviously a phony," and after Kennedy's election in 1960 (though pleased that the issue of having a Catholic in high office had finally been settled) the best David could find to say about him was that he was shrewd and charming—"a contemporary kind of British Tory."[3]

He even had something of a spiritual, though not a traditionally religious, awakening; "pagan mystic" perhaps came closest, with Hermann Hesse's *Siddhartha* (then hugely popular) the prototype, and Jung's collective unconscious the high-toned precursor. In David's view, Hesse accepted "much of Buddhism" but felt that "ultimately the Western conception of love as an active force modifies the detachment of Buddhist thinking." As he reached his thirtieth birthday, that classic passage point, David found that he'd been "much concerned" of late with "the paradox of consciousness and nonconsciousness, the reality beyond experience and beyond knowing." He still rejected any orthodox faith and was unmoved by any theology, any dictated creed or doctrine. He now called himself "an atheist with faith" and resonated profoundly to the notion that "the deepest reality can only be found intuitively and not rationally." None of which led David to believe that revolutionaries were wrong; the struggle for social change remained necessary because "until man has bread, he cannot have the insight that man does not live by bread alone."[4]

Several years before, he'd met Allen Ginsberg when personally delivering his copies of *Liberation*. Allen and his lover Peter Orlovsky were sitting around drinking cough syrup, and David boldly asked Allen why he hadn't been participating in various demonstrations. Allen undefensively replied that he should have been; later he referred to "the peaceful Genius of WRL." Thereafter they became somewhat friendly. One night David was on East Fourth Street with Peter and Allen when they saw a woman lying on the sidewalk, either drugged or drunk, her boyfriend brutally yanking one of her arms and yelling "Come on, you God damn bitch, get the fuck up!" David had been taught never to intervene when two people were fighting, but Allen walked directly up to the man and calmly said, "You don't want to do that"—as if, David later put it, "philosophically advising against a foolish chess move."

Allen then held out his hand and said, "I don't believe we've met." It worked. The man was thrown off guard, and Allen proceeded to offer the woman on the sidewalk a Fig Newton. She took it, got to her feet, and staggered off with her boyfriend. "An artful piece of work," David thought, "a bit of spiritual magic. Fearless, compassionate, spontaneous, and more deeply imprinted on my mind than any line from *Howl*." From then on, over the years, the two would occasionally see each other. At a party at Allen's once, Peter would start to pour water on David's head whenever he lit up a cigarette, but Allen would stop him. Peter claimed the technique had cured Allen of smoking—which it did for a while, until he found a new guru who smoked like a chimney. In general, David considered the Beats among his heroes: those "strange, disturbing holy men, who . . . have moved across the parched heart of the land, thundering illuminations and rain, ending the long spiritual torment and intellectual drought of this nation."

Another new hero was the psychoanalyst Otto Rank, who David read as affirming "a creative—not dangerous—unconscious," emphasizing that the mind "is but an aspect of the total reality" and the "voyage into self" lay far beyond the "individual ego of the Freudian." One certain fact, David decided, was that "there is no mystery of the physical world which does not point to a mystery beyond itself." He even had an astrological reading done. It underscored his "naturally introverted disposition," his intense, complex inner life, his great determination and willpower, his tendency to be overly suspicious and critical, and his frankness and directness—but coupled to a quick temper and a rather combative nature—all of which (except for the willpower) David found "extraordinarily accurate."[5]

David served as one of the major organizers for the 1961 mass protest against the annual civil defense drill in New York. In a nonstop series of meetings, speeches, and articles (among the most noteworthy was a two-part *Village Voice* series, "Neither Run nor Hide"), David proved a whirlwind organizer. The April 1961 demonstration drew a large crowd, some two thousand people (by then the issue of civil defense had become popular with liberals, too)—and that was the last time the authorities attempted such a drill in New York City. David himself was not only again arrested, but this time had to stand trial. The magistrate gave him and ten others the choice of a $50 fine or twenty-five days in jail. David chose jail, making him unable to reproach himself for being a "coward." Sent to Hart Island, a small piece of land off the east coast of the Bronx, he was assigned to a dorm with two men, one of them Ralph DiGia, a leading figure in the War Resisters League.[6]

David was put in a labor squad assigned to breaking up concrete and hauling it to a truck. A sizable number of the prison population were illiterate, so David and one other of the arrested peace demonstrators set up a class to teach them how to write and read. He found the students eager to learn and felt the class made good progress, though he decided that teaching was harder than hauling concrete. Except for time passing slowly, David, overall, didn't find his prison stay particularly onerous—"it's like a boys' camp with impolite counselors. Looking at it another way, Hart Island is a perfect example of Communism—everything is taken care of, including your freedom."

David and Barbara Deming started to see more of each other as their political views and activities increasingly converged between 1960 and 1962. In 1962, for example, she was one of a small group of signatories to the call issued from the Committee for May 10th—of which David was one of the prime movers—for national demonstrations against President Kennedy's eight-week resumption of nuclear bomb tests in the Pacific. Although they would never become consistently close friends and would later disagree sharply over several major issues, David always thought Barbara "a wonderful woman," and they became close enough for him to visit her once for a weekend in Wellfleet.[7]

David had been a political radical as far back as college, but Barbara, though a dozen years older, had until the late 1950s been largely apolitical, though vaguely liberal (pro-union and pro–black civil rights). Before then, as she later wrote, "I had the feeling that, if I entered the 'political' realm, I would become less truthful, keep less of a grasp on the *complexity* of truth—and also experience estrangement from people I cared for." But once activated by her trips to India and Cuba and by her study of Gandhi's writings, she never looked back.

The focus of her commitment would shift during the 1960s, initially centering on nonviolent protest for unilateral nuclear disarmament, then on the struggle for racial equality, and by the end of the decade on radical feminism and lesbian rights. But regardless of which issue currently captured her primary attention, she never simply dropped the concerns preceding nor her commitment to the consistent strategy of direct-action nonviolent protest. Indeed, she is today considered by some to be among the leading theorists of secular nonviolence.

Looking back, Barbara later wrote that the various struggles in which she took part "reverberated deeply a so-called 'apolitical' struggle I'd been waging on my own, in a lonely way, up until then, as a woman and a lesbian: the struggle to claim my life as my own." When she did get active, she did so with "such a passion, such a sense of urgency," because the Cuban or the black or the Vietnamese struggles, with "their demand for autonomy . . . was the very demand *I* had been trying to make."

She felt that she'd long been waging a crucial struggle with her father. He would constantly tell her how much he loved her—and he did—but would then add words along the line of "but you are a woman and have a destiny different from mine." To this Barbara would gradually learn to respond that "we are more alike—women and men are more alike—than you will acknowledge. And *I* am the one to say what my destiny is." What she did not ever do was to wish her father harm; "my own life would have been diminished"—a point essential to any understanding of the nonviolent struggle: "you are *not* our masters, and you *are* our brothers."

Barbara would also come to believe that nonviolent actions are by their nature androgynous. Two impulses long identified as belonging to different genders—the "masculine" impulse of self-assertion and the "feminine" impulse of sympathy—come together in any individual, regardless of gender, who adheres to nonviolence: "One asserts one's rights as a human being, but asserts them with consideration for the other." David was no less committed than Barbara to nonviolence, but throughout most of the 1960s, until the rise of the feminist movement, he emphasized a somewhat though not absolutely different goal than she: his concern centered more on the need to transform social institutions than individuals. "Revolution means, in my own view, the basic reorganization of the institutions of a society, a reorganization of the way that . . . [people] relate to those institutions, to the means of production, and to power." Neither Barbara nor David held to fixed concepts about nonviolence; the views of both evolved through time and experience.

In the ongoing process of her radicalization, Barbara joined an assortment of affiliated groups—the War Resisters League, the Committee for Non-Violent Action (CNVA), and the Peacemakers. Her first step—taken eagerly but nervously in August 1960—was to sign on for a sixteen-day training program in New London, Connecticut, which the Peacemakers sponsored. She initially felt disheartend upon arriving at the group's rented headquarters, an abandoned three-story tenement with plaster dropping from the ceiling, folding chairs, and a small number of sleeping cots (most of the attendees slept on the floor). Many in the group were already veterans of nonviolent protest, jailed for tax or draft refusal, for peaceful demonstrations against segregation, and for leafleting at war plants.[8]

But as the days went by, Barbara became increasingly enthralled by the diverse group of people who'd assembled for the training—and by the powerful way a commitment to nonviolence had changed their lives. "The candor and innocence," she later wrote, "of their actions give to these people—for all the very great differences among them—a likeness to each other. . . . They all share an extraordinary spontaneity— the sense that an individual *can* act and *has* weight. If no-one else will do it, then do it yourself." Barbara felt, she wrote A.J. Muste, "like one who had supposed himself a man without a country and then happened to land on his country's shores."

She decided to join the CNVA demonstration against the submarines armed with Polaris missiles (each with the capacity to carry a hydrogen-bomb warhead) then being built in the New London, Connecticut, shipyards. The CNVA conducted vigils, leafleting, and peace walks, with several of the more daring (not yet Barbara) actually boarding the subs and being carted off to jail. Subsequently, the temporary CNVA office in town was thoroughly trashed. After returning home, Barbara decided to write up her experiences in New London. She called the article "The Peacemakers," and the *Nation* accepted it for publication—the first in a series of Barbara's articles that would appear there. Along with much else, Barbara had finally begun to find her writer's voice through journalism based on her own experience.

The following year, in May 1961, she spent a week on the road with the CNVA-sponsored San Francisco–to–Moscow Walk for Peace, walking twenty-two miles the final day. She joined the group in Uniontown, Pennsylvania, when it numbered about thirty people, which swelled to over two thousand by the time it reached New York. She then spent another week in Alexandria, Virginia, participating in a vigil and fast in front of the CIA offices. On both occasions, she got little sleep—"these people," she wrote Carey McWilliams, editor of the *Nation*, "talk excitedly until late, then spring up at six in the morning!" Why walks and vigils instead of placing ads in newspapers or forming discussion groups? For Barbara the answer was: "we are not just mouthing words; we care enough to stir ourselves"—plus the added benefits of being able to recruit others along the way for the peace movement, as well as committing an act of "penance" for the country's knee-jerk waging of wars that killed millions in the process. She shared the conviction that the power of arms had to be supplanted by the power of persuasion. When she asked her fellow walkers if they felt there really was any hope for such a shift, she got variations of the same answer: "I don't operate on the basis of hope." I simply asked myself "what was right and what was wrong." In Barbara's gloss, "the truth . . . is the truth, and will not be mocked."[9]

Her own first arrest came after the United States, early in 1962, announced its resumption of nuclear testing. In response, Barbara and a small group of other women sat down in front of the Atomic Energy Commission building on Hudson Street in New York City. They were swiftly gathered up by the police, dumped into a paddy wagon, and taken to the Women's House of Detention, where they were strip-searched and arraigned. Barbara was made to undergo three such searches, leading her to conclude that the guards were looking for neither dope nor weapons, as they asserted, but for "our pride."[10]

Bailed out the next day, she spent the following morning, accompanied by her partner Mary Meigs and Elena and Edmund Wilson, in court on Centre Street. Barbara and four of the other demonstrators refused to plead guilty. The magistrate, "a bull-necked Irishman," as Edmund Wilson described him in his diary, unaccountably severed Barbara's case from the others, perhaps because, at age forty-five, she was considerably older, though Wilson thought the judge had "sized her up as a well-to-do woman of superior social position." He then "bullied" the remaining four "for all he was worth," telling them they had a right to their opinions but not a right to break the law, which he claimed they'd done by "obstructing traffic"—thus proving themselves "not Americans." He insisted that each of the four promise not to commit such a crime in the future—which they refused to do. The magistrate then sentenced them to thirty days in the workhouse.[11]

When Barbara's case came up, Mary wept, fearing that she'd get the same sentence as the other four. Barbara herself had fully expected to be sent to jail and had prepared a written statement in advance. She stood there, as Edmund Wilson described the scene, "like Joan of Arc, a pale slender figure alone before the judge." He never addressed her directly nor gave her a chance to speak. Instead, when her lawyer argued that it couldn't be proven that Barbara had obstructed traffic—that is, whether her legs had been inside or outside of a barrier demarcation—and asked that the case be dismissed, the judge declared that because "a doubt" did exist, he would grant the lawyer's request. Everyone was stunned at the unexpected verdict, and Barbara herself was "displeased" at having been treated more leniently than the other defendants.

Impressed by Barbara's presence at the two actions, A.J. Muste, one of CNVA's leaders, invited her early in 1962 to join the organization's Executive Committee. Through both her writing and her political work, Barbara was heading into the heart of the radical community. Mary, for her part, though admiring Barbara's growing commitment and the moral weight it drew out of her, wasn't temperamentally willing to match her political sense of purpose. Nor did she share Barbara's belief that everyone had a conscience, however buried, and that it could be discovered and cultivated; Mary equated conscience with guilt, as originally implanted by family.[12]

Along with politics, they would also argue about God, which Barbara—much like David—thought of as pure spirit, a notion that Mary resisted as much as she did the traditional image of a male personage, complete with long, white beard. Throughout their many talks on the subject, Barbara's mood would remain constant—"gentle, stubborn, profoundly searching," a "maddening calm" (to Mary) emanating from her, one annoyingly related to her "dogged will and absolute conviction of being in the right." Far from yielding to "the saint," but unable to match her relented arguments and feeling desperately cornered, Mary, by her own description, would sometimes snarl and snap. Yet she continued to admire Barbara's "serious face with its kind, mournful eyes," her "great patience," and her "searching and sensitive attention."

Another significant issue between them was their differing appetite for sex. Mary had, almost from the beginning, been somewhat alarmed at Barbara's ardor; her need for physical affection remained a constant, while Mary's diminished steadily and she grew more and more resistant, in the process becoming (by her own admission) somewhat "sulky" and resentful at their disparate needs. "Ours was the story," Mary later wrote, "of two bodies out of tune with each other." Barbara never fully fell out of love with her partners, but by 1962–63, the two women, after ten years of living together, had begun to draw apart.

During those same two years, Barbara's political activities continued to multiply. In 1962, following the abortive U.S. invasion of Cuba and the Kennedy-Khrushchev confrontation over Soviet missiles on that island, Barbara stepped up her advocacy for unilateral disarmament and was briefly arrested in a protest against atomic bomb tests. David, too, was outraged over the invasion. Even though he had "many disagreements" with the Castro government, he continued to support the Cuban Revolution and blamed the United States for forcing Cuba steadily "toward reliance on the Soviet Bloc." In the current crisis, David bent his energy toward persuading the Socialist Party to issue a forceful statement on the invasion that denounced Kennedy for reducing "the moral stature of this nation to that of the Soviet Union."

There was no basic difference, David argued, "between the events in Hungary and those in Cuba."

Barbara had become convinced that the issues of disarmament and black civil rights should properly be considered two parts of one struggle. She therefore decided to join CNVA's Nashville–to–Washington, D.C., biracial walk for peace. Many radicals thought it a mistake to combine the two issues, even though they were strong proponents of integration. They argued that those in the South who might otherwise be sympathetic to the peace movement would shy away if blacks were included. And blacks themselves, the argument went, would be harmed by the association, would hand their opponents the added ammunition of being called "unpatriotic." In fact, the walk ended up having, among the thirteen people who completed it, only one black participant.[13]

The ensuing prolonged argument over whether or not to link the two issues depressed Barbara. She felt it obvious that the same nonviolent strategy was common to both struggles and, furthermore, that they were naturally allied by their joint insistence that the country live up to the Declaration of Independence's statement that all men (that terminology still went unprotested in the early 1960s) were created equal and endowed with certain inalienable rights.

As late as 1964, in a lengthy letter to Muste and Dellinger, Barbara was still emphatically asking: *"Don't both movements perhaps stand in need of new help from each other?* . . . Hasn't the time come to try to define them much more clearly as part of *one* movement—a movement to try to bring into being (or more nearly into being) 'the beloved community,' a nonviolent world?" She argued that it was in the black struggle, above all, that one found "people awakened to the sharp sense that change is possible and necessary," a conviction that the peace movement was currently in need of. Besides, she felt that the peace movement was also a "freedom movement"—freedom from unemployment or demeaning employment, from the draft and war, from alignment with repressive regimes, and from the haunting fear of nuclear war.

When the 1962 march began in Nashville, to Barbara's consternation it passed right by a Student Nonviolent Coordinating Committee (SNCC) sit-in demonstration without even briefly pausing to show solidarity with the lunch-counter pickets. Yet two Fisk students who were members of SNCC did join the march for a time as it headed out of Nashville toward Knoxville. And as had been predicted by those opposing an integrated march, when Barbara tried to hand a leaflet to the white manager of a garage, he calmly told her that "they're going to shoot you a little farther down the line. They don't like niggers there, you see."

As if in confirmation, in Lebanon, a small town where they expected that night to sleep on the floor of a black church, a car full of young men slowed down near the marchers, and one of them leaned out to yell, "We're going to hang you all." Soon after, a second car sped by, and one of the occupants threw a Coke bottle at the marchers, hitting one of them in the ankle. Police cars also started driving by; one of the group cautioned against assuming that the police were concerned for their safety.

Arriving at the black Methodist church, members of the congregation started to pour in with a feast they'd prepared of fried chicken, peas, turnip greens, potato salad, and pie. Word about the march had spread through the local community, and soon the church filled up for a meeting. The minister spoke passionately about his hope that Lebanon would never forget what it had seen that day—the first integrated gathering of any kind that had occurred in the town. He told the congregants that they should no longer be fearful, that what they should be afraid of was continuing to be slaves.

The next day the marchers left for the town of Carthage, with warm waves of good-bye from much of the gathered Lebanon congregation. In Carthage, they had a similar welcome—a feast of food from the black community and a packed meeting inside the black church, complete with speeches and singing. But the first night after leaving Carthage, the marchers had their closest brush yet with violence. No one was present in the tiny one-room black church when they arrived, but someone appeared to say it was all right to sleep on the church floor. As they crawled into their sleeping bags, they suddenly heard a hail of rocks hitting the side of the building, one of them crashing through a window.

Stepping outside, they turned their flashlights on themselves to show they were unarmed, but the stones kept flying, and one of them hit the well-known pacifist Eric Weinberger on the side of his head, knocking him to the ground. Staggering up, he called out to his hidden assailants, "Why don't you come and talk with us?" Eventually seven or eight young working-class men emerged from the dark and started to exchange views. Several said that they might agree with some of the things the pacifists said about issues of peace and war, but they couldn't understand how they could be walking and sleeping with "a nigger." Then one of them asked the prototypical question: "Would you let a nigger marry your sister?" Yes, said a marcher who was himself a Southerner, but that decision, after all, would be entirely hers. Angry and disgusted, the entire group turned around and walked off.

But they came back, confirming Barbara's view that the success of nonviolence hinged on a combination of firmness with friendliness, and just as she had been beginning to wonder whether the two issues of race relations and pacifism *could* be discussed together. The talk then continued until one of the workmen said he had to be up early the next morning and should probably get some sleep. But before leaving, they shook hands with the Southern marcher who'd said he'd let his sister marry a black man. Barbara felt elated—and vindicated. She thought that maybe having a black man in their group *had* made it more difficult for their antagonists to listen to them on the question of nonviolence. But she decided that a black presence had also "snatched [the march] from the realm of the merely abstract," for the issue of war and peace "remains fundamentally the issue of whether or not one is going to be willing to respect one's fellow man."

As the new field secretary for the War Resisters League, David, beginning in October 1961, started to travel a good deal, with New England and then the Midwest as his initial points of concentration. He was a very skillful lecturer—passionate, lucid, not given to meandering, even funny—and his travels did help to expand WRL's membership and even led to the formation of several local affiliates. But after a lecture or discussion, David would be left feeling "really drained." For a respite, he needed to return to New York, usually after five or six weeks on the road, though on his initial trip his energy lasted for nearly two months. He got back to the city just before Christmas for a brief layover.

Paul Royce, his old love, had recently moved back to New York; the two of them reconnected and went to the theater together to see Genet's *The Balcony* and *The Blacks* (David's minimal comment: "Interesting"). David also picked up again with Alvin Ailey; he'd photographed

Alvin's company the previous summer, becoming so moved by the dancing that tears came to his eyes. Alvin and his troupe had recently climbed to the top of the ladder, getting rave reviews from, among others, John Martin, the dance critic for the *New York Times*.[14]

During his intervals in New York, David found time to do some more writing. He was beginning to get the reputation of being an astute political commentator, though he found the process of writing an "agony." Making it still more so, he thought of himself as something of a fraud: "I am always terrified that I shall be found out as a person who is not as expert, as clever, as I am taken for." He realized that he had a first-class intellect but felt it wasn't a "cultivated" one—meaning, apparently, that although he read widely, he consistently failed (in his view) to pursue a given theme in any depth; it was the price, he felt, of never having paid much attention to schoolwork.

Still, he began to get letters in response to various articles he'd written from as far away as California, Nebraska, and Europe. He also started to get offers from major publishing houses—Knopf, Macmillan, Dutton—to expand this or that article into a book or to collect his pieces for a volume. Seymour Krim, an influential writer and champion of the Beats, consistently urged David to do the latter.

Invited one night to a party at the then-famous Eighth Street Bookshop in the East Village, attended by, among many others, Allen Ginsberg and the unstable Carl Solomon, dedicatee of Ginsberg's *Howl*, During the party, David was taken aside by Eli Wilentz, one of the two brothers who owned the bookstore. He told David how impressed they'd been with the various pieces he'd written for the *Village Voice*; they felt that he represented "a fresh new voice," and urged him to collect his articles into a book.

The conversation flattered David but left him uneasy. He could acknowledge that all the encouragement he'd been getting provided *some* grounds for considering himself a writer, a long-sought dream that he hadn't ever fully allowed himself to entertain. He still resisted, insisting to himself that he "did not think clearly enough yet to carry off a book." But that was his old enemy, self-deprecation, whispering in his ear. In fact, his articles from the period are remarkable for their clarity and leanness, their candid, forceful, persuasive arguments.

Unusually self-aware, David recognized that what he called his "neurotic" reaction to encouragement was related to "a strange paradox."

In "defeat" he insisted to himself that he was superior to the general run of men, but in "victory" he was "plagued by a sense of gnawing doubt" and "of contempt for the others who have been deceived." In any case, it wouldn't be until 1970 that David would finally publish a collection of his essays—his first and, lamentably, only book. But at least in *The Village Voice Reader*, published in 1962, four of his essays were reprinted (no writer had more), and one was given the concluding spot.[15]

Though David avoided the idea of publishing his essays, he did begin to take notes for a planned book on a quite different subject—homosexuality. His working title was "The Gay Underground," and he intended to publish it under a pen name. David had made no secret about being gay, though he'd made neither a fuss nor a political cause out of his orientation. Either would have been difficult, for this was still pre-Stonewall. For a number of years, he'd spoken frankly about the subject even to his brother and to his parents. The new writing project had been triggered by a 1956 book his father had recommended: *Homosexuality: Disease or Way of Life?* It was the first of many works by Edmund Bergler, then a prominent psychiatrist who unequivocally came down—as did most psychiatrists of the day—on the side of "disease."[16]

David became "bitterly hostile" to the Bergler book and considered him "a fraud of sorts." He felt the book was basically "a load of nonsense," as well as inexcusably shoddy and inaccurate, and he mocked Bergler's notions that homosexuality always resulted from "a special psychic masochism" and was always possible to change. "Childhood background," David indignantly wrote his father, "is no excuse—the child (the child, mind you!) should have *chosen* differently!" He felt it was true that "many homosexuals seek punishment" but that was "primarily because they have contravened social mores and felt a deep sense of guilt [but] in a society where it was no sin, there would be no unconscious seeking for punishment." In response, David's father wrote him to say, "Surely there is room for at least a chapter in your book on the point that the violation of norms . . . takes its toll in human misery."

Though he considered Bergler "dangerous," David himself—here he was reflecting, not transcending, the ethos of the day—did agree that "homosexuality was a neurotic illness," not sin, not shameful, but not "healthy" either. Still, he wanted to refute most of Bergler, a wish that put David in the vanguard of a barely incipient movement, though he still couldn't "stand the gay world." He felt in a somewhat unique position to respond to Bergler, as "one of the few homosexuals whose life is integrated into normal society but who has never made any effort to hide." David apparently was unaware of *The Homosexual in America* (1951) by "Donald Webster Cory," the first positive nonfiction account of the gay male world. The author was actually the sociologist Edward Sagarin, who would later renounce the views in his own book.

David also wanted to examine, if not resolve, some of his own conflicted feelings on the subject. In these years a great many gay men weren't conflicted but rather shared the dominant view that homosexuality was rightly equated with pathology; those who could afford it presented themselves to a psychiatrist for "cure." David recognized what most therapists at the time ignored: that "they report only on the patients who come to them." What about himself? What about all those others who didn't go to therapists? Was it really logical to assume "that people who end up on the analyst's couch are a 'random sample' of the gay world?" He continued to object to making homosexuality "a way of life per se," to endure what for him was "the hell of the vibrant cha-cha life." In making this judgment, David was ignoring (or oblivious of) the large number of gay men who never or rarely participated in the bar or beach-party circuits. In any case, he felt that in choosing political involvement in a variety of social justice movements, which most gay people avoided, he'd rightly eschewed "escapism" and as a result "had made his life one that I would not for the world have missed. . . . There are very few people who find life as exciting as I do—my mild little crackup back in '58 notwithstanding."

Partial though David's appraisal of gay male life was, his insights into the mainstream view of homosexuality were keen, even when partly compromised by the time-bound assumptions he held regarding neurosis and normality. Despite his book's promise, he never got very far with it. Perhaps he was stymied by his doubts about whether he really was a writer. Perhaps his constant duties as field secretary for WRL—to say nothing of his ongoing commitment to *Liberation*, the Socialist Party, and a variety of other causes—left him little available time. The WRL alone kept him on the road attending gatherings and giving speeches for weeks at a time, often leaving him exhausted. Whatever the reasons, he let the promising book on homosexuality slide.

Yet he was hardly idle. After President Kennedy resumed atmospheric nuclear testing following the Soviet resumption in the fall of 1961, David played a major role in organizing one of the largest protest demonstrations that New York City had seen in some time—ten to fifteen thousand people—and he carried it off within twenty-four hours after Kennedy's announcement, rather than the usual three weeks it took to plan such events. He argued that socialists did not support the politics either of capitalism's military-industrial complex or of the totalitarian Soviet bloc. Furthermore, he chastised (though on the whole a staunch supporter) the burgeoning organization Students for a Democratic Society (SDS) for not being sufficiently anti-Communist, for the way at least some of its members apparently continued to believe, in their blanket dismissal of traditional anti-Communism, that the Soviet Union was sincerely interested in disarmament.[17]

David continued to write, though he confined himself mostly to short articles. His most significant pieces from the early 1960s were a defense of American Nazi leader George Lincoln Rockwell's right to free speech and his laudatory review of James Baldwin's collection of essays *The Fire Next Time*. In the Rockwell article, he also insisted that freedom of the press must extend to pornography—a matter over which he would later tangle with Barbara Deming. The Baldwin piece was a passionate one; David referred to the "appalling racial tyranny in this country" and argued that "the American Negro has less real human dignity granted him than the average citizen living under Soviet domination." By 1963 David was in no doubt that "as far as an area for action is concerned, civil rights is the major one . . . the front line . . . into which socialist energy should be directed."[18]

Barbara agreed with him. And like David, she did not, in the process of putting the black struggle at the top of her agenda, neglect her other political commitments. In another protest against atomic bomb tests, she was arrested (but not held). She also attended the HUAC hearings on Women Strike for Peace, one of the newer groups she'd joined, and she accompanied A.J. Muste to a five-day international conference— just fifty-five people from thirteen countries—in the hill town of

Broummana, Lebanon, to try to plan the initial projects for a World Peace Brigade for Nonviolent Action. The original idea had been Gandhi's; shortly before his assassination in 1948, he had called for such a meeting. The first project that emerged from the conference was a march into Northern Rhodesia (which in 1964 became Zambia) to protest the racist white government. The British stopped the marchers at the border. The nonviolent movement lacked the resources to sustain the World Peace Brigade, and it became inactive in 1964. (It would be reincarnated in 1981 as Peace Brigades International, and it continues to the present day.)[19]

The dramatic urgency of the black struggle within the United States itself did begin to occupy much of Barbara's attention. In early May 1963, she joined the demonstrations marking the inception of a full-scale assault against segregation in Birmingham. After walking half a block with a sign around her neck reading "All Men Are Brothers," she was arrested and jailed along with a group of protesters, most of them young black students. Even in jail, the authorities were appalled at the prospect of "integration" and immediately moved Barbara to the ward for white women, most of them imprisoned for drunkenness, "disorderly conduct," or prostitution. One guard openly suggested that her fellow prisoners rough Barbara up a little, and some of them did initially give her threatening looks. Though frightened, Barbara began to reach out to them. Most of the women in there were either sick (some had been deliberately deprived of their medicine) or in some kind of trouble, and they quickly responded to her friendly gestures. Toward the end of her stay, Barbara spoke openly to a few of them about how their own grievances logically put them in the streets "alongside the Negroes, petitioning those in power for the right to be treated like human beings."[20]

Barbara had been sentenced to six months, but after the case was appealed, she and others were released after six days. She checked into the Negro-owned Gaston Motel. The next day, the home of Rev. A.D. King, brother of Martin Luther King Jr., was bombed. Barbara rushed to the scene, and while she was viewing the destruction, another bomb wrecked part of the Gaston Motel. She began "to feel a sudden unpleasant catch in my stomach every time I step out into the street and see a white man. What is he going to do? So now I know what it is like. Now I am a Negro. Except that I can drive away from it."

And she did temporarily leave Birmingham, but returned in July for her trial, which brought no additional jail time. Back on the streets, Barbara witnessed Public Safety Commissioner "Bull" Connor's police turn their fire hoses on peaceful black demonstrators, the hoses so powerful that they stripped clothes from some of the people and bark from some of the trees—yet a few of the younger people still managed to leap high enough in the air, above the water, punctuating the sky with their FREEDOM! signs. Barbara went over to where the white reporters were gathered at the perimeter of the scene and asked one of them why he hadn't moved closer to get the full story. He barked, "No sense asking for trouble!" Not even in the name of freedom of the press? Barbara silently wondered.

She also attended several meetings in the packed Pilgrim Baptist Church and heard the prominent activist James Forman, Ralph Abernathy, an SCLC leader, and Martin Luther King Jr. encourage the crowd to be proud of who they were and the contributions they'd made to the country, to stick together during the demonstrations, and to be orderly throughout. She felt a special thrill when Martin Luther King—as if articulating her own earlier argument within the peace movement that the nonviolent pacifist struggle and the black struggle were as one—told the church audience that "we have a weapon that they can't handle. They don't know what to do with us when we are nonviolent. . . . You don't need to strike them in return, or curse them in return. Just keep going. Just keep presenting your body as a witness."

And Barbara did. She made the decision that she *would* march with the demonstrators—perhaps the murder of civil rights leader Medgar Evers the month before contributed to the decision—but then she temporarily got cold feet. Yet within a few days she managed to overcome her fear, thanks in large measure to the black community itself. As she moved more within it and black people embraced her as one of them, she caught something of their courage. One day she simply stepped off the curb and joined a group of demonstrators moving into the street. She found herself next to "a large, gentle woman" who'd brought along her three-year-old son. Barbara put a hand that she realized was trembling on the woman's shoulder. "Don't be afraid," the woman said. "I won't be," Barbara responded firmly, and taking the little boy by the hand, the three of them marched off together into the crowd.

Barbara's experiences in Birmingham led her to a whole new level of commitment to the black struggle. (Though Mary Meigs felt unable to participate directly, she sent SNCC a large contribution.) Barbara's primary moment of truth came in Albany, Georgia, which had been a key civil rights battleground since 1961. In October 1963, she joined the CNVA-sponsored Quebec-Washington-Guantanamo Peace Walk, which halted for two weeks in Atlanta after news arrived that President Kennedy, on November 22, 1963, had been assassinated in Dallas. After consultations all around, A.J. Muste and the activist leader Dave Dellinger advised from New York that the march pick up again, and thirty-six-year-old Brad Lyttle, the controversial, disciplined, and vigorous coordinator of CNVA, as well as (briefly) Dellinger himself, arrived to lead it.[21]

Barbara had originally intended to stay on the walk for three weeks, but by the time the group began to run into trouble as it headed out of Atlanta down to the town of Albany, 175 miles farther south, she "felt too tied to these people to be able to leave." As they moved into the Klan-dominated area surrounding Albany, signs of potentially dangerous confrontations began to appear. When they reached the town of Americus—where a month before local authorities had come close to executing four civil rights workers under a Reconstruction-era law against "seditious conspiracy"—Dellinger and Lyttle had to spend several days meeting with the town's officials to secure safe passage.

Barbara fretted that perhaps they'd passed through Americus *too* easily to mean anything to those who had to live there and struggle for their rights. Back in November, when they'd been briefly jailed in Macon for distributing leaflets and had begun a fast, a number of local people, black and white, had been drawn to the jail, and some of them had formed a picket line in front of it. In Americus, she worried, they would leave no mark but would pass through as privileged, untouchable transients.

But the larger town of Albany, which the marchers reached in early December, soon cured Barbara of her concerns. They were *not* about to be ignored or quickly passed through. For starters, local officials refused to let them even enter Albany without agreeing to comply with a variety of rigid restrictions, including marching on one street only—Oglethorpe, the line between the white and black communities—and refraining from passing out leaflets or other information. The marchers agreed—and then quickly proceeded to break the rules, walking down forbidden streets, carrying signs (END RACIAL DISCRIMINATION; LOVE, NOT HATE; and BREAD, NOT BOMBS), and passing out "inflammatory" material to onlookers.

They were arrested just as quickly. Or as Barbara later put it: "They throw us into jail—with the gesture of throwing us away. We serve our sentences and immediately turn up again, to repeat the act for which they arrested us." As each group was arrested, tried, and jailed, the news spread and others would show up, as if out of nowhere, to take their place. On December 23, the first group of fourteen was tried and jailed. Within days, six new recruits turned up from various parts of the country and stood outside the courthouse in the pouring rain to protest the sentences.

And so it went. The frustrated authorities terminated all sentences on January 15, 1964. Those released were soon back distributing leaflets and walking forbidden routes—and again were arrested. Dave Dellinger flew back down to Albany and spent eight days in jail. Ralph DiGia of the War Resisters League flew down and was also arrested. In *Prison Notes*, Barbara eloquently characterized the revolving process: "We assert: Here we are and we won't disappear. We assert at the same time, stubbornly: Our wills are our own. Those who hold power here are accustomed, like so many people, to treat others as though they were simply extensions of themselves; they think of 'their' Negroes, of their 'hands' at the mill. . . . We keep reminding them of the difference between their wishes and ours; we refuse to let them forget that they are imposing on us."

In the same way, the marchers, when arrested, refused to step meekly into the paddy wagons: they had to be carried—or dragged. Once in prison, most of those who were well enough fasted rather than eat the food put in front of them; several eventually had to be force-fed, but even then refused treatment as long as they could. As Barbara put it: "We let *them* do it." But she added, "certain tactics, such as 'going limp,' . . . [have] always been misunderstood to mean that our basic attitude is passive. The word coupled with 'passive' is forgotten— 'resistance.' It is also too bad that 'nonviolent action' describes merely what our actions are *not*; and in this term the word 'action' is forgotten."

Several blacks had been part of the walk for months, but two local black students now suddenly showed up in front of the jail and sang their hearts out in the rain, then returned to school before they could be arrested. The hope had been that a significant number of local blacks would participate, but for a time they remained wary. In 1961 and 1962, the militant new organization SNCC had helped to encourage the black community in Albany to engage in a series of demonstrations—the "Albany Movement"—and they'd been met with brutal beatings and imprisonment. That hadn't "defeated" their determination to end segregation, but it *had* succeeded, for a time, in a suspension of direct action. They'd learned that *they* would be the ones, after the SNCC students and marchers had passed through, left behind to face the wrath of Albany's white officialdom. Still, midway through the struggle, both the Albany Movement and the Albany Student Movement did bravely issue vigorous public statements on behalf of the walkers' civil liberties. It further convinced Barbara "that the struggle for rights for Negroes and the struggle for peace are properly speaking part of one and the same struggle."

Barbara was jailed on January 27, 1964, for what would be a month-long imprisonment. She frankly told her cellmates, most of them half her age, that she'd be unable to join those who planned to undertake full fasts; already thin, Barbara would only go so far as to eat half of one of the two meals served each day. Anything less, she feared, would lead to an early collapse and removal to a hospital. Barbara later heard that people closest to her were repelled at the very idea of hunger strikes. Her old love Vida Ginsberg "was altogether disgusted at the idea . . . fasting in public was like going to the bathroom in public." Even Mary Meigs criticized fasting as unfair to the officials responsible for the prisoners. Barbara agreed—to the limited extent that they'd put the prison doctor "in a painful position"; she counted it a "failure" on their part that they hadn't communicated with him better. Remarkably, given her depleted condition, she did manage to write Police Chief Laurie Pritchett in an effort to explain their fast: "It is a way of trying to communicate to you and to the other officials of this city that we are not concerned to win a personal victory in this struggle. We are concerned about what seem to us rights & wrongs. But we have no wish to harm anyone. We are very willing to bear the brunt of whatever suffering there has to be, ourselves." More remarkably still, she signed the letter, "Love to you."

Their steel cell contained only four bunks, with thin, filthy mattresses. The rest of them slept on the floor, only a single step possible in any direction. The cell also contained a small sink with cold water and a toilet with no cover. There was not even minimal privacy. No release from the cell was allowed day or night, not even for brief exercise. No meal hall existed; tin plates were simply shoved twice a day under the lowest bar. The only real light was a naked bulb hanging outside in the corridor, burning twenty-four hours a day. Noise was incessant. Pledges of love and flare-ups of anger were shouted from cell to cell, and the police were constantly cursing at top volume, banging their clubs along the bars, making sleep impossible or fleeting.

By coincidence, David, as the WRL's field secretary, had gone down to Athens, Georgia, a month earlier to give a scheduled lecture at the university on pacifism. By the time the Albany confrontation occurred, he was back in New York and immediately, along with Dick Gilpin, started working the phones on behalf of those who'd been jailed, even making calls to congressmen and senators, as well as to international figures, in an effort to find people in positions of prominence who might be able to put pressure on the Georgia authorities to release the prisoners. He felt especially worried about Barbara and Ralph DiGia, whom he knew were fasting; even though Barbara was taking some food, she'd been frail to begin with.

After nine days in lockup, the prisoners were finally brought to trial. Barbara was shocked at her own weakness when climbing the stairs into the courtroom, where she sat struggling not to faint. The judge sentenced the marchers to thirty days, with no time subtracted for the nine days already spent in jail. After the trial, four of the women, including Barbara, were moved into a different cell with slightly more space and given mattress covers. When Barbara tried to put hers on, she suddenly "felt my heart begin to stammer and all my remaining strength explode and give way." The city doctor showed up later in the day. He gave Barbara a vitamin pill but refused to examine her. Feeling steadily worse, she had a convulsion the next day and decided to eat part of breakfast as well as dinner. But for several days she lay in "a partial swoon, too weak even to wash," her dread of death growing. Then slowly she began to develop "a fragile equilibrium."

But she was still unable to sit up. A cellmate, frightened at the way

Barbara looked, begged the doctor to examine her. His reply: "She should expect to feel awful. . . . I don't know whether you're Communists or whether you're all crazy, but you're not Americans!" Trembling, he walked away. Barbara tried to comfort herself by remembering Gandhi's definition of nonviolence as "clinging to the truth," and by reminding herself that the action they'd taken in Albany had not been as "outsiders," that in the nuclear age "we were neighbors in a new sense, and we *have* to be able to talk with one another." But she felt that Albany's white population didn't "want people speaking freely, and for a simple reason: they [didn't] want Negroes to be able to speak out." So their peace *had* to "be disturbed; it [was] a false peace. And the order of which they speak is no true order; there are too many people for whose legitimate desires it allows no room."

Midway through their monthlong sentence, A.J. Muste, who'd himself been jailed numerous times, returned to Albany and was allowed to see the prisoners briefly. Nearing eighty, thin and pale, with little tufts of white hair, A.J. looked to Barbara as if he were "made of paper." He reported that he'd spoken with both Chief Pritchett and the city manager and had found Pritchett in particular to be "very rigid." But he added, trying to sound a hopeful note, that they were open to additional meetings and that the city manager seemed somewhat less hostile than the police chief.

After A.J. left, Barbara mulled over the "mistakes" they might have made that contributed to Pritchett being so unyielding in his belligerence. Perhaps they'd failed sufficiently to convey that the marchers had no wish to harm the white citizens of Albany. Certainly she, and A.J. as well, thought Brad Lyttle, before being jailed, had been mistaken in a speech that made angry reference to how costly to Albany the marchers could make their protest. Barbara also blamed herself and others for their laughter in court at some of the more grotesque remarks made by the city attorney. Laughing at opponents was no way to encourage reconciliation.

Barbara realized, of course, that "anyone would be a fool to count on securing justice by demonstrating friendliness alone." Refusal to cooperate with injustice was also essential. "We count," she wrote, "on the special effect that can be achieved when the two pressures—of friendliness and of disobedience—are exerted simultaneously." It was important to continually keep the two in balance: "The more un-cooperative we are, the more care we have to take to communicate friendliness too. It is hard . . . We cannot ever be sure of striking just the right balance." In her view, those employing nonviolence had to communicate "that we want no victory in the usual sense—are not concerned to see how much punishment we can deal out . . . if justice means anything, it means that those who have been opposing us will have rights too . . . refusal to hit back at any opponent or lie to him or trick him can inhibit him in his resort to violence, break the familiar circuit of vengeance and counter-vengeance."

Barbara wasn't naive, but she *was* visionary—saw as-yet-unfamiliar possibilities for what human beings might become and for the way they might interact with one another. Nor was David naive, though he had a less theoretical turn of mind than Barbara. Yet neither investigated in any depth (very few radical lefties ever have, Paul Goodman being one obvious exception) the suppositions about human nature that informed their beneficent assumptions regarding the efficacy of nonviolence. Nor has human nature, of course, ever been defined in a way that has remained stable for very long, quickly evolving in response to cultural shifts.

Those who champion biological explanations for human behavior, who insist that our actions are genetically and hormonally programmed—and thus intrinsic, unchanging, and universal—simply assume, despite limited empirical proof, that changes in cultural mores play an insignificant role in accounting for our "predetermined" actions. Those on the political right have all but uniformly subscribed to—but rarely examined—some version of Hobbes's characterization of human life in its natural state as "nasty, brutish, and short," a definition that has always served as an exemplary justification for elitist control of a dangerously immoral and combative populace.

Barbara never assumed that techniques of nonviolence could be counted on to work in all circumstances and with every individual; her mind was too subtle for that. Still, she did believe overall in its potency. Yet those who disagreed argued that she was, in several senses, "whistling Dixie." Yes, *perhaps* Gandhi had liberated India through nonviolence, but did he ever remotely convince dyed-in-the-wool British imperialists? Were other considerations the underlying reasons for British withdrawal—the unsustainable expense of empire or an attempt to try to outflank Indian Irreconcilables by transferring power to a new form (the Commonwealth) in order to retain it?

In arguing the efficacy of a friendly, patient, nonviolent response to adversarial rigidity, one that would ultimately move people toward uncomfortable reassessments, groups like the WRL could have cited in support of their position recent theorists of radical education, such as A.S. Neill, John Holt, Jonathan Kozol, or George Dennison, whose books and arguments were at the time so popular with the radical young. Not only were they not cited but, apparently, not read. This is curious, for the views of those advocating noncoercive, "free" schools closely paralleled and could have provided much positive reinforcement for many of the assumptions and arguments of those advocating nonviolence. Both movements contended that human nature was malleable and naturally drawn to affiliation and cooperation—rather than inherently aggressive and destructive.[22]

The peace movement might have been nourished and enhanced if made familiar with the findings A.S. Neill had offered decades earlier in his published accounts of the practices and results of his pioneering educational experiment, the Summerhill school. Generation after generation, despite the most damaging prior circumstances in which a child had been reared, Summerhill has demonstrated that if given enough time freed from rules, coercion, and adult interference, almost all the children were eventually able to discover their own real interests and to join responsibly in democratic community governance.

"Human nature," Neill and others in the "free schools" movement argued, might well be characterized to some limited extent by biological components, but is best defined by its overriding malleability. No left-wing movement—except, to some extent, the one during the 1960s—has yet paused to explore and debate the findings of such radical educators as to what human beings are or aren't capable of, though that is the obvious ground on which every effort at social change must succeed or fail. We debate instead such issues as why Marxian socialism (not Stalinist totalitarianism) has failed to take lasting hold in the United States, or why corporate capitalism, in its greediest, most corrupt form, has succeeded in blunting any sizable, sustained protest against its villainies.

Along with the findings of radical education, the sciences and social sciences of the last two decades have produced a significant body of supportive evidence that has also been ignored by political leftists, even though it provides crucial support for the view that greed, aggression, and combativeness are *not* biological in origin and that altruism, affiliation, and cooperation *are* innate ingredients of human nature. All of this may seem wholly irrelevant to understanding the course, say, of the peace movement, yet it might well be central to its analysis—and to any determination of what is feasible, what "human nature" will allow in the future.

Midway through her incarceration, Barbara feared that her stomach would rebel against the food—grits, bitter turnips, and black-eyed peas, over and over again—even though she ate little of it. On top of getting no exercise, her bowels were in a state of paralysis for several weeks, and she finally required a series of enemas. She also felt guilty that those of her cellmates who were fasting had to watch her attempts to eat, and she'd slide the tin plate into the corridor and around the corner so that they wouldn't have to look at it.[23]

After some three weeks had passed, most of the prisoners started to succumb to various debilitating illnesses. Writing on toilet paper, they tried to keep each other's spirits up by discussing favorite foods and trading wan little jokes: "Gingerbread with thick hot lemon sauce." "Man's most primitive urge is for gingerbread with heaps of whipped cream! Any other way, I'm sure, violates the collective soul." "The dinner of the week is fresh mushroom soup, quiche lorraine and raspberry sherbet with fancy cookies." "My recommendation for fasters: start out overweight, and have a slow metabolism!" Barbara put a quote from Blake on the wall:

> A robin redbreast in a cage
> Puts all heaven in a rage.

For the eight men (including Ralph DiGia, at forty-nine the oldest of the marchers; Barbara, three years younger, was second to Ralph) who'd been transferred to the Hole soon after sentencing, conditions were beyond any feints at humor. Squeezed into a filthy ten-by-twelve room already crowded with nine other prisoners and containing only six bunks (and no daylight), most of the limited sleeping was done on the floor, covered with unbelievably dirty mattresses.

Some of those in the Hole, and in the cells too, became so ill that Chief Pritchett began ordering selective force-feedings. In the cells, most talk and discussion had ceased. A.J. Muste and Dave Dellinger told Pritchett that they could no longer negotiate on behalf of those in jail; the prisoners themselves needed to express their collective will, and that in turn required one large meeting, with no police present. Pritchett agreed to let them congregate together in the widest section of the corridor. As they filed slow-motion into the space and gave each other frail embraces, Barbara was especially shocked at the changed appearance of the men, whom she hadn't seen since the trial.

One of the younger ones could barely speak; another, who Barbara had earlier thought had the look of an "impudent youth," now appeared as "a little anxious thin-lipped old man." Brad Lyttle's face, once brimming with energy and determination, now showed merely "a painful rigidity," with "only intellect and [a] stubbornly set will" apparent. Barbara herself must have been a similarly frightening apparition: when Dave Dellinger caught sight of her, he hugged her close and burst into tears.

Dellinger reported to the gathering that there seemed little awareness up north, and almost no publicity, about their ongoing struggle— let alone the fast that was taking place. The local Albany Movement itself had finally published statements in support of those in jail; from a long-range point of view that stand could erode the current power structure. But beyond that, Dellinger offered little hope that a continuation of the struggle would bring any decisive breakthrough. What he and A.J. needed to know was whether they wanted to serve out their sentences anyway.

Barbara found it difficult to speak, but she was among those who urged a continuation of the struggle in the name of possible long-term gains, especially for the black community. But more voices were heard on the other side of the argument, and for a time it seemed that a decisive vote to terminate was at hand. With her usual scrupulousness, Barbara worried that each side was trying to *coerce* the other—"and to force anyone into nonviolent struggle would be a contradiction in terms." In the upshot, it was decided to hold on for another week to show solidarity with an Albany Movement action then pending regarding voter registration, to see what would come of it.

Barbara felt relieved at the decision, but during the following days she felt for the first time "unutterably tired of being in here," felt it "harder than before to live through the hours"—a quite different feeling from her previous physical discomfort or bouts of fear and discouragement. She began to feel a stranger to herself, desolately unsure of who she was. Yet she held on.

As the days passed, A.J. reported that more reaction was coming in from prominent people. Norman Thomas, the liberal activist Norman Cousins, Congressman John Lindsay, and others had sent telegrams to the Albany authorities protesting the treatment of the prisoners. The Department of Justice had made inquiries. And one white Southerner had written a long letter of protest that appeared in the *Atlanta Constitution*. But as the days passed, there was also the steady physical deterioration among the inmates. Mary Suzuki, a young Canadian student who had become one of Barbara's favorite people, had grown "thin as cardboard" and coughed constantly. Another young woman had withdrawn entirely into herself, apparently asleep most of the time. And yet a third haunted Barbara with her haggard look and her yellow hair "plastered to the side of her head strangely, as though she had just been pulled up from the bottom of a well."

Even staunch Ray Robinson of Washington, D.C., Barbara's close black friend throughout the march—he was killed in 1973 during the Wounded Knee protest—finally had some candy and broke his fast. Only six women and five men continued to refuse food of any kind. And so it went. Nobody's health was improving. Yet when the day finally came (Barbara's twenty-seventh) when some sort of vague compromise was reached with the authorities about the route the marchers would take out of town, and their release seemed imminent, the bonds between them had grown so strong that it was painful to consider the prospect of parting. As Barbara later wrote to Mary Suzuki, "It's that we endured something together, of course, isn't it? But more than that, too—it's that together we were at least attempting an action that would speak to men's hearts. And so our own hearts more easily burst."

The marchers limped out of Albany on February 24, 1964, and headed to Koinonia Farm, a Christian farm community in Americus. Koinonia had been a haven for racial equality and had suffered bombs and bullets as a consequence. (It was later the birthplace of Habitat for Humanity, among other organizations.) There in the farm community the straggly band rested and recuperated for several weeks. Reports came to them that the Albany Movement's voter-registration demonstration had been well attended—with Chief Pritchett making no move to stop it or to arrest anyone. They were thrilled to hear that he "*could* be budged." Barbara believed they had also made the white people of Albany feel that "they could *not* put us from them. . . . We tried, however clumsily, to act out the truth that all men are kin to one another."

After gaining strength and making basic repairs to their bodies, some of the marchers, including Ray Robinson, Brad Lyttle, and Mary Suzuki, continued the Quebec-Washington-Guantanamo Walk, arriving in Miami on May 29. Then, in late October, six of them attempted to sail a small boat, *Spirit of Freedom*, to Havana, but the U.S. Coast Guard stood in their path and confiscated their boat.

As for a worn-out Barbara, she returned by bus to her home in Wellfleet, where, as she wrote Mary Suzuki, she sat for weeks and weeks "able to do little more than stare at the birds and the bushes." More than six months later, her health largely restored, she responded to Suzuki's question about what allows some people to treat others in such inhuman ways: "Isn't it, above all, fear for their *own* lives? And a crude feeling—often amounting, virtually, to a belief in magic—that they can make their own lives more secure and more abundant by cutting others off from them? Our faith is the opposite—that we are 'members one of the other.' And can only find our own lives if we recognize this and act upon it."

4

The Personal and the Political—the Early 1960s

David McReynolds had been a longtime supporter of the move-ment for black civil rights and had already spent a night in jail for attending a civil rights meeting. When Barbara had been in Birming-ham, David, as the WRL's field secretary, had been on a five-week speaking tour in Virginia, Florida, Louisiana, and North Carolina. It was his first time in the South since 1949, when he'd passed through and "with the courage or foolishness of the very young" had attempted every time he got on a bus to sit in the colored section.[1]

David had a knack for quickly sensing shifts in the cultural climate, and by the early 1960s he picked up on how militant younger blacks had become since 1949: "The Negro emerging now does not want to lose his blackness. And if he shakes my hand now, I gain the sense of touching a courage I do not see in myself and wonder at." David was also astonished that so many black churchgoers, despite "every wicked cruel thing we could do . . . have not yet given way to hatred, that their leaders still preach love, that in the hearts of their student leader-ship there is still somehow, despite everything, the conviction that the white man is the Negro's equal."

Yet David did feel that among the growing number of younger militants, nonviolence was wearing thin as a tactic and that contempt for Martin Luther King Jr. was growing. He felt no surprise at this, nor at the growth of the Black Muslim movement in the North; after all, "twenty million Americans are living in conditions which, in most cases, are far worse than those in Moscow." Given the stubbornness of most Southern whites in resisting change, David predicted that it was "inevitable that federal troops will finally have to be used." He was pleased to discover that a number of "courageous Southern whites"— including a friend from UCLA, Guy Carawan, the folksinger—now worked openly in the civil rights struggle and that within some of the larger cities, especially Atlanta and New Orleans, there was "a more relaxed interracial atmosphere than I generally find in the North."

David wrote up his experience on the WRL speaking tour for the *Village Voice*—a curious little piece entitled "Two Faces of Dixie." In it he labeled white Southern racism a "mental illness" and stated that "it is absolutely true that very few white Southerners want to grant the Negro his rights." But he also argued that after spending five weeks in the South, he'd come to realize that racism there was "more complex and more troubled" than most Northerners, himself included, had assumed. David omitted any specifics, but he may well have meant the increased involvement of at least some Southern whites, and the increased militancy of many younger blacks.[2]

Nor did David any longer feel, as he wrote in the *Voice* piece, that the North was entitled to congratulate itself to any degree: in his opinion life in Harlem "was no better and, perhaps, worse than it was twenty years ago," and Negroes were no "less demoralized and unemployed and subject to police brutality." David did well to underscore the fact that white Northern racism was far more profound than many liberals were willing to see or acknowledge. Yet bad though conditions in the North were, he was on somewhat less firm ground in equating them with the terror-riding Klan in the South or the "grandfather clauses" and poll taxes that all but uniformly denied blacks the right to vote.

More arguable still was David's view of Southern history—a view, it should quickly be added, shared by most professional historians of the day (meaning, mostly white men). Today it's no longer the consensus view that the South's "finest minds"—as David wrote in his *Voice* essay—knew that slavery was wrong, nor any longer agreed that the period of Reconstruction "was a period of horror" during which the North inflicted upon the South policies "so vengeful and destructive" as to affect the region for decades (true from the perspective of most whites, though certainly not most blacks). It's impossible, no matter how radical one's politics, ever to be entirely free of the mainstream assumptions of one's own day. In this, David was no exception—though more nearly so than the vast majority of his contemporaries.

After something of an internal struggle, the War Resisters League abandoned its single-minded focus on pacifism and wholeheartedly embraced the tactics of militant direct action and civil disobedience. (As far back as April 1961, David had forcefully defended such tactics in two articles in the *Voice*.) The WRL, moreover, now unambiguously aligned itself with a broadening range of political developments: the rebirth of student militancy, as represented by Students for a Democratic Society (SDS); mounting protest against escalating U.S. intervention in Vietnam (WRL was among the earliest critics of U.S. policy, staging in 1963 the first major antiwar protest); and the growing combativeness of the black struggle as epitomized by CORE and SNCC's intensifying shift from appeals to the national conscience and reliance on the power of redemptive love to an emphasis on self-reliance and self-defense.[3]

The entire WRL office was closed so that the staff and volunteers could join the August 28, 1963, March on Washington. The WRL had earlier released Bayard Rustin from his duties as executive secretary to allow him to work full-time on the historic event. Tom Kahn, Bayard's previous lover, and Norman Hill—both of them members of the Socialist Party—also contributed yeoman work. Bayard carried out his role as the march's primary organizer with remarkable skill—in all, some 250,000 people attended—but not before having to deal with some ugly efforts to remove him.[4]

Even though Bayard's homosexuality was well known within limited political circles, the racist senator Strom Thurmond, in an effort to discredit the march, revealed details of Bayard's arrest ten years earlier for homosexual behavior and had the statement that Rustin was a "sex pervert" read into the *Congressional Record*. Thurmond expected his revelations to ruin Rustin and besmirch the march, but the civil rights leadership, led by A. Philip Randolph, brushed off the attack and focused on praising Bayard's organizational skills. Behind the scenes, the conservative black leader Roy Wilkins, of the NAACP, demanded that Randolph, national leader of the march, remove Rustin from further participation.

Randolph refused. Bayard, he said, had "suffered enough." As early as 1960, he'd been forced to take a semi-covert role in the civil rights movement, even though, as Randolph put it, his contributions had far outweighed any private "error" he may have committed. Thurmond had waited too long to drop his bomb: the march was only a few weeks off and besides, by *triply* indicting Bayard as a communist, a draft dodger, and a homosexual, Thurmond had so overloaded his accusation that he'd given even devout black church leaders elbow room to persuade themselves that Bayard had been falsely accused of being homosexual.

The march itself overjoyed David. The bus he came down on—one of hundreds—arrived just as the huge gathering started down Constitution Avenue. As he eloquently described the scene in a letter to his old friend Vern Davidson, the crowd moved "from sidewalk to sidewalk, like a wall of black lava dotted with bits of white debris, carrying along an uprooted forest of placards and signs that seemed to float on top of the enormous, very slow moving mass of people." David believed that most of white Washington had been "scared shitless," certain that massive violence would break out—yet not one act of violence nor one arrest took place, which David thought "a miracle." That evening in D.C., the War Resisters League held a mammoth, joyful gathering, the hall filling up before the scheduled opening time, with a patient line of hopefuls stretched two deep all around the block.

A few weeks later, David was back in the Deep South, touring again for the League. He heard of Kennedy's assassination while speaking in Athens, Georgia, where Barbara and her group were imprisoned. David had never been a fan of Kennedy's, yet the news "stunned" him. He felt "considerable confidence" in Lyndon Johnson—which would change after he escalated the war in Vietnam—and predicted that Johnson "will make a strong President, and probably a good one."[5]

Soon after, in Chapel Hill, North Carolina, David and three friends (one white, the other two black) were arrested and jailed when they tried to eat together in a restaurant that "didn't serve Negroes"; when they refused to leave, the furious manager called the police. They'd been in jail only a short time when the four men heard singing outside the prison—"We Shall Not Be Moved," "We Shall Overcome," and other movement songs. Soon after, one of the guards abruptly told them that they were free to leave: someone had anonymously put up their bail. When they walked out of the jail, the crowd gathered outside broke into applause; after singing together for a while in the rain, they all marched off and walked two by two back to town.[6]

As had happened with the League in the late 1950s, the Socialist Party in the early to mid 1960s became rent with contention and potential division. At the center of it was Max Shachtman, whose Independent Socialist League (ISL) David had earlier worked so hard to incorporate into the SP. Shachtman, whom David described as "a man without morality but of great charisma," had been heading steadily toward the Right, supporting at every turn the Johnson administration. In doing so, he'd managed to alienate SNCC by backing the decision to seat only two delegates from the radical Mississippi Freedom Democratic Party at its national convention. He'd also refused to condemn the U.S. invasion of Cuba at the Bay of Pigs, and his growing alliance with George Meany and the AFL-CIO's most hawkish elements would essentially become pro-imperialist.

Much of the tension came to a head at the Socialist Party's national convention in Chicago in late May 1964, when David and others came out strongly against Shachtman's "realignment" plan. As David put it in a widely circulated memo, "The Realignment leadership tends to urge a softening of Civil Rights militancy in order not to damage chances of penetrating the 'official establishment' and influencing it." The memo also denounced those "sections of labor opposed to the kind of political and economic changes which must occur if the Negro is to become a full part of American society." An ally of David's put the matter even more strongly: "They urge us to go into the Democratic Party and try to take it over. An inevitable consequence of that is to ask the civil rights movement to 'hold back' in deference to the Democratic Party's need" to win the upcoming presidential election for Johnson over Goldwater.

David believed that the realignment move was just a cover for a general "flight to the right" on all questions, including opposition to the war in Vietnam. As he saw it, Shachtman had "scoffed at, derided, denigrated and dismissed" the party's foreign policy positions adopted at the SP's last convention in 1962. Though the 1964 convention refused to endorse the presidential candidates of either major party, David remained dissatisfied. He thought a more forceful stand against U.S. foreign policy in general should have been passed. And he was shocked when Norman Thomas, who shared many of his views, was greeted with scattered booing when he made an appearance at the convention.

Soon after, David made a dramatic decision. He resigned all the posts he held in the SP, including membership on the National Committee. Yet he retained his membership in the party; as a democratic socialist, he felt there was "nowhere else really to go." He even, in the spring of that year, went on a speaking tour under SP auspices to Indiana. But as the war deepened and the SP's opposition to it did not, David felt "deeply discouraged" about the party, more and more convinced that it was "completely irrelevant to everything which is going on at the present time."[7]

He drew a fuller picture of his position on Vietnam in a 1964 joint statement that he wrote and A.J. Muste cosigned. He began by reviewing some history. When the French had withdrawn from Indochina in 1954 and the Geneva Accords had been signed (but not by the United States), Francis Cardinal Spellman and other right-wingers successfully prevailed upon Ngo Dinh Diem, a devout Catholic living in the United States, to return to South Vietnam to take over the government from the discredited leader Bao Dai. Internationally supervised free elections were supposed to follow both in South and North Vietnam, but since everyone knew that Ho Chi Minh, leader of the struggle against the French, would easily win both elections, Diem flatly refused to hold them in the South. His rejection, coupled with increased corruption in the government and growing repression of the Buddhists, produced a resurgence of guerrilla war led by the National Front for the Liberation of South Vietnam (NLF), which initially was not, as most Americans were told and for too long believed, simply a Communist organization but a coalition of resistance groups.

The United States, in direct violation of the Geneva Accords, immediately moved to counter the NLF. Calling its troops "advisers" and insisting that a vast amount of military equipment was pouring into South Vietnam from the North to assist the rebels, the U.S. gradually escalated its involvement even before Johnson assumed the presidency.

The Diem regime fell in 1963, replaced at first by a military junta and then by General Nguyen Khanh. At this point, there had *not* been a massive intervention of troops and supplies from the North. The U.S. suppressed that fact to justify its growing presence, as it would later deny the full extent of its napalm bombing and strafing in Laos and Cambodia, as well as in Vietnam.[8]

David knew far more about recent U.S. foreign policy than did the vast majority of Americans, who simply accepted their government's rationale for its assorted interventions in support of dictatorships around the globe and ignored or shouted down those "unpatriotic" citizens who suggested alternate explanations. The true history of U.S. foreign policy in the years since World War II included the CIA's restoration in 1953 of the Shah of Iran to his throne to protect American oil interests, the 1954 invasion of Guatemala to overthrow a democratically elected government (and protect the interests of the United Fruit Company), and the impeccably consistent policy of our leaders to keep in power a long list of brutal anticommunist dictators including Somoza in Nicaragua, Batista in Cuba, Duvalier in Haiti, and Trujillo in the Dominican Republic. It was hardly surprising, therefore, that the U.S. supported a government in South Vietnam that refused elections and violently suppressed all opposition.

During this period of intense political engagement, David tried various ways of decreasing his stress. He realized how long it had been since he'd gone to the theater or a dance concert or a poetry reading and, in parallel, how much his drinking and smoking had increased. He decided to take up hatha yoga and began morning meditation based on Buddhist texts—which he could rarely manage for more than ten minutes, given his inability ever to make his mind "blank." Before long he was calling himself an "atheist with Buddhist leanings," even if the Buddhist part was confined to baby steps. And though no causal connection was claimed, love reentered his life after a long drought, in the form of one Peter Stafford.[9]

They'd first met in 1963 in Portland, Oregon, while David was on one of his speaking tours. Having read David's articles in the *Village Voice*, Pete was already an admirer and after David's speech asked if he'd join him and a friend at dinner. Pete, at twenty-four, ten years younger than David, was just over six feet tall and fair-complexioned, with long, flowing light brown hair. At first glance, he looked ungainly and homely. But at second glance, David found him "incredibly attractive" and "sexual without being aware of it (indeed precisely because not aware of it)." David was immediately smitten but assumed that Pete was straight and unavailable. They did have a second dinner together, but David never even thought to get Pete's phone number and address when he left Portland.

Nearly a year later, in the spring of 1964, Pete moved to New York to try to get a contract for his book in progress about psychedelic drugs. He had no other occupation and was living frugally on some limited funds he'd saved. David was astonished to get a phone call from him. The two began to meet often and soon learned more about each other. It turned out that Pete had spent the past three summers as a forest lookout, cut off from everything and everyone—and didn't seem to have minded a bit.[10]

Pete's family background was White Russian. He was an aristocrat on his mother's side, her father having owned a large estate just outside of Moscow, which he had to abandon when the revolution came. David felt that some of Pete's most prominent traits came from that "certain kind of Russian:—the thin, narrow features, the fervid, erratic imagination, the glory in ideas." On Pete's paternal side, the story was far more turbulent. His wealthy grandfather had left Pete some sort of trust fund amounting to half a million dollars, but which he could draw on only after his own father's death. It was unclear how much of the money had already been spent, for Pete's father was an abusive alcoholic who terrorized his family and then abandoned them when Pete was still a small child. All that Pete really remembered about him was cowering under the table "while things were being thrown about."

Pete had several traits in common with David's previous lover Paul Royce. He, too, was a would-be writer and didn't (while with David, that is) regard himself as homosexual. Pete described himself in a letter to David as "an awkward, cheerful, pleasant-innocent kind of guy." David thought him "lovely looking" and "sweet," and found himself filled with "joy and satisfaction and even peace" when they were together. He would "only say [that Pete] is my friend," feeling sure, though hoping otherwise, that the relationship wouldn't last very long.

("A day, an hour, a moment and it will be gone," he wrote his brother, "and to define the situation—at least to him—would be to bring it to an end.")

For three years prior to meeting Pete, David had been sharing his apartment with Tico, a Jamaican man who had strong feelings for him which David didn't reciprocate. They'd been on the verge of breaking up when, at the end of June, Pete asked if he could move in. David was delighted and immediately agreed, though he asked Pete to wait until the end of July; David had promised to spend the month with his family on the West Coast and, scrupulous as always, didn't want to hurt Tico needlessly or to give him the sense of being abruptly pushed out.

The trip to California proved depressing, and not simply because David missed Pete terribly (though he didn't dare say as much in a letter). For one thing, David felt guilty that he wasn't in Mississippi, where several friends of his had gone to take part in "Freedom Summer." For another, he found his parents looking considerably older, especially his father, who now had a heart condition and had withdrawn still further into a kind of dogmatic distance. The house, moreover, was stocked with things like Reader's Digest book condensations and stereo records featuring "music to dine by" and the like—not exactly David's cup of tea.

His sense of dislocation was further deepened when he sought out old friends from his Ocean Park days. He soon discovered that most of them had moved away and that "the sites of old joys"—like the Tropic Village—had been demolished. His beach shack on Ashland Avenue had also been torn down, leaving two blocks of vacant lots. But at least he found one old friend, the Communist Party leader Dorothy Healey, and they spent a couple of hours together—"really rather funny," he wrote Pete, "a member of the SP's National Committee [he hadn't yet resigned] and a member of the CP's National Committee in a random sort of chat."

David spent one weekend out in the desert visiting his paternal grandparents. Five years earlier, when both were eighty, they'd pulled up stakes in Glendale, built a modern house in Joshua Tree, a full hundred miles from L.A. (and family), and loaded it up with their anything-but-modern furniture. It had something to do with "the pioneering

87

spirit": in 1884, when five years old, they'd both left the Midwest with their parents and headed out to a largely unsettled California still primarily tied to Mexican culture.

Now in 1964, when David visited, Joshua Tree was spilling over with people, and he even managed to locate a gay bar. He usually avoided them, but he was curious to see what the locals looked like and was taken aback by their "normal" appearance; "I couldn't, for once, and for the life of me," he wrote Pete, "really tell the guys were homosexual except for the fact they were in the bar—jammed, crowded, jolly, tanned, open-faced, youthful, attractive."

The letters he wrote Pete were full of a sort of timid tenderness. In one, he put his feelings into caps so that Pete would be sure to notice: "I MISS YOU AND AM AFRAID TO TELL YOU. I NEED YOU, AND DON'T KNOW IF IT IS WISE TO LET YOU KNOW . . . I AM AFRAID YOU WILL CHANGE YOUR MIND, BE GONE, BE ELSEWHERE, WHEN I GET BACK."

Pete wrote back and reassured him: "How unsure and how touching—your fear that I'll run away just before you get back . . . because just as you need me, I need you. . . . You're a very special someone, Dave, an exception from the insensitivity of most, someone I immensely like and feel comfortable around." He added, appealingly, that his "immense admiration and respect alone" for David "wouldn't interest me very much in sharing a place. Rather it's the things you somehow feel ashamed or embarrassed or frightened to admit—the fact, for instance, that we're in a special sort of sense equals, that we try to reject a clinging to the half-good and pleasantly beautiful. I only like, as do you, those who know and admit that they are weak (as I am terribly so), who are innocent, gentle, guileless and compassionate, who need to be needed . . . we'll have to work on your self-assurance when you get here. . . . I think you should understand that I am one of the most celibate of men, that I hardly lead a wild sex life, that I don't generally go to bed with someone unless there are many connections going between us on various levels." If not exactly a declaration of love, this was far more than David had dreamed of.

As promised, Pete met him at the airport and soon moved in, though David still felt that before long he'd be "closed out by some woman." Even after they'd lived together for nine months, David wrote his gay friend and political comrade Vern Davidson "I still can't really believe it . . . the impossible dream we all have has been fulfilled for me." Yet he had to add—almost as a talisman—"all things will end, will close upon themselves and vanish."

He warned Pete that people would make immediate assumptions about the nature of their relationship, but Pete assured him that he'd thought it all through. A number of his "hip" friends in the Village had already warned him, strenuously, that he was making a terrible mistake. In the mid-1960s, interracial marriage was still able to cause a great deal of alarm among purportedly advanced "champions of freedom," but homosexuality was definitely beyond the pale.

Soon after arriving back home David suddenly—as is often the way with major depression—had an attack of profound terror, the first in six years. Knowing the signs, he wasn't as frightened as during the earlier events, but he was just as symptomatic—weak, sweating, excessively shaky and with "a sense of foreboding so great that one cannot be interested in food or sex or politics, a complete lack of interest in *anything*." He took three tranquilizers and slept for twelve hours. The next day he felt somewhat better, enough at a distance from the attack to start analyzing it.

He thought that perhaps "accumulated tension" had brought on the combined anxiety attack and depression, but it seemed more likely to him that it was due to "the situation with Peter." He simply couldn't get used to "having someone around who accepts me, wants to share things with me." Perhaps this was all part of "growing up, which requires being broken down in parts and shattered . . . learning to be committed even though you know you will later be shattered again when, as always, commitments fall through. Doubly so in a case like this, where not only are homosexual relationships unstable, but Peter isn't even in any proper sense a homosexual."

Pete shared most of David's political views and even before moving in had offered to do volunteer work for the War Resisters League. They were glad to have him. He did everything from some writing and mimeographing to serving a summons on the president of a longshoremen's union for trying to block the candidacies of two radical nominees for office. But center stage politically during this period was the pending presidential election.

In *Liberation* magazine, David and Dave Dellinger debated the election in late 1964. David argued for the importance of defeating

Goldwater, despite his uneasiness over Johnson's not yet fully crystal-lized policy about the scale of U.S. intervention in Vietnam and his awareness that "Johnson's business dealings were cheap and shoddy and immoral." As early as July 1964, the WRL had issued a memo call-ing for the unconditional withdrawal of all American troops from Indochina and also cosponsored a protest outside the Democratic Convention that drew some four hundred people.[11]

In this pre-election period, David did feel that it was important for Goldwater to be handed a decisive defeat. He thought Goldwater's "charm" and "decency" were real but that those qualities "would make him an excellent mayor of Phoenix, Arizona," not an excellent presi-dent. In David's view, Goldwater was "not really bright," and he was far too "old-fashioned, badly informed and often wrong." He had, as one example, managed to travel the South during his campaign "with-out saying a single clear word about segregation." Instead, he spoke of his bitter opposition to the Civil Rights Bill as an unwarranted inter-vention of the federal government into the rights of the states.

David was relieved when the November 1964 presidential election gave Johnson a landslide victory. But in the months that followed, satisfaction quickly gave way to profound disgruntlement on many fronts. Johnson soon became convinced that American involvement in Southeast Asia should be intensified; in 1965 he began a sustained bombing campaign against North Vietnam and a steady buildup of combat troops. By the end of the year, there would be nearly two hun-dred thousand American soldiers in South Vietnam—with more on the way.

When the first nationwide demonstration against the war came, on December 19, 1964, David served as coordinator for the protests and he joined Norman Thomas, A.J. Muste, and A. Philip Randolph in addressing the large crowd that assembled in New York City to de-nounce the U.S. presence in Indochina. Later that month, David also published a scathing piece in the *Village Voice* ("Vietnam Is Our Hun-gary") condemning the government's immorality in spreading false-hoods about the war. Along with much else, he called out Secretary of State Dean Rusk for reiterating the untruth that North Vietnam had been sending in "massive shipments" of arms to supply the National Liberation Front (NLF), when he knew perfectly well that only a trickle had come in that way. Most (the *New York Times* put the figure at 75 percent, *Business Week* at 90 percent) of the NLF's weapons were captured American-made stock. The public was also being constantly told that South Vietnam was a democracy, when in fact it was an incompetent dictatorship and no free elections had ever been held there—and if they had been, the Communist leader Ho Chi Minh, a national hero because of his earlier victory over the French, would have won them.

Not that David held any brief for the NLF; he was quick to acknowledge that it—like the United States—was spreading terror and if successful would establish a repressive Communist regime. David was among the very few activists on any side of an argument during this period who would refuse to deny evidence that contradicted his own position. He also chastised an "intellectual community" whose primary concern to date seemed to be that an escalation of the war might cost American lives. David's rejoinder was that as of the close of 1964, just over two hundred American lives had been lost—versus 79,000 Vietnamese. He caustically pointed this out to George Kennan, who in late November had argued in the *New York Times Magazine* that we ought not be too critical of our government lest we endanger the U.S. soldiers risking their lives (shades of the same twenty-first-century arguments made about the wars in Iraq and Afghanistan!).

At the same time, black civil rights groups and student organizations like SDS were becoming more militant. This would lead to further divisions within pacifist and socialist ranks about what their appropriate response should be to groups like the Black Panthers and to individuals like the SNCC leaders H. Rap Brown or Stokely Carmichael—who probably didn't much care, as peace and socialist organizations had small memberships and little direct influence. The WRL had a mere three thousand people who received its literature and only two thousand who were actual members; the figures for the Socialist Party were still lower. Even *Liberation*, probably the leading left-wing publication, had a limited subscription list, and its board of editors was becoming torn by disagreements.

David became deeply troubled by these developments and increasingly active in regard to them, constantly flying off to give speeches and attend meetings. In May 1965, he despairingly wrote in a letter, "I am now almost paralyzed by Johnson. I will say only that what the Nazis were in the 40's to most of the world, and what the Communists were in the 50's, the U.S. is today . . . the depth of my bitterness just now is such that it is best I shift off politics"—that is, in the letter, not in life.[12]

But at least David could turn to the comfort of his relationship with Pete, which served as an enormous source of disbelieving pleasure and consolation for him. It also brought out David's lyrical strain; when, in February 1965, he was out at the University of California at Berkeley, where he addressed a crowd of a thousand students on the steps of Sproul Hall, he found time to send Pete tender messages: "Come softly here, into this shelter where harshness is only voice deep. Put out your hand, lay here beside me, and do not disdain my tongue, which will speak a better language when it is silenced against your body."

But there were tensions in the relationship too. After they'd been together a year and a half, Pete took a three-week vacation to California and hinted that he might soon go back there for good. He didn't, but when David returned from an out-of-town speaking engagement in September 1965, he found Pete, his girlfriend (about whom David had earlier been informed), and another young man naked in bed. David tried for a casual approach: as he wrote his brother, "Pete is very relaxed," he "makes sex into something very simple, which it should be." Besides, he told himself, it's Pete's apartment too. But David couldn't stick with the offhand approach for more than a few days— not when another young woman seemed about to move in, someone Pete had earlier had an affair with, and not when, as David arrived at the apartment, she was having sex in the back room with the same young man he'd earlier seen naked.

David's surface acceptance cracked; he felt "so excluded, so lonely" that he broke down and cried, though later, typically, he blamed himself for being "so hard to live with." Was what he'd witnessed, he asked himself, any "worse than homosexual orgies?" After all, he knew that Pete wasn't to any degree hustling him—he was "one of the most fundamentally decent people I've ever known. We remain mysterious and important to one another."

But he did have to admit that Pete was often reluctant to have sex with him and was only uninhibited in bed "when he is feeling very joyous or a little drunk" or stoned on pot. David decided he'd try to take his friend Allen Ginsberg as a model: Allen and his lover Peter Orlovsky were still together because "Ginsberg has had to learn to make it with women, since Orlovsky 'digs girls.' " David told himself that he, too, must have a buried heterosexual drive; after all, he did strongly believe that if heterosexuals repressed their homosexual urges, then the same is true in reverse.

He felt that "oddly enough the freedom of the last two years" had left him wanting to move beyond homosexuality, though not beyond Peter, to move more deeply, which would mean "not the abandoning of homosexuality but the ability to accept women as sexual persons." And he wanted to accept himself as capable—as he felt everyone was—of "stepping beyond homosexuality." He felt it was late in his life, at thirty-seven, "to step beyond anything . . . but one can always strive toward openings. . . . It is as if, having for the first time in my life entered a relationship where I did not feel guilt, and where the act is playful and not the using of one person by another, . . . [I can see sexuality] as a form of communication to be more widely engaged in."

David wasn't advocating casual sex—he'd had twenty years of experience with strangers and found it generally unsatisfying—but rather was trying to duplicate what most "baffled" him about Peter, "the a-sexuality of his drives." It wasn't gender or age that determined Peter's choices "but simply whether he likes the person and whether he feels like 'communicating' in that way. There is, for him, no sense of jealousy because there is nothing exclusive in the action." Sex wasn't urgent for Peter; he saw it as one means to the important end of deepening a relationship with someone he liked.

In straining to reach that new ideal, David was doing his best—a brave attempt in someone approaching forty—to accept the latest wave of cultural change, even if he did lag behind the new generation in belatedly acknowledging that women were sexual beings. In particular, he was slow to adopt the as yet barely articulated countercultural challenge to the standard view that homosexuality and heterosexuality were separate categories of being, airtight containers that never touched, let alone combined, in an individual.

He did manage a few rounds of heterosexuality; in fact, he'd had one or two earlier. But even with the help of peyote, willpower proved unable to overcome his deeply imprinted orientation. As he wrote his parents, with remarkable frankness, "I am too old now, and have gone through far too much, to make the adjustments that I might have wanted when I was younger." But from knowing Peter, he had, unlike most of his generation, become converted to the view that sexual exclusivity of any kind was itself the neurosis that needed challenging.

He'd also learned from Peter that "everyone is both masculine and feminine," as defined by then-current standards, that if he was "strong" in some ways, especially in regard to "aggressiveness," he was "also weak in many ways"—thus acknowledging that "weakness is not necessarily feminine." To the contrary, he believed that women "were generally the stronger partner but that the men appear stronger." He supposed, but wasn't sure, that his drive "to dominate and control is the male element . . . I could never leave anyone alone."

And that, as he was well aware, included Peter, who with his small inheritance had been buying, in David's ascetic opinion, too much "stuff," including a tape deck and a Nikon camera. It was, David somewhat peevishly wrote Peter, "like things moving in. Not books or poetry or flowers or thoughts or people, but things. And with them, barriers and cautions and window bars." His own preference was for "material humility."

But it wasn't Peter's preference; he didn't consider a tape deck bourgeois luxury. He resented David for trying to dictate a particular lifestyle to him. His own beliefs and standards were close to David's but not identical. By November 1966, Peter had concluded, with some reluctance, that at least a tentative parting of the ways had become necessary. He'd earlier told David that he needed to have a place of his own, an "office," and that he'd succeeded in renting a place on Thirteenth Street. But David was wholly unprepared, on returning to the apartment one evening, to find that Peter, without further notice, had completely moved out—clothes, books, everything. David was awash in grief and repentance.

Peter came by a few days later, and he and David both broke down; they tried to understand what had happened or might be going to happen. David characteristically and immediately put the blame entirely on himself, on his jealousy and possessiveness, his inhospitable treatment of Peter's friends—all of which he felt sure had made Peter believe that he was being "forced into an exclusive homosexual relationship." David tried to explain that his bad behavior was at root due to his own "deep sense of unworthiness"; he'd found it nearly impossible to believe that "anyone could love me for myself." So he'd simultaneously tried to possess Peter utterly and at the same time tried to drive him away. He'd been, in his own eyes, "spiteful and difficult," unconsciously trying to test Peter, to see if he really cared enough to hang around. But now he saw that "people can take only so much of that." Nobody wanted to be "suffocated."

It was obvious to them both that "things aren't over," but precisely where they stood or were likely to go wasn't at all clear. David was determined to fight "for a second chance," which he wisely understood to mean sitting still, leaving Peter alone, and minding his own business—"and that will be hard." But he hoped that he was angry enough with himself to stick to his resolution. Even if he failed, he self-deprecatingly insisted that *he* was "the barrier" to closeness and he *had* to try to change. He explicitly rejected the notion that he was being too hard on himself, but he was. If Peter felt trapped, then David himself had to have made some contribution, for relationships always represent some sort of mutual conspiracy, however unconscious.

For a time, he and Peter saw each other with some frequency and pleasantness, but the intervals gradually lengthened. David had hoped that Peter's Thirteenth Street place would not become his home, but within the year it did. Still, their relationship, however tenuous, wasn't entirely over. As late as 1968, David felt that "within limits and in a complex way, Peter and I remain linked." But he had to rein in his feelings with great care. If he pressed to any degree, Peter retreated. If he sought in any sense to possess him, he vanished. Though counter to his temperament, David tried to simply be there; that would maximize the chance but not guarantee that Pete would stay around. David knew that the situation had become "immature, unstable, neurotic" and comforted himself with the dubious conclusion that those qualities characterized "most situations, to a greater or lesser extent." The final dissolution came when Pete left New York in 1969.

Barbara's home life had become no less unstable. Trouble had arrived in the person of twenty-three-year-old Marie-Claire Blais, a French-Canadian writer who'd already published three novels, the first, *La Belle Bête*, when she was twenty. On coming to the United States in the spring of 1963 on a Guggenheim Fellowship, she'd initially settled in a shabby basement apartment in Cambridge, Massachusetts. Edmund Wilson, who was at work on his book *O Canada!*, which included a chapter on Quebeçois writers, had recommended her for the Guggenheim and had met her for the first time in Montreal just before her departure for the States.[13]

He and his wife, Elena, had invited Marie-Claire to dinner in Montreal, with Edmund expecting—from what he'd heard about her poverty-stricken working-class background—"a big tall rather coarse-featured country girl." He was startled to find instead "an attractive little woman, with well-developed breasts but tiny hands and feet, a sharp nose, a very small mouth and deep-thinking, gray-green eyes, with the good quiet manners and the very pure French" that he supposed she'd learned from having been schooled for twelve years in a convent. She was "perfectly self-possessed" and had an "unusual simplicity and directness that are the signs of a remarkable person."

Edmund, however, was not a particularly keen observer of women. His wife, Elena, had far more insight. When Edmund went to their house in Talcottville, New York, in the fall of 1963—a place where he could write without interruption—Elena invited Marie-Claire to their other place in Wellfleet on Cape Cod for a week. But it didn't take that long for Elena to tire of her. It wasn't a matter of Marie-Claire's English still being rudimentary but more that she talked incessantly and hyper-emotionally, her chief subjects being suffering and death. She found everything *angoissant*—full of anguish—and wore Elena out with her worries and confessions. Elena wasn't at all convinced that everything Marie-Claire told her was true—she was, after all, a novelist and given to flights of imaginative fantasy.

It should be said on Marie-Claire's behalf that she was still very young, poor, not yet secure as a writer, had come from a fairly wretched, gloomy background (though accounts of it vary widely, one portraying her mother as a teacher), and had been steeped in her Jansenist convent in a theology that emphasized original sin and human depravity. For her part, M-C (as everyone soon referred to her) found Elena enchanting and, with her strong features and high cheekbones, "stunningly beautiful." She did strenuously object, however, to Elena's view, which would change over time, that a woman's primary concern should be to support her husband. Not that M-C was any less taken with Edmund—who, with his "powerful intellect and physical presence," reminded her of Winston Churchill—but his formidable intellect and "masculine vanity" made her shyer in his presence than in

Elena's. Besides, Edmund kept pointing to the weaknesses in M-C's writing style, kept telling her that "it must be tighter . . . trim, trim, the flow needs to be more sustained, controlled."

On one of M-C's several subsequent visits to Cape Cod, where she often stayed with other acquaintances as well as the Wilsons, she was introduced to Mary Meigs and Barbara, who was recuperating in Well-fleet between trips to the South to join protest demonstrations. Before making the introduction, Edmund cautioned M-C (at least as she describes it) that these were two "extraordinary" women. Earlier, Edmund had decided that he was "in love" with Mary and that "the only valid relationships" were those between men and women. According to M-C, Edmund insisted that "love between people of the same sex" is "like a glove made for the left hand worn on the right."

Mary was instantly smitten with M-C. In some ways, Mary thought her like Barbara. Both "remind me that I am less entire than they are." They "have, in a sense, already gone through the eye [of the needle], have lost themselves and saved themselves, while I seem, in the tradition of my family, to protect myself. . . . I have always been plagued by the sense of the shortness of my attention-span and my ability to be distracted." M-C preferred older women to those her own age, and she returned Mary's interest.

On a walk together in the woods, Mary accidentally let go of a branch that hit M-C in the eye, making it difficult for her to read or write for several months. Whether primarily out of guilt or using her guilt as an excuse, Mary decided to offer M-C the use of the small "yellow house" on her Wellfleet property (she and Barbara had long shared the larger "red house"). M-C—whom Elena had quickly summed up as "attaching herself to women" and not letting go—gratefully accepted Mary's offer. Before long she was taking her meals with Mary and Barbara, and by the end of 1964 had become (as Barbara put it in a letter) "in effect a member of our family."

And that three-way relationship held for roughly the next six years. Edmund thought that M-C functioned essentially as a daughter to Mary and Barbara, but the subject of erotic love between women was not one of his literary specialties. Elena, to the contrary, decided that M-C was *"un petit champignon de femme fatale,"* who'd "got her hooks into Mary while Barbara was away freedom-marching in the South." Rumors began to fly in the Wellfleet artistic community that while living in Quebec, M-C had provoked a good deal of "hostility." For her part, M-C was telling people that Elena was being remarkably "forbearing" about the number of hours M-C spent alone with Edmund (in fact, according to Edmund's diary, they'd thus far been alone in his study for exactly one quarter of an hour, to discuss her writing). Elena herself refused any longer to be alone in M-C's company; other people stopped asking her out when they invited Mary and Barbara.

Over the years, the situation between the three women became far more complex than any outsider could grasp—or that can be fully deciphered even now. Barbara herself at one point actually fell in love with M-C, who told Barbara that she reciprocated her feelings, and the two of them did have sex, though rarely. In Barbara's view, "for the most part our days are calm and affectionate," and their lives together "seemed to be working." She generously believed that although M-C was capable of "a lot of pretending, neither of them ever *intended* to hurt each other," even if M-C did insist to Mary that Barbara was "terrorizing" her. At the same time, as was always the case with people she cared for deeply, Barbara never fell out of love with Mary, who, well before M-C appeared on the scene, no longer felt the same about Barbara.

What would eventually emerge from these emotional entanglements was a primary bond between Mary and M-C, while Barbara in 1967 fell in love with a then-married woman, Jane Gapen. Neither of those bonds would ever break. Between Barbara and Mary, a brief period of mutual accusation would follow, but within a few years the two would reconstitute a devoted, lifelong friendship. Even when recriminations were still in progress, Mary never ceased to admire Barbara, going so far as to call her a "saint." In her autobiography, *Lily Briscoe*, Mary later itemized Barbara's many qualities: "her serious face with her kind, mournful eyes, . . . her dogged will, . . . [her] earnest moral weight, . . . [her] searching and sensitive attention," the "fortunate mechanism" that "prevents her from ever being spiteful, stops her from repeating gossip or believing the mean things that people say about each other, [her] steadfastness of love, . . . and [her] refined unconcern for everything, except for what is essential to the work."

But by "saint," Mary didn't mean some plaster cast paragon, one without human faults. In her autobiography, Mary enumerated those as well. Despite Barbara's rather startling appearance—nearly six feet tall, her gestures "slightly theatrical," with a deep voice and long arms in "continuous motion"—Barbara barely noticed "how she dresses." If she liked a piece of clothing, which usually meant some "shapeless loden coat and baggy pants," she would wear them until they fell to pieces. This annoyed Mary, who was *not* indifferent to fashion or to how others judged her appearance.

Barbara's lack of concern carried over into household matters. Like M-C, she paid only occasional attention to cleaning the house or cooking meals—until Mary, who liked everything neat and tidy, would explode. Thinking her behavior "perfectly innocent," Barbara would be surprised by Mary's "gratuitous aggression" but would earnestly set about doing housework. That would last for only a week or so before she again stopped doing chores in favor of working on an article or disappearing on a protest march. Mary did understand that all this was a matter of Barbara's "maddening" simplicity—and her own attraction to "wifely" duties.

Barbara's indifference to disarray and to what she ate and wore were in Mary's eyes less important than Barbara's unawareness of her impact on other people, her inability to see that "with all her delicate perceptions and conscience," she failed to understand "how much weight her passion, her longing or her sense of moral rightness put on others." Neither Mary nor M-C minimized the importance of Barbara's political work—in fact, Mary often admired it—but they felt that being "life-directed by conscience" came at the expense of "art," a price they were unwilling to pay. As M-C put it, "artists also have a right to exist . . . the personal action of writing is itself something."

Mary sometimes joined Barbara in political protest, like refusing to pay her taxes, and admitted to being envious of Barbara's ability to "keep doing good and believing in herself." She acknowledged that when Barbara had first become involved with the Committee for Non-Violent Action, her initial response had been mocking. But not only did it soon turn to respect, Mary herself joined the CNVA, bought the Voluntown Farm in Connecticut for the group, and for a time attended meetings, rang doorbells, and handed out leaflets.

But after a while, she admitted to herself that she simply didn't enjoy such activities or understand how anyone could. She wanted only to "remain attentive to my own rhythms, to the messages that I received when I kept very still." People in CNVA kept telling her that the more one participated, the more commitment grew; but in Mary's case, she felt "so much less committed" through time that she ended up shedding almost all of her ties to pacifism and political activism.

Unlike Mary, who'd made a considerable effort to become political, M-C abstractly professed appreciation for Barbara's activities ("I believe that her life is truly aligned with a plan of action devoted to the greater good") but did not claim to understand her. "This is the difference between us, myself being an egoist, and she transforming her ego into useful and rigorous action. . . . [I have] a life path so different from hers . . . I no longer want to be bothered by her." M-C's main concern was that Barbara's political involvement could prove a danger to her and Mary. The "menacing letters" Barbara received left M-C fearing "that they would burn down our house or something of the sort. . . . It scares me. I have no courage when it comes to these things," especially because "I myself am so difficult, a handful of a thousand demons. . . . It is not easy to live with Joan of Arc in her place." Yet while refusing to get involved in Barbara's political activities and expressing resentment at what she sometimes experienced as Barbara exerting "immense pressure, and oppression too," for her to get involved, M-C still claimed to have "great admiration" for Barbara's "work . . . of which certain aspects touch on heroism and sainthood."

When their life together finally ended, Mary and Barbara exchanged long, deeply honest letters to each other. Mary fully acknowledged her own "capricious alter ego nourished by the petty circumstances of every day." But she also felt for the first time fully able to express her view that it was impossible to take "a moderate position" with Barbara, that she was so persuasive an arguer and so convinced that social change was possible and that "anyone who wasn't with her was against her," that Mary sometimes felt squeezed "into a defenceless corner."

Barbara was shocked at Mary's description of her. Most people told her that she was an "intense listener" who could be counted on always to acknowledge opponents' arguments and, above all, their humanity. Barbara did agree that she could sometimes be rigidly principled, yet the image Mary and M-C held of her was at the same time painful to learn. Far from denying the inadequacies they pointed out, Barbara felt "I should have been able to sense it, too, and that I didn't is a horror to me and makes me doubt myself in a new way I never have before."

She thought back to the times when she went off to the South or elsewhere and "feeling scared," she wrote Mary, "tried to draw closer to you, each time in the process, driving you further off. I do finally recognize that the mere fact that I felt impelled to take these actions made me, as you put it the other day, strange to you, so how *could* you turn toward me?" Barbara was perhaps too quick to internalize Mary's indictment, seeming to forget (as Mary had not) Mary's own contributions to the deterioration in their relationship—like withdrawing sexually or dropping out from and sometimes scorning any activist form of political commitment. Though Barbara had no trouble admitting to the "blemishes" in her character, she exempted her political activism. She felt that her ethical principles required no amendment or apology. She held firmly to her political convictions and would soon discover that they applied to areas of injustice previously outside her vision.

McReynolds family portrait—from left to right: Charles, David, Martin, Elizabeth, and Elizabeth Anne.

David cuts a cake during an event of the Temperance Council, youth division of the Women's Christian Temperance Union, at Clifton's Cafeteria in Los Angeles, 1947/1948. Brother Martin is on David's right.

David with mother Elizabeth and sister Elizabeth Anne outside his Ashland Avenue house in Ocean Park on the day of David's graduation from UCLA. The family apparently found him asleep when they arrived.

Portrait of Barbara in Japan, 1959.

Barbara and the artist Mary Meigs (above) were lovers from 1954 to 1972.

The leading figure in the U.S. pacifist movement, A.J. Muste had a powerful influence on both Barbara Deming and David McReynolds.

NEW YORK PUBLIC LIBRARY

David first met Alvin Ailey in the notorious "queer" bathroom on the UCLA campus in 1949. They became good friends and David credits Ailey with greatly helping him reduce his self-hatred based on being gay.

WAR RESISTERS LEAGUE

David met Bayard Rustin in 1953. When Rustin was imprisoned "on morals" (homosexuality) charges that year, twenty-three-year-old David, although still coming to terms with his own homosexuality, was one of Bayard's few visitors in the Los Angeles County Jail.

Vida Ginsberg was a Bennington College senior when she met Barbara in 1941. This photograph was taken on the grounds outside the library at Bennington. Vida was one of the great loves of Barbara's life; the two were romantically involved for seven years. In 1948, Barbara's younger brother Quentin ("Chip")—with Vida's encouragement and Barbara's knowledge—began courting Vida. They were married in 1949.

David met the writer Peter Stafford (above) in 1963. The two were romantically involved for several years in New York.

DAVE MCREYNOLDS

VOTE

FOR CONGRESS 19 C.D.
Peace and Freedom Party

MC REYNOLDS FOR CONGRESS COMMITTEE
4 BETHUNE STREET. N.Y.C. 243-9812

In 1958, David, at the age of twenty-nine, was drafted to run on the Socialist Party ticket for Congress, from the 19th District (the Lower East Side of Manhattan). His candidacy marked the first time in more than twenty years that the party had entered a congressional race in the district.

WAR RESISTERS LEAGUE

On November 6, 1965, David, forth from left, was one of five men who publicly burned their draft cards at an anti-war demonstration in Union Square; they were among the first to do so following a law passed earlier in the year that made it a felony for anyone to knowingly destroy or mutilate his selective service registration certificate.

ED HEDEMAN

In 1969, at the height of the protests against the war in Vietnam, the National Office of the War Resisters League (WRL) on Beekman Street in lower Manhattan was raided and ransacked. The perpetrators were never found but many believed the FBI was responsible.

Barbara at a civil rights demonstration.

Barbara at a New York lesbian poetry reading.

5

David and the New Left

Nineteen sixty-five was a momentous year. President Lyndon Johnson began a sustained bombing campaign against North Vietnam and sent in the first *acknowledged* American combat troops, bringing the number of Americans in Indochina to some two hundred thousand, with more on the way. Johnson's actions led to mounting opposition within the United States, as well as shifting the focus of the peace movement and its flagship organization, the War Resisters League, to direct-action—but nonviolent—protest against further U.S. involvement in Vietnam. That year also saw the civil rights march from Selma to Montgomery—and on "Bloody Sunday," the spectacle of mounted police trampling and clubbing peaceful marchers attempting to cross the Pettus Bridge. That sickening sight led President Johnson to announce that he would soon present voting rights legislation to the Congress.[1]

The same year also saw a growing hostility between substantial segments of the New Left and the previous generation's social democratic Old Left, now clustered around Irving Howe's *Dissent* and SANE, the cautious, liberal antinuclear organization that counseled negotiations rather than immediate withdrawal from Vietnam. Late in 1964, Students for a Democratic Society (SDS), the leading white student group, called for a massive rally in the spring of 1965 to protest U.S.

involvement in Vietnam. Because SDS rejected what it called the Old Left's knee-jerk anticommunism, its call was open-ended: anyone was invited to participate in the rally, regardless of political affiliation. But segments of the peace movement, including some of its leading figures, Muste, Rustin, and Norman Thomas, long associated with a policy of noncooperation with communists (as was David), weren't thrilled with SDS's "indiscriminate" inclusiveness; they supported the call but questioned the involvement of CP members.

Socialists Michael Harrington and Bayard Rustin became particular targets of scorn from younger radicals—Harrington for his earlier criticism of SDS's 1962 foundational Port Huron Statement and for his belief (increasingly shared by Rustin) that a coalition of church, labor, civil rights, and liberal movements aimed at reforming the Democratic Party was the best vehicle for achieving social change. Rustin, in addition, recommended that street demonstrations be stopped and in 1964 had supported the "compromise" at the Democratic Convention that offered the Mississippi Freedom Democratic Party only two seats.

David McReynolds had long been close to Rustin (he was never close to Harrington or felt at all indebted to him). As far back as 1953, when Rustin had been imprisoned on morals (homosexuality) charges, twenty-three-year-old McReynolds, still coming to terms with his own homosexuality, had been one of Bayard's few visitors in the Los Angeles County Jail. Many other radicals of the day, except for A. Philip Randolph, turned their backs on Rustin. A.J. Muste, something of a mentor to Bayard in the Fellowship of Reconciliation (a church-oriented group concerned with issues of social justice), treated his arrest as a personal betrayal and persuaded the organization to fire Bayard as a staff member.[2]

The secular pacifists in WRL reacted quite differently. Rustin had been serving on its governing board and offered his resignation—but the board turned it down. Some of its members, led by Roy Finch, a onetime reporter for the *New York Herald Tribune*, then moved to hire Rustin as a staff member. That proved a tougher sell. Finch was supported by many of WRL's leading figures, including Dave Dellinger, Ralph DiGia (who, like Finch, leaned more toward anarchism than socialism), and the working-class Igal Roodenko, who lived in the same Mott Street tenement as Rustin and was also gay, though at the time not "out."

The opposition was again led by A.J.Muste. Finch cleverly waited until Muste was out of town before presenting the hiring proposal to the advisory council, which passed it by a 15–5 vote—this at a time when McCarthyism was a feared force in the country and when homosexuals were widely viewed as security risks. After Muste returned, he led a hard-fought battle on the Executive Committee to veto the hiring of Rustin but ultimately lost 6–4. An exasperated Muste promptly resigned from the committee. A considerable time would have to pass before he and Rustin could manage enough of a reconciliation to allow them to work together again.

Rustin's achievements over the dozen years that had led up to the 1963 March on Washington had been extraordinary, but the March was probably the greatest of his accomplishments. Though Bayard was kept behind the scenes because of his "degenerate" history (his rift with Martin Luther King Jr. was "shattering" to him), his remarkable organizational skills were what made the March a huge success. Still, by 1965, David and others had become increasingly disquieted by some of Rustin's apparent political shifts. In January of that year, he resigned as executive secretary of WRL and became head of the recently inaugurated A. Philip Randolph Institute in New York City, which focused on black issues and where Bayard would remain for the rest of his life. Secular radicals weren't reassured about Rustin's shifting views when they discovered that the Institute's largest donor was George Meany, president of the AFL-CIO and a man well known for his opposition to radical causes of any kind.

At about the same time Rustin resigned from the League, he published what became a famous (to some, infamous) article, "From Protest to Politics," in which he argued that blacks should resist the growing appeal of black nationalism and move beyond civil rights demonstrations in order to concentrate on transforming the Democratic Party into an instrument of progressive change—the same position taken by Mike Harrington and by the Socialist Party's Max Shachtman.

Dave Dellinger—now editor-in-chief of *Liberation* (which, despite its small circulation, remained influential on the radical left)—and longtime activist Staughton Lynd separately attacked Rustin in the magazine's pages. Lynd's piece was by far the more caustic of the two. He described Rustin's article as an elitist attempt to discredit SNCC's radicalism and accused him of being in favor of American policy in

Vietnam, calling him a lackey of capitalism. That was too much for David (and for Harrington, Irving Howe, and Norman Thomas, as well). Even though David agreed with Staughton Lynd (who he thought "a very good person, very good guy") about Bayard's seeming shift from radicalism to liberalism, he felt that Lynd's attack was far too polemical in tone and too sweeping in its indictment.[3]

David defended Rustin both in *Liberation* and in *New Politics*. He argued that Lynd's attack on Bayard amounted to the wholesale maligning of a man who'd made many remarkable contributions to the fight for social justice and had many times risked his life and endured beatings and prison for the movement. He also argued against Lynd's accusation that Bayard had become a supporter of Lyndon Johnson's war in Vietnam. The evidence, David insisted, didn't support such a charge, which was much more accurately leveled, David felt, at James Farmer, who'd engineered the repeal of a CORE resolution against the war, and Roy Wilkins, the conservative head of the NAACP, who'd long kept that organization on the sidelines of foreign policy debates.[4]

Yet Lynd, it could be argued, proved a better prognosticator than David. Rustin's criticism of the war did become more muted over time. It's true that he moved only so far as to support the liberal view that urged negotiations rather than unilateral U.S. withdrawal, his earlier position. It's also true that by late 1966 Bayard became mostly silent on the war—even as he increasingly lashed out at the radical Left, in particular at SDS and SNCC, for "romanticizing" the National Liberation Front (NLF) and for being wholly uncritical of its record of atrocities and its firm allegiance to communism.[5]

David himself was in general favorably disposed toward the New Left, though he agreed that it was willfully ignorant of the long and necessary struggle against Soviet-style totalitarian communism and that it *did* romanticize the NLF. He himself didn't "see the NLF as angels," and he often spoke out—in a *Village Voice* article, for example— against "the violence and terrorism" used by the NLF in Vietnam, even though he felt that the NLF's excesses "did not justify the massive, sustained and deliberate violence the American government has unleashed against the Vietnamese people."

To underscore his displeasure with the Lynd/Dellinger attack on Bayard—and also because he felt that *Liberation* had of late taken too "uncritical an approach towards the New Left" and hadn't sounded "a more distinctly pacifist voice"—David resigned his position as associate editor of the magazine. He'd long felt ambivalent about Dellinger. He remembered Bayard's telling him when he first went to work for *Liberation* back in 1957 that he "would find Dave less than fully honest." And he had. As he once privately wrote, he regretted that Dellinger "always has to position himself to the left of everyone else" and described him as "not my favorite person." David recalled a *Liberation* meeting after Dellinger took the helm of the magazine, during which "A.J. [Muste] looked almost lost, realizing that he was 'trapped with Dellinger'—that without him the magazine couldn't move ahead, but that it had drifted in directions A.J. wasn't comfortable with."

Yet if David had some misgivings about Dellinger's character, he nonetheless felt that he was "a very brave man—remarkably courageous, very warm, very human . . . a good and decent man." David also sensed that Dellinger may have had a bit of homosexual experience, and that it might have been with Bayard Rustin. He was wrong about the Rustin part but correct about the rest. In his autobiography, *From Yale to Jail*, Dellinger makes one brief, cryptic comment about having had a single homosexual contact in the late sixties or seventies. But though he minimized his experience, he consistently and staunchly defended homosexuality in public, writing at one point that "it ill behooves any of us to be self-righteous about other people's actions in this area."

His autobiography *did* downplay his activity in "this area." A section of his private papers, previously closed to researchers, makes clear for the first time that Dellinger had, as far back as college, fallen in love with his roommate but was "so prejudiced and fearful about homosexuality that it would never have occurred to me that we 'decent' people would have expressed our love sexually." As a middle-aged man, though, he had several passionate and sexual affairs with younger men, while admitting, in a letter to one of them, that he had (like David McReynolds) "negative relations to so many who announce themselves as gay—the old 'swish' syndrome."

In that sense he didn't identify as "gay," but he did consider himself "and everyone else not deterred by fear, conditioning or opportunism to be basically bi-sexual." In another letter to one of his younger lovers, he was more explicit still: "I have no gender preference at all, which presumably makes me bi-sexual. . . . [I] have had some of my best experiences with men and women at the same time." Had Dellinger made any of this knowledge public during his lifetime, it would have come as a great shock (though his wife, Elizabeth Peterson, had sensed—but apparently never made much of the fact—that her husband was erotically drawn to other men). Most people—not knowing much if any ancient Greek history—did and do equate the kind of physical courage Dellinger displayed with macho heterosexuality.

On another matter, David felt that *Liberation*, under Dellinger's editorship, had shifted to a position he called "fraternal hostility toward the Socialist Party." To some extent, he shared that attitude; he, too, had become distressed at the SP's failure "to provide significant leadership" or "to play an initiating role" in protesting the war in Vietnam. Also, he agreed with Dellinger's sympathy for the New Left but felt the magazine had become too uncritically its champion.

He thought that when Bayard and Roy Finch had been on the magazine's editorial board, they'd created a better balance among different points of view. What was needed, in David's opinion, was a stronger endorsement of pacifism and a less automatic enthusiasm for the New Left: *Liberation* should be "a bridge between the wisdoms and follies of the Old Left and the insights and follies of the New Left." But he wasn't hopeful that the magazine could change emphasis. He didn't find Dellinger "intellectually perceptive" and thought him excessively "committed to a permanently naïve and revolutionary view of the world."

Unlike so many others, left or right, David's political positions were usually nuanced, and he was also able freely to admit that he'd made some "terribly wrong" judgments in the past—his support, for instance, of Johnson's candidacy in 1964. As he once succinctly put it, "the first lesson in politics . . . and radical politics is no different, is that you *must* accept compromise and coalition . . . radicals also choose 'lesser evils.' The debate is never over whether or not one makes compromises, but only over whether the compromises were truly necessary, whether the course chosen was the least evil of many possible evils." The true pacifist task, he felt, "is that of building revolutionary values. To others we will have to leave the task of building revolutionary organizations."

Similarly, his devotion to nonviolence required the admission that in some few cases—opposition to Hitler, say, or the violent uprising in Hungary in 1956—the pacifist approach might well have failed. (On this, Barbara Deming fully agreed with David.) In parallel, he stayed in the Socialist Party but openly lamented ("I am very pessimistic" about the party, he wrote in 1966) some of its current twists and turns. There were several effective SP affiliates around the country, but in David's view, the party as a whole—especially as represented by its paper, *New America*, controlled by Max Shachtman's clique—hadn't adopted a strong enough position against the war and was insufficiently friendly toward the New Left. These stances made it difficult to recruit new members or to increase the party's influence. Earlier, David had worked diligently for years to build a dominant left caucus, but he didn't have the time or energy to attempt a second such effort.[6]

In a 1966 "Memo to a Non-Existent Caucus," David described at length his current unhappiness with the party. Despite the strong position taken by the majority at previous national conventions, Max Shachtman, "the intellectual rallying point for the most extreme elements in the party's right wing," had succeeded in preventing the SP as a whole from denouncing the war in Vietnam "with precision and vigor"—and had also helped to destroy the party's left-wing youth movement (YPSL) just as a mass student radical movement was emerging nationwide.

To the standard argument that we owed it to the Vietnamese, after all the havoc we'd wrought in their country, to help repair the damage, not to just pack up and leave, David would reply that our continuing presence—"a capitalist state, acting in its own imperial interests"—would repeat "the whole pattern it had established in other developing countries," namely to support an "exploitative military dictatorship." After all, it had been "U.S. policy which put Lon Nol in power and laid the basis for the Khmer Rouge victory." David considered all the talk about establishing a democratic government in South Vietnam as fraudulent nonsense. He himself had always felt that "a Vietnamese multi-party system" was a pipe dream.

David wrote directly to Shachtman suggesting a public debate on these issues; Shachtman peremptorily refused. He explained why in a letter to another SP member: David had "attacked" him at the SP's 1960 convention, and subsequently in a circular, on the "purely personal" grounds of his integrity—the attack "slanderous, defamatory, groundless and unprovoked." David wasn't in the habit of assaulting persons rather than policies, and he wrote Shachtman that he didn't know what he was referring to and asked him to make public the offending circular. He got no reply. Shachtman had perhaps heard about David's reputation as a superb debater, and he refused any future political or personal contact as "neither possible nor desirable." David had no choice but to accept the rejection, but he continued to decry Shachtman's failure to denounce the Vietnam War and his avoidance of "a public dialogue on his position."

The Socialist Party's refusal to issue a clear-cut call for withdrawal, supporting instead negotiations or a cease-fire followed by negotiations, continued in the face of the "massive brutality" of American actions. David fully acknowledged that the NLF was controlled by Communists and that if it took power in South Vietnam, its members would be likely to prevent free elections, but, he wrote, we had "prevented free elections in 1956 and have never permitted them since that time." David considered President Johnson's new "peace offensive" a fraud, because he'd demanded as a precondition that the NLF lay down its arms and cease to covet South Vietnam. But David and others in the pacifist movement wrote to their contacts in Hanoi urging some kind of response to Johnson in order to prevent him from claiming that the NLF wasn't interested in ending the conflict. At the same time, it wasn't the WRL position to support the NLF; David and most other pacifists condemned violence on *all* sides. They supported the right of the Vietnamese people to reach whatever decision *they* chose, regardless of what it was.[7]

In any case, David decided that until the SP could add its voice unequivocally to the call for withdrawal from Vietnam, he would spend nearly all his own time working for the War Resisters League (at a salary of $81.04 per week), which early on had fully denounced the war. To that end, he stepped up his speaking schedule, crisscrossing the country—though he disliked flying—doing lectures and teach-ins, joining demonstrations and conferences, risking arrest and jail time—all aimed at pushing a peace agenda.

During 1965 alone, five to ten young men seeking advice about draft resistance passed through the WRL office every week, and Ralph DiGia worked especially hard to provide them with counseling. Congress had passed a law making it illegal to burn a draft card, but in November of that year, at a major rally in New York's Union Square, David had been one of five men to thumb their noses at the law and burn their cards. Quite accidentally, he alone of the group was spared a prison sentence; at thirty-six, David was over draft age and the government felt it might lose all five cases if one of them proved flawed. Though Norman Thomas didn't regard draft card burnings as particularly useful, he did fiercely oppose the war—in November 1965, at age eighty-one, increasingly arthritic and partially blind, he helped to organize and spoke to great effect at the massive antiwar rally in D.C., calling for negotiations and an end to the bombing of North Vietnam. But Thomas was a conciliator by nature. He saw his role, as he wrote David, as trying to "reach the unconverted and those who do want—as I do—successfully to oppose communist expansion. . . . I am pro-peace as a condition for a true democracy, not pro-communist or pro-Vietcong."

In the spring of 1967, during the first truly massive Vietnam protest in New York at Central Park's Sheep Meadow, another burning of draft cards was planned. But SANE and most of the Old Left were horrified. "My God!" David angrily responded. "People might think the movement was serious about stopping the war!" But the moderates refused to give in, and a compromise was finally agreed to: the card burning would take place before the main rally began so that the two events would be clearly separated. It was an absurd compromise, in David's view: no one would be fooled by burning the cards ten minutes earlier.

To prevent the police from arresting those planning the incineration, David, the writer Grace Paley, and a number of others formed a human chain around them. David would later come to feel that these individual acts of resistance weren't effective on a political level, though they did help "to penetrate the consciousness of some Americans and give them a sense of the immorality of what we are doing in Vietnam, which may in time lead them to political action."

He also recognized that the movement for withdrawal from Vietnam still represented, in 1966, only "a very small section of the population"; his estimate was 10 to 15 percent. The numbers would grow,

David predicted, as more and more American soldiers were killed and as it also became increasingly clear that the "war on poverty" at home and the "Freedom Budget" (a comprehensive plan for full employment) would fall by the wayside, supplanted by the federal government's concentration on issues relating to Southeast Asia.

David felt it his duty to continue to speak out and thus, he hoped, augment the ranks of the disaffected. He'd thought of himself as a radical before the war, yet it radicalized him further. The war was currently "the great issue of conscience," and David felt that its barbarity, "now approaching genocide," was *not* balanced out by Johnson's earlier accomplishments on the domestic front. Yet he never argued that treating civilian populations as objects of war was a uniquely savage American phenomenon; instead he viewed mass slaughter as widespread among nations—"a symbol of the sickness of civilization in the twentieth century." He was well aware—as SDS militants who uncritically supported the NLF were not—that Ho Chi Minh and his comrades were rumored to have killed thousands of peasants during the period of forced collectivization during the 1950s.

David also spent a good bit of time in Europe and Japan, attending a weeklong meeting of the War Resisters League International (WRI) in Rome, where he urged European peace movement members to increase pressures on their governments to oppose Johnson's policies in Vietnam and thereby force his isolation internationally. He also made contacts abroad with various socialist leaders. Though David had resigned from the offices he held in the SP at home, he'd retained his membership, forming, along with others, the left-wing Debs Caucus in the hope of eventually recapturing the party. The WRI conference in Rome produced a statement expressing opposition to "the brutal war in Vietnam" and reminding the world that international law laid down at the Nuremberg Trials had insisted that individuals had "a legal obligation to refuse service in a war such as that in Vietnam: a war in which prisoners are tortured and killed, civilian areas bombed, gas and napalm widely used, and the crops deliberately destroyed with chemicals."[8]

A second statement/petition was addressed to key members of all socialist parties on the eve of the 65th Annual Conference of the British Labour Party in October 1966, declaring that the British Labour government "is the only non-fascist government in Europe giving open and public support to the American actions in Vietnam." The statement also addressed the assurances given by President Johnson and the British foreign secretary that the Americans "seek to negotiate" and that it was Hanoi and the NLF that have "been stubborn and difficult" and "will not compromise."

The truth, the statement argued, was that "America has yet to show any serious interest in negotiating the central issue—the withdrawal of its troops"—nor had it shown "any willingness to negotiate directly with the National Liberation Front." Without ignoring or excusing "the terrorism" of the NLF, the statement also pointed out that such terrorism "pales into insignificance when ranged against the actions of the American forces in Vietnam" in their use of torture, napalm, and gas and their willingness to poison crops and crush the Buddhist opposition. The following year (1967) when David landed in London, he was detained at Gatwick Airport for seven and a half hours; all the documents he had with him, including confidential minutes of the War Resisters International, were confiscated; and he was threatened with deportation. Lord Fenner Brockway's protest to the Home Office finally secured his release.

David even managed nearly a week in Saigon, with his British friend Peggy Duff, a tough, nonaligned socialist. While there, they talked with some of the leading Buddhist figures, including Thich Tri Quang. David found their position "difficult to understand": they seemed to want all "external forces" removed from Vietnam yet also seemed afraid to call directly for the complete withdrawal of American troops— perhaps because they couldn't be sure whether they were talking to covert CIA agents, the press, or members of the peace movement. David wrote Norman Thomas that on balance his conclusion was "that the Buddhists are not prepared to call for the withdrawal of the Americans," even though when they talked to him and Peggy "they laid heavy stress on the need for all external forces to be removed from Vietnam."

Back home again, David wrote and circulated a series of memos to key figures in the WRL in which he argued for certain positions and principles for the League to adopt. For one, he argued in favor of attempting to impeach President Johnson, who in his focus on Indochina had by now largely lost interest in his own Great Society programs. This marked an about-face for David. Earlier he'd argued that such an attempt would be "politically unrealistic . . . and irrelevant." Moreover, an impeachment campaign would imply that Johnson alone was responsible for the war in Vietnam, thus overlooking the fact that it had been started before his presidency and "that the Pentagon, the State Department, big business—the entire establishment—shapes American foreign policy."[9]

His reasons for shifting positions on impeachment included Johnson's current success in pinning opposition to the war on "certain fringe elements," thereby ignoring the stated opposition by the chair of the Senate Foreign Relations Committee, the majority leader in the Senate, and "some of the most experienced and able Senators," like J. William Fulbright and Mike Mansfield, as well as "a whole range of intellectuals" who weren't pacifists. And when the "Spring Mobilization" demonstration took place in 1967 in New York City, it drew some three hundred thousand demonstrators—hardly a "fringe" crowd. David had also decided to support impeachment because Johnson was trying to persuade the country of his sincere desire for peace and had made "an enormous show" of his efforts to negotiate with Hanoi, whereas in truth he'd attached such rigid preconditions to negotiation that the NLF couldn't possibly accept them. Its own tentative moves toward negotiations had been ignored or sabotaged by the Johnson administration.

David also cited the general distrust of Johnson—the "sense of unease about his personality"—and the fact that "it is virtually impossible to organize an effective political attack on a whole system." It was far easier to focus on "a concrete symbol." In support of that contention, David claimed that "Birmingham was able to go into revolt against racism because of Bull Connor"—a dubious conclusion, given the long-standing mistreatment of the black community and the likelihood that resistance would have broken out even if a Bull Connor had never existed.

David was always quick to acknowledge his mistakes—indeed he tended to exaggerate them: his record for astute judgments far outbalanced the errors. He claimed that he wasn't "under any illusion that Johnson can be removed by an impeachment campaign," but then why divert energy and resources to it? David's answer was to predict that if Nixon was elected in 1968, "he might well be able, despite all of his talk of escalation, to bring the conflict to a close much more swiftly than Johnson could"—which would prove to be another of David's mistaken judgments.

Liberation published David's original memo "Impeachment of President Johnson" in its December 1966 issue, and Dwight Macdonald gave it a favorable review in *Esquire*. But Norman Thomas, for one, thought David's arguments for impeachment unpersuasive. Two thirds of the Senate, Thomas wrote him, would never convict Johnson, and if they somehow did, he'd be replaced by Hubert Humphrey, who was committed to the same policies. David gradually backed off, with the claim that limitations on his time made it impossible for him to move ahead and actually organize an impeachment campaign.

David was on firmer ground when he argued for the WRL taking on the members of the Committee for Non-Violent Action (CNVA, the group Barbara Deming had been primarily affiliated with, was dissolving) and continuing its publication, *Win*. A general consensus quickly developed that any or all individual CNVA members should be welcomed into the League and that *Win* magazine should not be allowed to die. The particular value of *Win* was that it hadn't become a house organ but spoke in general for the radical pacifist and antiwar movements and also had been favorably disposed toward the New Left.[10]

It was decided that *Win* would continue to have a wholly independent editorial board but that WRL would sponsor the magazine, though its financing left to future discussions. The League already had a house organ, the *WRL News*, which appeared every two months and in recent years had expanded from two to six pages. It would be maintained as a bulletin for the membership, which had doubled in the past five years, most of the new members being younger people. Over the same period, the League had developed three local WRL-affiliated groups; previously there had been none. As the war in Indochina continued to expand, so did the fortunes of the League.

The case was different for CNVA. Most of the blame for its pending extinction was put on Brad Lyttle, its recently resigned head. Though he'd made substantial contributions to the peace movement, it was pretty widely agreed that Brad's rigid personality turned many people off. David for one had never taken to Brad, regarding him as a loose cannon—he'd once invited Brad to talk about disarmament to a local socialist group, but Brad instead spent the evening talking about the importance of the orgasm (the "sexual revolution" had come of age); David thought the unannounced shift in topic bizarre.[11]

Brad subsequently accused David of deliberately blocking him from becoming a key figure in the pacifist movement. David was "utterly baffled" by the charge. He'd assumed that with the demise of CNVA, Brad would be hired as a staff person at the League. The fact that he wasn't had nothing to do with opposition from David. Certainly Brad's energy and his competence were never in question; whatever you asked him to do, he'd somehow accomplish it. And in truth he never got the credit he deserves for his contributions to the peace movement. It was Brad who constructed the platform in Union Square for the 1965 draft card burning and Brad who could get police and sound permits—to David, "mysterious things"—on short notice. Alas, it was also Brad who worked out a mathematical chart (though no one had requested it) proving to *his* satisfaction that a nuclear war was inevitable.

Because he thought Brad was paranoid, David *had* tried to avoid working with him. And several times in the past he'd contested Brad's views. He denied, for example, Brad's contention that claiming rights under the First and Fifth amendments was "somehow an evasion of our obligations as pacifists." Several years back, moreover, Brad—apparently repelled by the now-commonplace, stale repetitions of "Off the Pigs!"—had published a piece in the *CNVA Bulletin* denouncing the New York peace leadership for questioning the judgment of the riot squad in attacking a peaceful antinuke protest in Times Square. Brad declared that the police had been "almost free of any blame." David agreed with Brad "that we should consider the police as human" but suggested that the peace leadership "also be considered with the same charity." David could himself be stubborn and uncompromising when arguing a political point, but unlike Brad, he was rarely rigid—impervious to counterarguments or evidence.

In February 1967, A.J. Muste died of heart failure at the age of eighty-two. In an obituary published in *Liberation*, Dave Dellinger wrote that A.J. had "left a heritage in which his radical personal commitment and an insistence on the necessity for nonviolent revolution were combined with a deep respect for those with whom he differed politically or philosophically." The latter phrase, "deep respect," was also of profound importance to David and to Barbara Deming. When she and David met at Muste's memorial they spontaneously embraced, their affection and "deep respect" for each other intact, despite serious disagreements in the past (and more to come).

Both Barbara and David spoke at the memorial. She'd planned her speech in advance and movingly recalled the trip that six of them, including A.J., had made the previous year to Saigon to protest the war in front of the American Embassy. Barbara had been fearful, both for herself and for the very frail A.J., that they would be arrested by General Nguyen Cao Ky's police and roughly handled. And they were detained, spending considerable time, on a broiling hot day, sitting in a paddy wagon in the direct sun. Barbara looked across at A.J., and he looked back at her with "a sparkling smile" and with a sudden lighting up of his eyes: "It's a good life!" he said.

David hadn't planned to speak at Muste's memorial service, but after two Quakers had made "sweet comments"—"it was obvious none of them even knew the man"—David did get up and, upset at Muste's death and hardly able to speak, managed to say that Muste "wasn't a saint but a difficult, stubborn man who had the courage to be himself and somehow to love us." At the time of A.J.'s death, he held no posts in the peace movement and was in that sense not irreplaceable. As David put it, he "was the leader but not the boss." But David also felt that "it is foolish for anyone to think that A.J. can be replaced. He was a great man, such as one is fortunate to encounter in a lifetime, and immeasurably fortunate if one can say he was an associate and co-worker."

But greatness did not simply rub off on anyone connected to Muste. There was no question that A.J.'s authority would pass to Dave Dellinger, whom David considered his "political opponent." More anarchist than socialist, Dellinger was less critical of aspects of the New Left than David, though the two men did agree on much. He predicted that Dellinger "cannot, I think, hold onto his new position (an informal position, a kind of spiritual position almost) because I think he lacks the inner greatness for it and pragmatically because he has no power base. A magazine [*Liberation*] is not a power base."[12]

It was during this tumultuous period that David finally faced the fact that Peter wasn't ever going to return to the apartment, though he'd left behind a sleeping bag, kites, and considerable clothing. David wrote to him and gently asked him to remove the items, making it clear at the same time that he still loved him and would welcome his return. "I said once that while you didn't belong to me, I did belong to you. . . . I can't imagine not being delighted to see you."

When Pete ignored David's first letter, David went to Pete's apartment late one night, woke him, and deposited a load of his things. He later apologized, explaining that his brusque gesture had resulted from his own "'divided' view" of himself. On the one hand he felt "I am dirt, no one of value could respect me or really love the true me and, to compensate for that, the opposite conviction that 'I am secretly a pure Christ, a great man, a genius.'" Despite suffering periodic episodes of depression, David's confident, even formidable exterior gave little hint of his troubled, lonely side. Yet low moods weren't a steady state. As he wrote his parents, he was at a point in his life when he felt "mostly happy" and content.

When his spirits did sink, he tended to self-medicate with heavy drinking, and his consumption began to worry him. He kept thinking that he should see a therapist, but didn't—mostly because, from tales he'd heard, the therapist would be likely to lay all of his emotional problems at the doorstep of his homosexuality. "I would just make no headway with anyone who wanted me to suppress one aspect of loving."[13]

In those years—still pre-Stonewall—that *was* the standard view in the world of psychiatry: homosexuality was equated with pathology. Homosexuality itself wasn't the reason for David's discontent, but rather his unresolved attitude toward it—all but inevitable given the official view at the time. The hostile, punishing climate of the day ensured that most gay people would internalize a negative view of themselves, and the imprinting was so deep that even after liberation began, they continued to feel varying degrees of shame. David was more self-accepting than many, but even late in life, he still felt that he would "probably go to my grave with a sense of guilt about homosexuality." Early imprinting doesn't easily give way with a shift in public opinion, and participation in liberatory sloganeering and actions is more a tactic for changing one's self-image than in itself magical transfiguration.

David would periodically claim complete satisfaction with his orientation, but his discomfort with being homosexual in fact remained an undercurrent. He'd long been certain that "it isn't a sin, it isn't a crime," but he tended to believe—like most of his generation—that it did represent "neurosis." Though he'd been promiscuous when younger, David had come to regard that as "degrading," and he currently had sex less often and with fewer people. He toyed with the idea of entering therapy because he did want "to move beyond" homosexuality, to expand his options. He strongly believed—and in this he was way ahead of his time—that the real issue was exclusivity, that the rigid categories of "gay" *or* "straight" served to mask the reality that everyone felt erotic attraction to both men and women ("any man who is not potentially able . . . to have relations with another man is fully as neurotic as the homosexual who cannot relate to women").

By the 1960s there had already been support for David's contentions in the work of Alfred Kinsey. As early as 1948, Kinsey had concluded—and his findings have never been successfully challenged—that nearly one third of "straight" men had had, as adults, sex to orgasm with another man. Kinsey was widely denounced for his "fraudulent" claims, and he lost much of his funding. Much later, in 1979, William Masters and Virginia Johnson, in their book *Homosexuality in Perspective*, would add evidence to support Kinsey's conclusions. Their in-depth studies of groups of gay and straight people—some of the latter overtly homophobic—both insistent on their exclusive orientation, were nonetheless found to have pronounced fantasies about having sex with people whose gender contradicted their conscious, stated preference.

But the still-prevalent view in the 1960s was that homosexuality resulted from a particular family pattern: a close-binding, suffocating mother and a distant or hostile father. David rejected that theory. His own father could indeed be detached and was entirely gone during the war years, thus denying David the presumed-to-be-necessary male figure to identify with. But his mother didn't match up at all with the "smother mother" central to the theory.[14]

Even so, David didn't adopt the counterview that homosexuality was biological in origin. He still felt that his orientation had been environmentally, not genetically, produced, and as proof pointed to the fact (which he observed from personal experience) that family background played no ascertainable role in a prison setting, where "*most* men will become homosexual" in the absence of women. As an adult—but by then he was pretty much formed—David had many friends who were women, and he'd also had a few unsatisfying heterosexual experiences. With neither biology nor environment providing him with conclusive answers, nor some combination of the two, David was left essentially theoryless—an empty space that down to the present day has yet to be filled with persuasive evidence. Of course, a fully convincing explanation for exclusive heterosexuality has also proved elusive. Possibly the transgender experience may have much to tell us about the fluidity of both gender identification and sexual desire.

Part of David's ongoing shame resulted from his tendency to conflate same-gender sex with the gay social scene—meaning that segment of the subculture that he saw on his occasional visits to bars or parties. In those settings (and the heterosexual equivalents weren't much different), he found the predominant superficiality repellent; he hated all the small talk about "keeping tidy houses, adoring their mothers, talking about the latest plays, and worrying because their hair is receding."

He did make an effort to connect with what was then the tiny segment of the gay population attempting to organize politically. As early as 1965, when the East Coast Homophile Organizations (ECHO) met in New York City, David attended the conference, even though he didn't believe "in setting up organizations of homosexuals as if they were some kind of minority that was unique." But he did get the Executive Committee of WRL—unheard of for an organization dominated by straight people—to sponsor his bisexual friend Paul Goodman as an official speaker at the ECHO conference. Some one hundred people attended Paul's speech, and David thought it "very good," especially because Goodman argued that those who were "exempted from family life" by virtue of being homosexual, "ought therefore to shoulder other social obligations . . . something outside of themselves or else [they] would dry up."

But Goodman was talking to a crowd that believed (as Frank Kameny, one of its leaders, put it in denouncing the New Left), "You are not going to cure . . . society's prejudices by leading the homosexual into a rejection of society's values." It's no wonder that David saw the all-white conferees (about one-third lesbian) as "very quiet, sedate, everyone looking terribly respectable" (the men wore suits and ties). In his view, the crowd "could easily have passed for some sort of Junior Chamber of Commerce types." No, decidedly not David's cup of tea.

But he didn't seem to realize that in attending such a public confer-ence, these pioneering men and women were in fact putting themselves at personal risk—to say nothing of losing their jobs and apartments if their attendance became known—and CBS did televise a few bits and pieces of the conference. When the Stonewall riots erupted four years later, in 1969, David would find himself stunned. "That crowd was the last crowd I would have expected to have a rebellion." "God bless 'em!" he added.

The year 1967 saw President Johnson further increase the number of American troops in Vietnam. He had never asked Congress for a dec-laration of war—which the Constitution required—and yet he contin-ued to pour soldiers into the region. The "domino theory" became his administration's all-purpose justification: if Communism wasn't con-tained in Vietnam, then all the countries in Southeast Asia would be-come its victim. Until 1968, the majority of Americans continued to support Johnson's policy, as well as his weak rationale for it (including Max Shachtman and his followers, who continued to move steadily to the right).

Yet in denying Vietnam the determination of its own destiny, in refusing any negotiations that included the NLF, and in tabling his own once-promising domestic agenda (though he'd earlier insisted that both "guns and butter" were possible), Johnson was continuing to swell the now-substantial opposition to his policies. In 1967, Mar-tin Luther King Jr. bravely spoke out against the war, though a sig-nificant number of black leaders had advised him against taking such a controversial stand. King called the war the "symptom of a far deeper malady within the American spirit." Michael Harrington had early opposed the war and its escalation, but as SDS reached the pinnacle of its influence and increasingly championed the communist NLF, he, along with Rustin and the circle around Irving Howe and his maga-zine, *Dissent*, publicly denounced—and caricatured—the youthful pro-testers of the New Left. Harrington claimed that they were "turning from a non-ideological radicalism to a vulgar Marxism mixed with more than a little middle-class petulance."[15]

David and Harrington had been acquainted as far back as the early 1950s, when both had been active in the youth section of the SP. They'd often worked together but had never become close. And by

1967, they'd become considerably at odds politically, even while retaining respect for each other and while still in agreement on a number of public positions. Though Harrington was finally moving away from his mentor, Max Shachtman, he and others helped Shachtman organize a new group called Negotiations Now. It positioned itself as an alternative to those—like David—calling for immediate withdrawal. David primarily had Harrington in mind when he wrote an article, "A Letter to the Men of My Generation," for the *Village Voice*, in which he began by making it clear that, contrary to the Shachtmanite effort to brand him as pro-Communist, he "loathed" the politics of the NLF even as he saluted its courage in standing up to the American juggernaut.

He then went on to scorn Negotiations Now for insisting that the American public would not support withdrawal ("what have we left to negotiate, except the roads our troops will follow as they withdraw?"). He had urged nonviolent civil disobedience at home because he believed that was the best tactic for reaching the conscience of America— "not through bombs and terror." Many young protesters held older leftists in contempt, David argued, because they had failed to put their bodies on the line and take risks. He urged that his generation join hundreds of other New Yorkers, himself included, the following week in sitting down and physically blocking access to the Induction Center in Manhattan.[16]

In the next issue of the *Voice*, Harrington responded. It was true, he acknowledged, that he "cannot participate in some of the demonstrations" against "the evil war in Vietnam" because the New Left was insufficiently opposed to Vietnamese communism; here he was again equating fringe groups, like the DuBois Clubs or Progressive Labor, with the whole of the New Left. He also ridiculed "middle-class activists . . . who regard venting their alienation from American society as more important than stopping the bloodshed in Vietnam"—without revealing how he'd managed to evaluate their motives. Yet Harrington did acknowledge that "many of the cadres of the NLF are moved by a genuine nationalism and thirst for social justice and not by admiration for totalitarianism. . . ." He also honorably confessed to "being emotionally dissatisfied with my own position. This war is so ugly and horrible that I want to do something more personal, more involved. . . ."

Yet in contrast to David's support for civil disobedience, Harrington believed that rising sentiment against the war "has come about in spite of, and not because of, tactics of civil disruption" such as the "kamikaze" attempts to block access to induction centers. He labeled such actions as "anti-libertarianism and elitism," and predicted that they "will alienate people from the anti-war cause. . . ."

David's response was conciliatory but firm: "I think it a tragedy if the one or two NLF flags that do appear in mass peace demonstrations are what keep him [Harrington] out of the line of march." David insisted that "at the core of radical politics, and not incidental to it, is a sense of morality." He agreed with Harrington that the triumph of the NLF might indeed establish a totalitarian regime. It might also be true that calling for unilateral withdrawal could alienate the public and prolong the war. But "we cannot really predict the results of our acts and . . . for the radical, it is essential to judge the value of the act itself." And he was in no doubt that peaceful protests against the war *were* moral acts.

6

Protesting the War in Vietnam

During Dave Dellinger's 1966 trip to North Vietnam, he approached the authorities there to see if he could arrange for additional visits from members of the U.S. peace movement. They not only agreed but urged him to organize the trips as soon as possible. The first one, in December/January 1966–67, lasted for eleven days and consisted of four women: Diane Nash Bevel, a well-known figure in SNCC; Pat Griffith, a Far East specialist; Grace Mora Newman, sister of one of the three GIs who'd refused assignment to Vietnam and were serving long prison sentences; and Barbara Deming.[1]

Barbara, like Dellinger before her, was horrified at what she saw. Everywhere they went—and they were shown a large sampling of villages and cities—she witnessed similar wreckage from U.S. bombing raids on *non*-military targets, despite the government's insistence that it aimed solely at military sites. Either the skill of the pilots was woefully inadequate, or the U.S. government was lying about a deliberate "war of terror against the civilian population." Schools, churches, hospitals, and homes everywhere lay in rubble. In the town of Phu Ly, which had a prewar population of nearly eight thousand, not a single building had been left standing and there were no inhabitants. When bombing South Vietnam, the weapon of choice was napalm. In the North, it was often pellet bombs, specifically designed for people, not buildings. Estimating the number of *civilians* killed or maimed to date, Barbara put the figure (later confirmed) at close to a million—not to mention those, homeless or orphaned, who wandered the streets.[2]

On returning to the States and angrily making her observations public, the government began to issue statements designed to discredit the four women. It claimed, for example, that Vietnamese antiaircraft fire had caused most of the damage the women had witnessed. The claim outraged Barbara: "We are supposed to believe, apparently," that these people were "infinitely stupid—clearly an inferior race—because they could day after day fire off antiaircraft which would miss and fall back, damaging their own buildings, and they could persist in this clumsily, day after day . . ." Harrison Salisbury, the respected *New York Times* reporter, was in North Vietnam at the same time as the four women and he, too, reported seeing bomb craters much too deep to be accounted for by antiaircraft fire.

To counter the government, Barbara utilized whatever media opportunities came her way. These included the *Today* show, where the feminist writer Andrea Dworkin, for one, thought she was "strong, vital, and gentle: speech pared down to its essential content: simple, true and firm." But along with encouragement, Barbara received a stream of hostile letters. Among the less ugly ones, Barbara was asked why *we* should get out of Vietnam, but not the Communists, too. "Isn't it because the Communists live there?" Barbara replied. "They are Vietnamese; so where could they go? President Eisenhower himself estimated that if the elections were held which the Geneva Accords of 1954 had promised (and which we prevented), at least 80% of the Vietnamese would have voted for Ho Chi Minh—who is a Communist."

During the winter of 1967, Barbara went on a speaking tour to talk about her experiences in North Vietnam and to share her fear "that we Americans are on our way to becoming the *world's* bullies, all while the majority of us are confident in our hearts that we are a well-intentioned people and therefore incapable of atrocities." After describing the devastation she'd witnessed, Barbara would urge her listeners to take a series of actions: to refuse to pay taxes, or at least the 10 percent added to the telephone bill that went directly to paying for the war; to refuse to buy government bonds or to work in places that produced napalm and the like; and to boycott companies like Dow Chemical that manufactured the weapons of destruction.

Good-size crowds turned out to hear her. Paralleling the onset of bombing North Vietnam in 1965, the pace of antiwar protest had also begun to escalate. And paralleling the U.S. government's campaign of disinformation, two consortiums sprang up—the Underground Press Syndicate and the Liberation News Service—to share and disseminate more reliable reporting. With the spread of information about the war's mounting horrors came larger crowds at antiwar demonstrations. Martin Luther King Jr.'s open expression of support—*on moral grounds*— for protesting the war in the spring of 1967 increased the crowds still further.

During Barbara's speaking tour, some member of her audiences always rose to denounce her arguments as "disloyal," to which she would respond that "they are profoundly the opposite." If one's leaders were taking the country down a road that "is both ignoble and utterly reckless, . . . surely the role of loyalty is to try to prevent this." She would add that we owed loyalty to our government only if "it serves the interests of our people," and she'd ask in what way the conflict in Vietnam met that requirement. Far from serving our interests, she would argue, our leaders were wasting our resources, wasting "all the money that should be doing something about our cities, doing something about poverty, doing something about the pollution of our air and water." On top of which the government was sending increasing numbers of our young men—"particularly from the poor and exploited among us"—to be killed or maimed. Besides, we owed loyalty "to people everywhere," not just to those in the United States, and she urged her audiences to recall that the Declaration of Independence stated, "*All* men are endowed with certain inalienable rights."

Back in April 1966, Barbara has also joined a six-person trip to Saigon that had included A.J. Muste and Brad Lyttle. She thought such a trip "particularly right and necessary—to protest the war on the very spot where it was being waged." Initially she'd felt "much too scared" to accept the invitation. Many people thought that physical courage came automatically to Barbara. It didn't, nor did it to David McReynolds; both had to engage in an intense inner struggle to overcome their fear. Nonetheless, Barbara's keen interest in the trip had led her to attend the planning meetings. Mary Christiansen, a woman Barbara had met earlier, had been one of the first volunteers to go to Saigon, and at one of the meetings Barbara asked her directly if she wasn't frightened. "I hadn't really thought about that yet," Mary said. That seemed to Barbara exactly the right response—to think first about whether an action was important enough to take, and then later about how to cope with one's anxiety. And that was how she'd gotten herself to join the group.[3]

Not that her fears simply evaporated. Up until the time she was due to leave, Barbara found herself dwelling on the odds of getting killed in Saigon. It was only when she walked up to the rest of the group at the airport terminal that her fear ebbed and was replaced by "a very peculiar kind of joy." And that was the larger lesson she learned, or relearned: "to borrow the extra courage from one another that we sometimes needed." And toward the end of her trip to Saigon, she did need it. When their group held an outdoor meeting to protest the war, they were attacked by some paid students, arrested, and deported.

Barbara had long been convinced that unless more people moved from "words of dissent to acts of disobedience," the protest to stop the war would have no effect on government policy. To that end, it was essential always to stand together in support of "*whomever* is singled out for punishment." This wasn't an easy task, for the movement was composed of a variety of individuals and no one felt entirely comfortable with everybody else. In Barbara's view, people always needed to be frank with one another when they disagreed, but her plea was "that we not begin to be afraid of any of us and, in a panic, try to wish any of us out of the picture. We will need every one of us. We are all part of one another."

Her words proved applicable to two other major actions she joined in the months after returning from Saigon. The first was in front of the Pentagon on October 21, 1967, a gathering in which David McReynolds also participated (as he had in an earlier Speak-Out there). The Defense Department had severely restricted previous demonstrations at the Pentagon, but a large crowd was expected at this one, and just before leaving for Washington, D.C., David warned his parents that he "may well be jailed there."[4]

Months of planning preceded the demonstration, in some of which (the trip from Wellfleet to New York City was a difficult one) Barbara participated. In David's later view, Dave Dellinger—who did do a prodigious amount of work for the event—has too exclusively been given the credit for it, and Norma Becker and Sid Peck, who worked behind the scenes, have been given too little. In any case, the planning sessions were often contentious, particularly between "Yippie" leaders Abbie Hoffman and Jerry Rubin on one side and their critics on the other. At one point, a split was narrowly averted by Barbara's suggestion that the event be divided into two parts—the demonstration in front of the Lincoln Memorial, for which a legal permit had been secured, and which wouldn't involve acts of civil disobedience, and then a march to the Pentagon, where the government would be directly confronted.

The demonstration drew some hundred thousand people at the Lincoln Memorial, the largest antiwar protest to date, but only half that number then went to the Pentagon. After nightfall, the Pentagon crowd moved to the lawn in front of the building, apparently prepared to spend the night. Young men began to burn their draft cards, which flickered in the darkness, yet the police seemed unwilling to interfere. David had fully expected to be arrested and had come prepared with a toothbrush, a few chocolate bars, and a book to read. But since some time had passed and the cops seemed willing to let the protesters sit there freezing all night, and since he was already nursing a cold, David decided to leave the Pentagon grounds and head back to Manhattan. Soon after he left, the police and the marshals, preceded by tear gas, suddenly descended on the crowd with their clubs flailing. They shut down the sound system and made nearly seven hundred arrests, with fifty prisoners receiving jail sentences. Barbara and Dellinger were among those arrested.

Dellinger was one of many demonstrators badly bloodied by the MPs and marshals, and J. Edgar Hoover had him put on the FBI's notorious "watch list." The clashes between the troops and the protesters continued until the permit for the demonstration expired at midnight the following evening. Dellinger declared a triumph for mass civil disobedience and said that the time had come to apply the same tactics to the upcoming 1968 national political conventions. The widespread publicity given the protest may not have resulted in converting any or many hawks, but at least it spread the word about resistance to the war. Barbara subsequently worked with a group of young peace activists in Hyannis, near her Wellfleet home. When they were jailed, Barbara, joined by Mary Meigs, stood in front of the prison protesting.

The second major national action Barbara participated in during that period was the Poor People's Campaign initiated by Martin Luther King Jr. shortly before his assassination on April 4, 1968. Five weeks after King's death, the Poor People's Campaign built what came to be known as "Resurrection City" in the nation's capital. Barbara had joined the campaign at its starting point at the Lorraine Motel in Memphis, where King had been murdered the month before, and walked from there to the encampment in Washington, D.C. While on the road, the walkers, almost all of them blacks, with a scattering of white radicals, often slept in municipal gyms where the loud voices bounced off the walls and allowed only a few hours of sleep each night.[5]

The living was still harder when they arrived in Resurrection City. Barbara stayed for a full three weeks; the City lasted six weeks in all. It rained so often that the plywood shelters leaked and mud was omnipresent, sometimes thick enough to pull off shoes. There was no garbage collection; water was available only from a few fountains and outdoor taps; the food supply consisted primarily of bologna sandwiches; the police periodically sprayed Mace at random, sometimes enough to blind and choke people for long periods; the public address system was relentlessly loud, its babble of announcements and instructions lost in repetition; and civility in general was at a low ebb.

The population of the City was much more diverse than during the march from Memphis. Poor black people were joined by poor white people, Native Americans, Mexican Americans, and Puerto Ricans— precisely the mix that the organizers had intended in the hope of creating Poor People's Power. But solidarity failed to materialize, replaced instead by ethnic antagonisms and the outbreak of near-constant fights. It was difficult to see that the encampment was producing anything of significance, and more than a few residents got fed up and left.

No confrontation with the government ever happened, and yet Barbara agreed with Southern Christian Leadership Conference (SCLC) leader James Bevel that the encampment should be seen as an opening shot, a necessary "clearing up of our minds." Still, when the government closed Resurrection City down, Barbara felt there should have been a major confrontation. Instead, the SCLC leadership chose to negotiate with the government to ensure that the city be evacuated as quietly as possible. Barbara felt offended that SCLC's ministerial leadership, so used to being listened *to*, had failed to pay attention to the wishes of the actual participants in the Poor People's Campaign.

She believed that if they had, the city's residents would have chosen "to stage a demonstration that would not have been quickly forgotten by this country."

Barbara's active participation in the black and antiwar struggles did much to clarify her theoretical understanding of the deeper issues involved in employing nonviolent tactics. She produced a major essay, "On Revolution and Equilibrium," which had a powerful impact on many who read it. In the essay, Barbara began with the assertion that she felt no need to judge those—particularly some offshoots of SDS or the current leadership of SNCC and CORE—who currently could find no way to avoid using violent means to combat the violence employed against blacks or the Vietnamese people. Rather than judging those who'd come to such a conclusion, Barbara focused on a set of trenchant questions: If nonviolent campaigns had to date produced only slight gains for blacks (which she didn't dispute) did that mean "nonviolent tactics were the wrong tactics to employ," or had many of those leading the battle underestimated "the difficulties of the terrain before them? Did they lack at the start a sufficiently radical vision? Can those who have now turned from reliance upon nonviolence say surely that resort to violence over those same years would have brought greater gains?"[6]

The recent black-led rioting in many U.S. cities—the "counterviolence of the victimized," Dave Dellinger named it—had succeeded in bringing out the troops and in inflicting many injuries among the rioters, but what gains had it yielded? Barbara's answer was none, beyond increasing the recognition among the oppressed that the enemy didn't consist solely of those few who ran the show, but rather "a whole system." That gain in awareness was worth having, but it came at the expense of caricaturing nonviolent action as an impotent appeal to conscience. Barbara agreed that in the past the nonviolent peace movement had too often confined itself to petition and had spoken too glibly of "loving" one's opponents.

But contrary to Stokely Carmichael, one of SNCC's leaders, Barbara argued that the choice wasn't simply between a humble appeal to conscience on the one hand or a resort to violence on the other. There was power *in* nonviolence, "and to speak to conscience one need not be meek." The most effective actions resorted simultaneously to the power of direct action *and* to engaged the conscience. If nonviolent actions had failed to produce greater gains, too much—just as Carmichael charged—had been expected from those in power, too many had relied on a demeaning appeal to brutal opponents "to love one's fellow human beings."

In Barbara's view, more emphasis needed to be put on the power "one discovers when one refuses any longer simply to do another's will." One had to use words less and exert force more—nonviolent force. Gandhi's *satyagraha*, after all, meant "*clinging* to the truth." As Barbara put it, "One doesn't just say 'if we are customers in this store, it's wrong that we're never hired here' but refuses to be a customer any longer. One doesn't just say, 'I don't believe in this war' but refuses to put on a uniform. One doesn't just say 'the use of napalm is atrocious' but refuses to pay for it by refusing to pay one's taxes, and so on and so on. . . . There is a good deal more involved here than a moral appeal. It should be acknowledged . . . that we, too, rely upon force. When, for example, we sit down and refuse to move, we force others to cope somehow with all these bodies."

But then how did that separate the tactics of the peace movement from the war movement? Barbara's answer was "that those committed to a nonviolent discipline refuse to injure the antagonist. . . . The man who acts violently forces another to do *his* will. . . . He tears another away from himself, pushes him around, often willing to break him, to kill him. The man who acts nonviolently insists upon acting out his *own* will, refuses to act out another's—but in this way only, exerts force upon the other, not tearing him away from himself but tearing from him only that which is not properly his own, the strength which has been loaned to him by all those who have been giving him obedience."

But Barbara herself found those distinctions "a little too neat." She was well aware that in "any serious nonviolent struggle, one has to resort to obstructive action. When we block access to buildings, block traffic, block shipments, it can be charged that we go a little further than refusing obedience and impose upon the freedom of action of others." She thought there was some justice to the charge but continued to feel that it was "appropriate to speak of nonviolent obstruction," and she reverted to her earlier distinction "as the definitive one: the person committed to nonviolent action refuses to injure the antagonist. It is quite possible to frustrate another's action without doing him injury. And some freedoms are basic freedoms, some are not. To impose upon another man's freedom to kill . . . is not to violate his person in a fundamental way."

The heart of her argument, Barbara felt, rested on solid ground: "We can put *more* pressure on the antagonist for whom we show human concern. It is precisely solicitude for his person *in combination with* a stubborn interference with his actions that can give us a very special degree of control (precisely in our acting both with love, if you will—in the sense that we respect his human rights—and truthfulness, in the sense that we act out fully our objections to his violating *our* right). We put upon him two pressures—the pressure of our defiance of him and the pressure of our respect for his life—and it happens that in combination these two pressures are uniquely effective."

As was often the case, in public as well as private matters, Barbara was her own subtlest critic. She questioned her own formulation about frustrating "another's action without doing him injury," foretelling possible objections to it. In staging an action of massive obstruction in a city, for example, she acknowledged "the risk that we will prevent some emergency call from being answered"—like preventing a doctor's car or an ambulance from getting through in time to save a patient's life. To avoid such potential catastrophes, Barbara urged that such situations be anticipated and carefully planned for, but she recognized that not every contingency could be predicted.

This isn't to say that Barbara anticipated *all* possible criticisms of her position. When she wrote, for example, that "the antagonist cannot take the interference with his actions personally, because his person is not threatened," it seems reasonable to ask for a definition of "his *person.*" Doesn't "person" include one's values and understanding of the world? Wouldn't a confirmed segregationist, convinced that God had created blacks as inferior beings, feel that in assaulting the very basis of his belief system, his *person* was being violated? As Barbara put it, "the whole subject [of pacifism] is infinitely complex." If some flaws or omissions exist in her argument, she remains entitled to being called, as at least one historian has, one of the few "major theorists" of nonviolence during the mid-twentieth century.

Barbara's personal life had become less stable than her political views. She, Mary Meigs, and Marie-Claire had continued to live together in Wellfleet, and the atmosphere was often one of ease, when, as Mary put it, "our need for love and attention is satisfied, times of harmonious equilibrium . . ." Barbara, too, felt "that for the most part our days are calm and affectionate." Often they read silently during meals, Marie-Claire fascinated by Émile Durkheim's study of suicide, a natural match, given her preoccupation with suffering and morbidity. But even Marie-Claire found it "very amusing" when one night, after they'd drunk a fair amount of wine, she and Barbara "did imitations of all the people at Wellfleet." She felt compelled to add that "when she wants, [Barbara] can be very funny," implying that she rarely wanted.[7]

During the early years together, Barbara had even, for a time, felt herself in love with M-C, who insisted (falsely, Barbara felt) that she had similar feelings. M-C would leave flowers and little notes on Barbara's bed—"the most important thing in my life is the three of us, and if one suffers, the other suffers too." It was M-C who first suggested to Barbara (through Mary) that she "would like to lie next to her," and it was M-C, according to Barbara, who initiated a sexual relationship with her. But when the time came that M-C no longer wanted to have sex with Barbara, she again sent that message through Mary. More than a decade later, Barbara still felt some bitterness toward M-C—not because sex between them had ended but because M-C kept using Mary as a go-between instead of directly and honestly expressing her feelings to Barbara.

M-C was much more open when describing her feelings to a close friend in Canada: "how useless, vain, absurd and incommunicable it has become between me and B[arbara] . . . her virtue, her courage . . . tears me apart, I feel irritated, enraged and malicious to not have these qualities in myself." She felt that at first she'd "imposed upon myself as a job" admiration for Barbara's political activities, but that "has considerably diminished during our life together." In fact, as early as 1967, when Barbara was in prison in Washington, M-C had resented interruptions by journalists and telephone calls: "solitude is taken away once more." M-C also feared that Barbara's political activities might put her at risk of being deported.

Mary Meigs—who, by her own honest self-assessment, had "a sharp tongue" and was given to "gratuitous fits of bad temper"—was the most outspoken of the three about the growing strain between them. Marie-Claire preferred to act dreamily as if unaware of daily, passing matters, yet she managed to tell Mary that Barbara was "terrorizing" her (details unspecified), and Mary repeated the charge to Barbara. She was stunned at the accusation. Blaming herself, she decided that her wish to be alone again with Mary must have gotten communicated—though she'd never fooled herself about the fact that Mary had begun to draw away from her even before M-C appeared on the scene. In any case, Barbara was as unlikely an emotional "terrorist" as imaginable, and even M-C referred to her as "a noble and tender woman." Barbara was wise enough to realize that each of the three was "seeing things in her way—and shocked to learn how the other sees things."

Yet Barbara does seem to have been trying hard to "tread carefully." There's only a single (known) instance in which she'd ever been openly negative about Marie-Claire (and never about Mary, whom she continued to love). When Edmund Wilson, in Barbara's presence, once referred to M-C as "that little bitch," Barbara responded that M-C was more complicated than that—was "a little *witch*." Edmund— and many others it appears in the artistic community at Wellfleet— had grown ever less fond of Marie-Claire; as an irritable Edmund put it, she "believes that everything clusters around her" and "has really settled down to suffering as a way of life, [which] . . . involves making other people suffer." Nor did he any longer rank her novels as exceptional, demoting them to "monotonous and rather phantasmal."

Edmund always retained his deep affection for Mary Meigs and felt the need at one point to warn her that she might "find herself in the middle of a Balzac novel." He once asked her directly "whether she had a fine grip on her money." Mary assured him that she did and that, besides, M-C cared nothing about money. "This is natural," Edmund acidly wrote in his diary, since Marie-Claire was "spending hers." He told Barbara that he'd warned Mary directly about M-C, to which Barbara responded, "You can't warn somebody in love." Edmund predicted that Barbara, who could be naively trusting, would end up being the one "left out in the cold."

Fortunately for Barbara, she'd by chance run into Jane Watrous (now Jane Verlaine), someone she'd distantly known at Bennington when she was a senior and Jane a freshman. Back in college, Jane had been smitten by Barbara's beauty, talent, and "insurmountable melancholy." She'd been "overwhelmed by my feelings of love . . . [but] at any opportunity to speak . . . I simply lost my voice, it squeaked." She'd never let Barbara know of her attraction because Barbara and Vida Ginsberg were at the time so obviously in love.

Jane considered herself bisexual, though she recognized that Barbara believed that "you're one or the other." In the years following Bennington, Jane had married Oscar Verlaine, who worked in the school system as a psychological tester and considered himself an expert on human behavior. The couple had moved to Dillsboro, North Carolina, but within a few years the marriage had begun to disintegrate. Periodically both she and Oscar would bring up divorce, yet they'd stayed together, unhappily, because of their two children, George, age thirteen in 1969, and Mimi, age eleven.[8]

Jane and Barbara began to write often and to see each other when the geographical distance could be overcome. As early as 1967, Oscar and Barbara met, and Barbara believed that "though he is a bully, he is also in a lot of ways a sensitive man." But once he realized that she and his wife had become emotionally and sexually involved, the bully took over. He told Jane that he considered her relationship with Barbara "monstrous," that she was "a disgusting queer," "mentally ill," and "unfit" to be a mother. Barbara had much earlier learned to dismiss such charges about herself and for some time had regarded homosexuality as a perfectly normal phenomenon. Yet she now told Jane that if "deep in yourself you are persuaded by O [Oscar], by the others, then ask me boldly to be simply your friend again, and that's what I'll be. It would be hard, but it would be possible. . . . Don't allow yourself to be coerced by me in any way."

Jane and Oscar separated, but Jane began to fear that he was "dangerous," in the sense of being determined to take the children from her. He didn't seem to *want* the children but did seem resolved, in Barbara's words, "to make life awful for a while for everybody." Jane felt it was "only right" to let Oscar see the children after they divorced, but she feared that he was prepared to demand complete custody of them. By now Jane and Barbara were certain that they were in love and wanted to live together—but *with* the children.

Barbara felt that once Jane and Oscar were divorced, he'd no longer view her "as in some sense his property" and would no longer be likely to threaten legal action about the children. Still, she caught Jane's sense of alarm. She applied to Oscar the same sympathetic understanding—

the opponent, the Other, should always be treated as a human being—which she tried to bring to all her contacts and to her political encounters as well.

And for a time Oscar seemed to respond. When Barbara offered to lend him money to prevent his having to sell property at a loss, he accepted. Yet he kept seesawing back and forth about going to court to win custody of the children. And when Barbara invited Jane, George, and Mimi to spend the summer of 1969 with her in Maine, Oscar exploded, writing Jane a vicious letter denouncing her as "evil," calling her "a homosexual prostitute to Barbara Deming," and accusing her of "having betrayed all, even your own children."

He wasn't alone. Various "friends" of Jane's and Barbara's took to reciting the same litany: Are you sure you won't harm the children? Isn't a father figure essential to their healthy maturation? Both women were afraid there might be some truth to those questions, and they had to overcome the fear that being raised by two women wasn't an optimal situation. Barbara comforted them both by arguing that the lack of father figure in fact amounted to "the lack of a patriarchal brainwasher." But they remained fearful that if it came to a court battle, they were likely to lose the children. The women's movement in 1969 was much less strong in the South than in the North, and even their own Southern lawyer was "not really on our side" (they eventually got some help from a New York City lawyer). But to keep the fight out of the courts, they essentially ended up paying Oscar "what amounted to ransom."

Knowing that Barbara and Jane intended to live together, Mary Meigs, under pressure from Marie-Claire, decided to break up the household at Wellfleet. M-C had previously claimed to love her rather austere country life with Mary and Barbara but had lately been talking angrily about (in Mary's words) "the sacrifice of her youth, as though it had been imposed on her by her pitiless friends." Into the mix, also, went the fact that M-C had fallen in love with another woman, Andrée, and wanted the three of them to live together in Brittany, which for two years they did, Mary later blaming herself for "the zombie-state that paralyzed my will." "With whom else in all the world," Barbara wrote Mary, "could she have found the kind of home-and-yet-freedom she has found with you?"

By the time the breakups began all around, Mary and Barbara had long since felt sure, and as it turned out accurately, that the bond between the two of them was "permanent and unshakeable." Barbara wanted Jane to understand that in spite of being "in the very midst of the greatest happiness I have ever felt," she still felt pain about Mary's falling out of love with her some years before and also at the imminent breakup: "fifteen years, fifteen years—no, they don't drop off one like clothes. It's one's own skin that one leaves behind." As a parting gift, Mary stunned Barbara with the generous-hearted present of a small house in Maine.

By the fall of 1969, after "a scary and exhausting fight," and a lonely one, Oscar finally agreed—thanks to the payment of money—that Jane could have custody of the children. Along with Barbara, Mimi, and George, she found an old farmhouse near Monticello, about two hours from New York City, with twenty-one beautiful acres of woodland and pastures. When Barbara went to collect her furniture from Wellfleet, neither M-C nor Mary appeared, which hurt her very deeply. The Monticello house needed a lot of repair, and all hands worked diligently at it for months. By the end of the year, it was livable, and Barbara reported to a friend that she'd "never felt in such harmony with another person. (With the kids too)." An extra blessing was that the two women held similar political views.

If the upheavals in Barbara's life during 1968–69 kept her from being as active in movement work as she'd previously been, David's activities, if anything, picked up speed. In 1968 alone, he led a losing faction fight within the Socialist Party to prevent the Shachtmanites from gaining control of the Executive Committee; helped to organize a Peace and Freedom Party (P&FP)—which had seventy thousand members in California alone—for New York State; successfully argued for the WRL to sponsor *Win* magazine, which would become influential; and even ran for Congress on the P&FP ticket. Overworked, he became tired and depressed, again started drinking too much, and again gave thought to seeing a therapist. But when he went back to exercise and meditation, he felt a good deal better within weeks, though his sense of well-being would continue to waver.[9]

In the face of SDS's growing militancy and the rise of Black Power nationalism, David began to refer to himself as a "conservative radical." At one meeting of the Peace and Freedom Party, for example, attended by "the usual mishmash of ultra radicals who want to burn things down," he actually lost his temper when a "revolutionary" black man started heckling him, while he was giving the main speech of the evening, about the need to start shooting cops. Startled at his loss of control, David blamed his outburst on buried racism: "How close to the surface this is in all of us."[10]

Although recent polls revealed that roughly 80 percent of blacks still favored integration over separatism, David believed that the polls didn't register "the intensity of hatred" that existed. In New York, black nationalists had formed a splinter party—Freedom and Peace (F&P)—that reordered the priorities of the national Peace and Freedom Party and gave the party's black caucus an automatic 50 percent vote.

F&P nominated a black militant, Herman Ferguson, to run for the U.S. Senate and then drafted David to run on its ticket for the Senate spot. Remarkably, the Black Panthers pledged him unconditional support—quite a testimony to his long record of activism against racism. "Politics on the Left are rougher now than they used to be," David wrote his parents, "and I would just as soon not be where I now find myself." Indeed, a heated series of maneuvers and threats followed, and David bowed out of the Senate race and ran instead for a seat in the House—with Eldridge Cleaver, the P&FP candidate for president, who'd often asserted that nonviolence was no longer an acceptable tactic for blacks. David met Cleaver and found him "impressive and likeable" (though his opinion would soon change) and David rationalized running on the same ticket with him because he "is genuinely committed to building a radical coalition of blacks and whites" (an opinion that would also change).

David believed that black self-assertion was essential. "Do not ask the black man to love us now," he wrote in an essay. "He cannot. Whatever psychic energy he has will be directed toward loving himself, his people, his potentiality. Accept his hatred as a step toward his own liberation." At the same time, David felt that in the face of such hatred, "we should not flee . . . there must not be any more applause or twittering amongst ourselves when we are called 'honkies' and written off as 'scum.'"

But he also felt that by itself black nationalism wasn't enough, that it "wasn't even radical, despite its talk of guns and violence" but rather "potentially very reactionary by breaking into bits and pieces the blacks, the poor whites, the Jews, etc., who need a certain unity of action to really get at the system itself." He feared that "the Black Power movement takes the Negro out of politics." He felt sure that a revolution without violence could not be achieved by whites alone, but he was unhappily aware that "the courage and endurance required to build such a coalition was lacking on all sides." Yet without such a coalition of blacks and whites, he predicted, "there will be death in the ghetto in which a few cops and many black children will die . . . before the iron fist of white fear closes in" and produces a frightening backlash.

In David's view, the "one element of health" in the rise of Black Power was "the sense of dignity the slum Negro has come to feel as a result." But he felt that although the newest set of black believers, personified by H. Rap Brown (a prominent figure in both SNCC and the Black Panther Party), *did* speak for the agony of the ghetto, Brown could not speak to it: "He has no program nor any direction" except that which the embittered, frustrated mobs that had been rioting in cities across the country had already taken.

He thought it illogical for some believers in black power to have "made the Arabs special objects of support even though in some areas of the Arab world blacks are still enslaved and the Arabs historically were *the* slave traders in Africa." The call for separatism, moreover, had in David's mind "strong support from the most racist elements in the white community because they see it as one of the easiest ways of disposing of an otherwise impossible situation." But only whites controlled "enough capital to tear down ghettos and rebuild them. We didn't ask for the power, but we have the power, and if we fail to use it, we then do become guilty for the communal violence that lies ahead."

A few weeks before the election, yet another racial conflict opened up in the Ocean Hill–Brownsville school district in Brooklyn, which was overwhelmingly black. Local parents had blamed the schools for their children's failure, and a decentralization agreement had been reached, with control over the schools passing to the community. The new community board promptly transferred a group of nineteen white teachers and administrators and refused to reinstate them. That led the United Federation of Teachers (UFT) to go out on strike late in September 1968. The Shachtmanites (David cursed the day he'd led the effort to bring them into the SP) supported the strike. So did Mike Harrington, though somewhat reluctantly. David was vehemently against it. He blamed the UFT for refusing to accept the inevitable: that the schools in the district would be run by the local (black) community. He even advocated that the UFT picket line be crossed, the locks on the school doors busted, and the kids allowed to return to class. The struggle in Ocean Hill–Brownsville would drag on well after the fall election, with the UFT ultimately winning its demand for reinstatement.

Five people ended up running for the House of Representatives from District 19. David ran on a platform calling, among other things, for immediate withdrawal from Vietnam, amnesty for all war resisters, an end of the draft, elimination of the CIA, and withdrawal from the space race until "we have dealt with poverty and slums." He wryly noted that the P&F Party posters referred to him as "Dave"—an attempt, he humorously suggested, "to humanize someone who appears so remote and distant to most people."

The *Village Voice* threw its support to David, whom it characterized, accurately, as having "a passion for democracy, faith in reason and tolerance, and an implacable opposition to violence and dehumanization." But the P&F Party could allocate less than $5,000 to the race, and no one was under any illusion that David would poll more than a few thousand votes. And in fact, his vote tally came in at a little under 5 percent. On the national level, David considered Nixon a dangerous, unreliable man and was horrified at his victory.

At the 1968 WRL convention, the division was generational, not racial (since so few blacks were members). The younger people at the convention opted for nude swimming during the day; David had no objection to the nudity but felt that "a small group [was] imposing a decision on the larger group." He asked himself, "Am I getting square in my old age?" and answered, "Very possibly." That answer may have shown admirable self-deprecation, but wasn't really true when compared to the attitudes of many other older lefties, like Mike Harrington. At the annual Socialist Party convention in July 1968, for example, David led the losing left-wing opposition, and Harrington continued his lukewarm support of Max Shachtman. When the Shachtmanites won control of the national committee at the convention, they elected Harrington chairman of the party, even though in practice they largely ignored him.

Harrington and Shachtman continued to share the view that labor remained the central ingredient and focus of the needed effort to remake the Democratic Party—though unlike Shachtman, Harrington welcomed the "conscience constituency," which apparently included people like David, as an ally in that effort. And whereas Shachtman sweepingly denounced the New Left, Harrington was much more muted in his criticism, rejecting SDS's "moral" opposition to liberals still trying to work within the system. He also—again, unlike Shachtman—moved ever closer to SDS's position on the war in Southeast Asia, and by 1969 he would finally abandon his support of negotiations in favor of U.S. withdrawal.

David agreed more fully with SDS and had for some time. Like the New Left, he stressed the importance of being loyal to one's own sense of right and wrong, not to the state's definition. And he opposed the manipulations and maneuvers of mainstream politics—like Shachtman's attempt to "capture" and reform the Democratic Party (in fact, he ended up joining it and defending its policies). David also agreed with SDS in dismissing the argument that the war in Vietnam had to continue simply because we were already involved. Yet he never became an uncritical supporter of the New Left. As someone who despised totalitarianism of any kind, David thought SDS's dismissal of anticommunism too blithe and its tendency to embrace the "old hacks" of the CP too encompassing.

David's aversion to Stalinism was, if possible, further heightened in the summer of 1968 by his accidental presence during the Soviet invasion of Czechoslovakia. He'd gone to Europe to attend two conferences, one in Vienna (the War Resisters International) and the other in Ljubljana, Yugoslavia (the International Confederation for Disarmament and Peace). There was a four-day interval between the two, and David, curious to see what many on the left called "presently existing socialism," decided to spend the time vacationing in Prague. On his last scheduled evening, August 20, he roamed the city until 2:30 A.M. and then got up at 6:30 to catch his flight to Yugoslavia.[11]

When he went downstairs in his hotel for coffee, he immediately sensed a crisis in the air. Looking out the window, he saw Soviet tanks rolling by in the streets and Russian troop carriers lining the road. He learned that all flights had been canceled, and going outside he saw small, quiet groups of Czechs weeping openly. By noon organized resistance to the Soviet invasion had begun, and by evening underground papers began to appear. When David walked toward the center of town, he discovered that the Czechs had built a barricade to try to stop the tanks—"a fantastic tangle of burned-out streetcars, buses, trucks, and debris."

Over the next two days, David saw, with immense admiration, a proliferation of nonviolent actions. The Czechs, under Alexander Dubček, had enjoyed some eight months of uncensored press and radio, and they now peppered the city with manifestos, leaflets, and papers. Posters supporting Dubček, who'd been arrested, were draped everywhere over buildings, trams, and cars, and the Czech national flag was displayed in many windows. Groups of Czechs surrounded nearly every Russian tank or troop carrier—not to throw rocks but to argue and plead with Russian soldiers. Thousands of people clogged the main street headed into Wenceslas Square. On August 23, the American embassy notified American citizens in Prague that a special train would be leaving for Vienna at 5:00 P.M. David got on it and reluctantly headed for his conference in Yugoslavia. The Soviet occupation of Czechoslovakia would last until 1990.

7

The Late 1960s—Militancy and the Emergence of Feminism and Gay Liberation

The bloody attacks by police on protesters at the 1968 Democratic Party convention in Chicago were followed in 1969–70 by the "conspiracy" trial of the so-called Chicago Eight. The trial was a parody of justice, and its verdicts were later reversed, but the two events together seemed to catalyze the antiwar movement's shift away from the principles of nonviolence. Dave Dellinger, one of the Chicago Eight, himself wavered between orthodox pacifism and the violent resistance championed by Tom Hayden, one of the younger generation's leaders.[1]

Neither David nor Barbara was in Chicago during the convention. David certainly didn't feel that the Democratic Party was *his* party but did believe it had the right to hold a convention and had disapproved of the demonstrations; both of them were predictably dismayed at the violence that had taken place. Though Barbara followed events closely, she was temporarily preoccupied with inhabiting a new life. As for David, at thirty-nine he felt confused about the amount of violence that suddenly seemed everywhere. "Why are they carrying guns? Why are they rioting and throwing fire bombs? . . . My protection is in making friends with these, the armed youth, even as I try to disarm them."

David was referring in particular to the sudden rise out of SDS of the Weather Underground and the various factions of the Revolutionary Youth Movement—all committed to violent resistance to the war in Vietnam. David feared that someone would shoot a cop, and then repression would come down hard. He never doubted that President-elect Nixon was capable of it, even eager for it. He had, after all, continued Johnson's policy "of trying to win a war by simply demolishing populations that get in his way." In David's view, this was "criminal insanity": "Johnson and Nixon between them have killed more people than any combination of Soviet leaders since Stalin. . . ."

Then in December 1969 came the police murder in Chicago of Black Panther leaders Fred Hampton and Mark Clark, followed soon after by the killing of four students at Kent State University during antiwar protests. These events made David feel "increasingly doubtful we can find a nonviolent solution. Hour by hour the chances of a democratic resolution of the conflict—the impeachment of Nixon and Agnew—slip away and crisis deepens." David was still drinking at the time, and he had a strong sense of fear that at any moment the thin door of his apartment might be smashed in.[2]

When the Socialist Party convened at its biannual convention a month after the Kent State shootings, it seemed to David reasonable to hope that an unequivocal statement would *finally* emerge condemning the war in Vietnam. But quite the opposite happened. With the help of Mike Harrington, the Shachtmanites extended their control. David called Harrington "the gutless wonder of the socialist movement . . . the war is still, in his mind, tragic, but it is still impossible for him to choke out the words 'get out,' even in a whisper." A resolution calling for the U.S. unilaterally to withdraw from the conflict was defeated by a resounding three-to-one margin. What passed instead was an openly prowar declaration describing the situation in Vietnam as "one of democracy versus totalitarian communism."

This was too much for David, and even Harrington later backtracked, thus leading Shachtman to cut off all ties with him. David remained a member of the party's left-wing Debs Caucus but, given all the years he'd devoted to the SP and the hopes he'd once had for it, he felt deeply saddened by its conservative stance. This was especially true now that portions of the labor movement, led by Walter Reuther, had rejected George Meany's leadership and moved into the antiwar column. David continued to bend his energy to bringing the Vietnam war to a close.

In May 1971, he was again in D.C., this time for two weeks, to march on the Justice Department and to participate in a sit-in on the steps of the Capitol. David worried beforehand that there would be violence. He knew and trusted Abbie Hoffman but thought Jerry Rubin was "on a permanent ego trip." Most of all David worried about another "Yippie" leader, Rennie Davis, who he found "so reserved" and enigmatic that David never felt sure *what* Davis had in mind or was going to do. There was even a widespread rumor that might be a government agent instructed to provoke a bloodbath. But Davis was *not* an agent and did not—unlike the police—engage in violent actions.

During the demonstration, David felt "terrified at the triple row of cops in front of us with their clubs at the ready." As it turned out, he wasn't one of the many who got bloodied. Thousands of others did get arrested on the steps of Congress, as Congressman Ron Dellums was addressing the crowd, and David himself did end up in jail again. This time the protesters were housed in an indoor stadium (the Coliseum), and David was sleepless during his thirty hours there—the crowd was so large that there was no space on the floor at night, he had no blanket, and it was too cold to sleep anyway.

But the whole action heartened him. Some of the "kids" in jail with him were so obnoxious that he "wanted to hit them over the head" (possible for a pacifist to fantasize but not to act on), but most of them he found "beautiful." There was also "massive support from the black community" for the demonstrations, which allowed David to harbor the hope that the movement might again become "black and white together." He came out of the whole experience "deeply moved, even shaken." The Socialist Party paper opposed *all* the demonstrations and, as David put it, "honored me twice by mentioning me as one of the villains."[3]

Barbara, too, was part of the "Mayday" actions in the Capitol, marking her return to active involvement with the movement. She took part in a piece of guerrilla theater planned by the National Peace Action Coalition and it was she who suggested that a symbol be designed to represent the peaceful nature of the demonstration—a square with a stylized dove of peace on it and the words PRACTICE NONVIOLENCE. Barbara also took part in guerrilla theater planned by the People's

Coalition: the group dressed themselves in sackcloth, rubbed their faces in ashes or dirt, painted trickles of blood at the corners of their eyes or mouths, and then went weeping and wailing through the Senate office building. After initially feigning her tears, Barbara, to her own astonishment, began to cry real ones. Like David, she ended up in jail—a playing field without shelter, latrines, or, until the night of the first day, food—but like him, she returned to Monticello "filled with new hopes" that centered on the younger generation of activists. She was enthralled at the celebratory way each new wave of arrested people was greeted, with intense warmth and energy—blankets tossed high, until one of the prisoners yelled out, "Remember those with asthma!"—and with the constant effort to dialogue with the police and MPs guarding them.[4]

Jail, as usual, was uncomfortable. At one point, they were gassed without warning when the outdoor wire fence they'd been leaning on began to buckle. But as Barbara wrote to her friend, Tracy Mygatt, a pioneering figure in the peace movement, people looked out for one another, and everyone she had contact with seemed committed to militant nonviolence—after three years, Barbara wrote, in which the majority of youths, she'd feared, had turned sharply away from any such commitment. She told Tracy, "It was one of the happiest times I have ever spent, because of these companions. Full of noise, of exploding energy, of irreverence for present authority."

It deeply touched her that they were also full of "amazing carefulness" toward others; they befriended cops and MPs, "and the MPs ended by collecting hundreds of dollars of bail" for them. "Don't believe the mass media about the young protestors," Barbara warned Tracy, "they are not at all, as charged, just out to tear down. They are determined to build a new society—a more loving one. And they don't depend on leaders!—another very hopeful note. They act in small affinity groups—the groups of course in touch with each other—and improvising as they go."

The previous year and a half for Barbara had been consumed by the many adjustments involved in shifting houses and partners and by the protracted ups and downs of the custody battle with Oscar. That had finally ended with the decision to leave it up to the two children to decide which parent to live with, and they swiftly chose Jane— and Barbara. Then came seemingly endless months of scraping and painting, scraping and painting, to make their new home livable. Despite all the hard work, Barbara had never felt happier, convinced that she had finally found her soul mate.

But some adjustments did have to be made—not only with Jane, but with Mary Meigs as well. Jane held honesty in as high esteem as Barbara did and felt it necessary to let her know that they placed different value on sexuality. Barbara had always welcomed and felt comfortable with sex, but Jane admitted to a tendency to avoid it, to go through periods when she wanted to retreat even from affection. She didn't pretend to understand why but thought it might have to do with feeling "unworthy" and also "a kind of exhaustion of the last few years." She felt ashamed of her resistance to someone she "adored" and who "keeps seeing my best self." But there it was. At the least she wanted Barbara to know "that I don't equal your enthusiasm" for sex and at times do "feel your love as a kind of pressure." How the two women worked out this difference between them is unknown, but some modus operandi must have been found, because they stayed together, and happily.[5]

As for Mary Meigs, Barbara was shocked and angry at the accusations Mary sent hurtling after her in the months following her departure. Mary repeated her earlier charge that Barbara had all but molested Marie-Claire, forcing her sexual attentions on the unwilling younger woman. Barbara was initially horrified at the indictment, knowing full well that M-C had declared herself in love with her and had initiated sex between them. But the more she thought about it, she wrote Mary, the more she became convinced that she *had* "pressed my attention (love is actually the word) upon M-C in ways with which she couldn't cope. She should have told me this herself—not left it to you to tell me. . . . But I should have been able to sense it, too, and that I didn't is a horror to me, and makes me doubt myself in a new way I never have before." Still, Barbara remained incensed at Mary's additional charge that she had made M-C "feel stupid." "How *could* I," Barbara replied in anguish, "as God knows I never thought of her as stupid."

Then there was Mary's somewhat incoherent indictment about money—something about Barbara taking for granted her benevolence. But Barbara had merely been indifferent about money, just as she was about keeping a neat house or maintaining a conventional appearance.

"Isn't it true," she plaintively wrote Mary, "that you and I have always seen things very differently (and money matters very much so)?" But it was nonetheless painful to Barbara that Mary now felt "used," making Barbara feel "that I let you . . . spend too much money on me." Still, Barbara couldn't see that, overall, "either of us deserves very deep reproaches." It was her profound wish that "on some relaxed day in the future, we'll find ourselves friends."

Within the year, the two women had patched things up—and they stayed patched. They became once again each other's most devoted friend. Barbara felt that on the whole "we were all three trying with all the energy and imagination we had to make life possible for one another." And Barbara further believed that "we almost had managed it, that to an extraordinary degree we had succeeded, that each of us suffered—and sometimes very much—but that the care we showed for one another made this always bearable. . . ." Before long, Mary—her laughter all but coming through the pages of a letter—confessed that her real money problems were with Marie-Claire, who owed her in excess of $20,000, "which she had no intentions or means, of repaying"— but should Mary, she reported, "owe her a penny for anything I have to pay right away."[6]

When Mary visited Barbara and Jane early in 1971, all three got along splendidly. After Mary left, Barbara wrote her a touching letter: "How happy I was to see you. What a complicated happiness. That even includes still an element of pain. For even though my life with Jane now is everything I want . . . your life and mine were joined so deeply for so long—and I care for you so—that in spite of all, *something* in me aches still at our having separated. And yet and yet—as I said to you—I do really feel now that our lives are joined again, in some mysterious and subtle way that strengthens us both. . . ."

In 1971, David joined a small group that visited Hanoi. At the time he arrived, he was deeply sympathetic to the Buddhist monks who'd recently led enormous mass demonstrations in Hue, and had, just over the border in South Vietnam, succeeded in shutting down the city for a time. The U.S.—playing the role of "Wrong Way" Corrigan to the hilt—had of course failed to back the Buddhists and had instead helped to clear the streets. In going to Hanoi, David knew perfectly well that he was entering the stronghold of the Communists, sworn enemies of the Buddhists. When the group landed in Hanoi, David had his camera with him and asked if he could take photographs, expecting that instead the camera would be confiscated. Their guide gave him permission, and he took pictures of anything he wanted throughout his stay.

The guide told David that he'd already seen some of his pictures in *Win* magazine. That sent David's head spinning. It turned out that Hanoi, through the International Control Commission, regularly received *Win*, and people read it, including the bylines. David quickly surmised that his occasional reference in the magazine's pages to his homosexuality was also well known—though no mention of it was ever made during his stay. Nor was David foolish enough, as he traveled around and saw women holding hands with women and men with men, to conflate friendship with sexuality.

But the sight *was* one aspect of the country's effect on him. Political dissent might be totally absent in North Vietnam, and he was well aware that repression was real and continuous, yet he couldn't help but be greatly impressed by the gentleness with which people treated each other. "The realities on the ground," as he put it, did something to modify his previously (in his words) "rigid anti-communism." But he was no dupe; he remained well aware that there were "damned good reasons" for "decent, independent radicals" to regard Communism as anathema. The thirty-five years since the war ended have confirmed David's worst fears about Communism. Vietnam in 2011 is a country marked by a security system that crushes dissent and has done little to improve the lot of most of its people, to combat endemic corruption, or to deal with widespread environmental disasters—none of which excuses the role earlier played by the U.S. in defoliating Vietnam's forests with Agent Orange, directly spraying millions of its people with dioxin, and killing several million more.[7]

On September 2, 1971, nearly four months after the Mayday demonstrations, David headed off to a WRL conference in Athens, Georgia. So did Barbara. But she never arrived. Through no fault of her own, her car was hit in a terrible accident that very nearly took her life. Suffering from multiple injuries—both lungs collapsed, and even her ability to see was compromised—she was hospitalized for the better part of four months and then laid up as an invalid at home for nearly a year. Having just gotten her life with Jane and the children on a solid footing, the ground was knocked out from under her again.

She was in considerable pain for a prolonged period, unable even to read or write. The days seemed interminable, but Barbara was a brave patient and did little complaining. After three months, the various machines that had been attached to her were removed and she underwent surgery. Following that, the doctors put her in a body cast for many more months. They kept changing the cast and once put it on so tightly around one of her ankles that she "felt as though some giant hand had hold of me by that ankle and was squeezing it." After the body cast was finally removed, Barbara had to learn to walk all over again. Once able to leave the hospital for home, more people could visit her, which provided some distraction and comfort. But for several more months she remained attached to some "monstrously awful contraption"; inactivity being contrary to her nature, the long days were "dark and painful."[8]

By the beginning of 1972, more than six months after the accident, she was able, with one eye only, to write and read for short periods while still flat on her back. Jane had kept Mary Meigs informed throughout the lengthy convalescence, and Mary, still in Brittany, wrote that "it seems to me no one has ever been patienter & braver than my old Bobbie" and wished her "inexhaustible resources for the dragging-on of your ordeal." And drag on it did. Nearly a year after the accident, Barbara remained on crutches and suffered from a tenacious bladder infection. But her eyesight had much improved and she was at last able to sit down in front of a typewriter and send off full letters (in contrast to her earlier short, "quivery" notes) to personal and political friends.

Mid-August 1972 marked Barbara's return to a limited degree of activism. In the pending presidential election, with McGovern running against Nixon, Barbara opposed both David's recommendation that the antiwar movement's "confrontation tactics" would be counterproductive during the campaign and Dave Dellinger's refusal to endorse McGovern. She felt that "resistance activities" had to continue in case McGovern diluted his promise to end the war, but she also felt that the antiwar movement had created McGovern's candidacy, that he represented its views to a significant degree, and that people should be urged to vote for him. Dellinger insisted "that this struggle will be best served by the left refusing to play the traditional electoral game"—to which Barbara responded, "I say DAMN ALL THOSE LABELS! I say DAMN what we may have decided about all elections before this. If there is at least a significant opportunity here to end the war . . . let us try to SEIZE IT."

Disagreement aside, Barbara traveled twice to New York City to be with Dave Dellinger and others as they began a monthlong fast to protest the war. Dellinger would continue his fast even while traveling to Hanoi the following month, where for the fourth straight year he and the Committee of Liaison secured the release of a few American POWs. On the final day of the fast, David McReynolds, too, went uptown to support the hunger strikers. Over the thirty-day period, they'd had only water, not a morsel of food, and David noted that Dellinger "has lost a great deal of weight."

The month after Nixon's landslide victory over George McGovern in the November presidential election, Barbara wrote Dellinger about her profound fears for the future. True, the Democratic Party had shifted to the left in nominating McGovern, but the prowar sentiment in the country as a whole had remained high enough to give Nixon his landslide, a seeming mandate to reject peace negotiations and to escalate the bombing still further. It is "so criminal," Barbara wrote another friend, "that no words can begin to speak of it." She felt that Nixon, in his insistence on victory, might even turn to atomic weaponry.[9]

Barbara realized that there was now no chance of a nationwide strike against the war, but being "an incurable optimist—though the kind who is never surprised when things go wrong," she joined a large delegation that went to the Capitol to talk with individual congressmen in the hope, misplaced as it turned out, of persuading them that Congress should use its power to cut off funding for the war. She and others also resurrected an idea they'd presented to the Vietnamese back in 1967: to permit the recruitment of several hundred American women to live and work in scattered towns and villages in Vietnam in the hope that their presence might somewhat stay the government's hand or at least trouble the minds of American pilots, who currently dropped their bombs according to maps without place-names on them—to avoid any suggestion that the indistinct landscape far below was inhabited by human beings. Still lacking physical stamina, Barbara hadn't yet volunteered for Vietnam herself, "but if it will ever help just to add one other presence—I will volunteer at once." As in 1967, though, the Vietnamese turned down the offer, fearing that allowing in foreign volunteers would open the door for China to send volunteers of its own—and the Chinese were widely distrusted in Vietnam.

Meanwhile, the War Resisters League had become stronger in membership and donations than ever before in its fifty-year history. Whereas the league had previously had only a New York office, it was now a national organization with strong local chapters and lots of affiliated young people. At the 1972 annual convention, as David put it, "We had more than just our usual Jews, agnostics and unorthodox. We now have Catholics, and two Mennonites came." That same month of October, Mike Harrington finally announced his resignation from the Socialist Party, which, in his words, "is today doing the work of Richard Nixon." Because Harrington had refused an outright break with the Shachtmanites until after David and most of the left-wing faction had left the party, David felt little sympathy for him: "If Mike had aligned with us earlier, we would not have lost the fight." He was "too late" and "too timid."[10]

It was also in October 1972 that Peter Stafford, now thirty-three, finally left New York for the West Coast. Though he'd moved out of David's apartment way back in 1966, the two men had, in a desultory, undefined way, continued to see each other occasionally and, even less frequently, to have sex. Up until roughly 1970, David had gone on blaming himself for the failure of their relationship: "I, who am so quick to state love," he wrote Pete, "did so perfect a job of killing it, no? Of withering it, demanding upon it, attacking it, until now there is also the loneliness of knowing I am this alone because of myself. . . ."[11]

Always hard on himself, David in 1970 had had a particularly troubling year. Though he usually slept late, for a time he now woke up regularly between five and six A.M. "with intense flowing dreams, sometimes nightmares . . ." He'd get up, take a drink and a Miltown (then a bestselling mild tranquilizer) and fall back into a deep sleep, but wake up still feeling weary. He continued to promise himself, as he had for several years now, that he would exercise regularly, lose his growing (at age forty-one) potbelly, stop smoking, drinking, and taking Miltown, and enter therapy. But his resolution had never held for long. He even started to feel "trapped" in New York and to "hate" his

WRL job. Perhaps worst of all, he "hated" himself, because too many people had a high opinion of him and he thought he was unworthy of their admiration, was an "impostor." David was headed into an emotional crisis, but it would smolder for a while longer.

It was held off in part by the "ego-elation" of having his essays, *We Have Been Invaded by the 21st Century*, published in 1970 by Praeger, and in paperback the following year by the prestigious Grove Press, with an introduction by his friend Paul Goodman. But the improvement in his spirits didn't last long. When he and Pete had lived together, his days had been "filled with a joy" he'd never known before, but that period of his life now seemed very far away. His depression got to the point where he even let his parents know that "My soul is often deeply troubled, lonely, and even desperate." At the same time, he asked them if they'd "ever realized that non-Christians can be profoundly religious" or if they understood that he did "accept Jesus even as I reject Christianity" and that he got comfort as well from "the teachings from the East."

For occasional sex, David relied on the then-popular subway johns and the public baths; they were easy and impersonal, though with Pete he'd had something far more satisfying. He felt convinced that henceforth he'd be desolately alone, resistant to fully opening himself up again to another person. By the time Pete left New York in 1972, his own life had taken a downturn, and he was no longer the ebullient, confident young man David had fallen for. Pete had worked hard for two years on a book about Richard Nixon, which David had "never thought very good," and he'd been unable to get it published. At thirty-three, Pete, in David's opinion, "has been slowly falling apart, drinking far too much, touched with that pasty look . . . tending to shout or laugh but without the gentleness I had known." David had at last reached the point where he no longer felt in love; to that extent, his long-standing anguish about Pete had greatly diminished by the time he departed.

David wasn't able to find any alternative sense of comfort in the increasingly visible—and political—gay community that had arisen following the 1969 Stonewall riots. He did believe that "the openness of homosexuals is permanent" and welcomed that development. Yet he continued to find gay humor "brittle and lacerating," a means of masking, not expressing, authentic feelings. He found no corresponding need in his own nature. Besides, he still felt that the gay world wasn't "a happy one" (not that he romanticized the straight world either) and thought Mart Crowley's play *The Boys in the Band* accurately represented the misery of homosexual life—just as he thought Edward Albee's *Who's Afraid of Virginia Woolf?* was a faithful depiction of most of the straight world.[12]

But he wasn't immune to the shifts in gay consciousness and behavior that were under way. He tried to stay open to them and began to wonder, for example, "if my comments against (or feelings against) very swish homosexuals don't reveal grave inner problems in myself." And he tried to learn more about the new gay world (he'd previously gone to a meeting of the small pre-Stonewall homophile organization the Mattachine Society but hadn't been impressed).

In 1973 he went to a performance of Jonathan Ned Katz's new gay liberation documentary play, *Coming Out!* It deeply embarrassed him, and it took an act of will to remain in the theater. "Item 8," it turned out, consisted of a real-life dialogue between Seymour Krim and David that had been printed in the *Village Voice* way back in 1959, with Krim arguing that homosexuals "would become militant" one day and David arguing that "they never would." It gave him some comfort to remember that when the *Voice* had originally printed the dialogue, Lorraine Hansberry, author of *A Raisin in the Sun*, spotted David on a Greenwich Village street one day, told him that "she appreciated my appeal for tolerance," and invited him over to her apartment for a New Year's Eve party.

At the close of "Item 8," the actors onstage moved toward "David," raised their fists at him and chanted "Gay Power!" Then they lifted him up "like a log" and carried him offstage. David found the scene "very painful to watch" and felt that even though his own words had been used, the depiction wasn't fair. He wanted to shout out, "But you don't know about gay society when I was younger. . . . Where were you all when we risked arrest to keep our bars open in Los Angeles, etc." Anyway, he was "glad Krim won that debate and I lost it."

Seeing one of the actors outside the theater later, David told him his reaction to the scene, and the actor passed it on to author Katz. He wrote David that he was "sorry about that pain, but at the same time think that debate is an important and dramatic scene in the play." David responded at some length. He wrote Katz that the quotes from his debate with Seymour Krim had been "accurate enough," but that the scene had left out his "appeal to erase the arbitrary lines of judgment by which we categorized people, something which Lorraine Hansberry saw at once when she read it and which Krim also saw."

What was also left out, he felt, was "the background for my bitterness toward gay society," gay then meaning something substantially different from what it means today. Also absent from the scene, he wrote Katz, "was the fact that we queers defended our beach bars from the police, refusing to turn tail and run when the cops came in—the Hollywood faggot bars could be closed down by simply leaving a squad car out front with a flashing light." David graciously added that "a writer cannot defend himself from his own words" and he gave Katz permission to reprint the debate in future productions of the play and in its published version.

It didn't help that David's father continued now and then to make homophobic comments in his letters. "I don't know what to say after all these years," David wearily responded to one letter. He couldn't imagine that "God believes people should be weeded out and dropped into hell or sent up toward heaven on the basis of which orifice they use for the sexual act, or which sex they choose for it." He charged Christians in general—meaning his father in particular—with "their excessive fear" of sex and a lack of "sensual delight in it." In David's view, Christians were apparently convinced "that sex is only possible if a preacher cites the proper cabalistic words and should be done only if babies will result." David realized that he'd "never fully escape a certain guilt over homosexuality, because my early culture taught me it was wrong. But the painful guilts of early years have given way for the most part and, in the new society being shaped around us and under us, the homosexual feels much more security and far less guilt."[13]

The advent of gay liberation also had an impact on Barbara. She enthusiastically joined a Gay Activists Alliance demonstration in front of City Hall demanding passage of a bill against discrimination in housing and employment. It failed, as it would many times in the ensuing years. She shared an umbrella against the cold rain with Marcia—the then-famous Marcia P. Johnson, a pioneering transgender figure, who Barbara thought was a transvestite, based on her mini skirt and "high make-up." One of the cops kept glancing at Marcia "with a glazed and fearful eye, quite obviously scared to allow Marcia membership in the human race . . . but no doubt *any* of us."

Barbara's mother, Katherine, was among the first to know that her daughter had come out as a lesbian. Barbara had written her to say, "We do have a right to exist—we just begin to tell ourselves and each other. To exist without pretending that we don't . . . pretending not to be ourselves has made us all feel a little bit insane." She expressed her appreciation that when her mother had first discussed homosexuality with her years before, she did so without condemning "it to me as anything ugly." As a young woman, Barbara had struggled for a time with the idea "that she really should marry a man," but she counted herself lucky that she "never succeeded in that effort . . . I never could have led the life I wanted to . . . I would have led *his* life." She'd gradually stopped "disrespecting" herself as a lesbian—except that "one does live in society, and if one can't speak what one is, one's self-respect is not complete." Still, finally speaking publicly the words "I am a lesbian" was "one of the most difficult acts" Barbara had ever done. She dedicated her 1974 collection of essays "To all those seeking the courage to assert 'I am'—and especially to my lesbian sisters."[14]

Barbara's mother didn't receive news of the dedication with particular grace, though she did reassure Barbara of her love and told her not to "worry about it." Still, her mother's own socialization as a "respectable" woman dictated that she disapprove of any public "flaunting" of one's private life. Katherine expressed her regret to Barbara "that this has become a movement. I don't see how it can do any good to anyone." Barbara knew that her mother had done the best she could and didn't press her for any further gesture of support or affirmation. Yet Barbara noticed that thereafter her mother became "very much more tender with me."

Barbara did voice her newly discovered militancy in a lengthy exchange of letters with Brad Lyttle, the longtime radical pacifist. Brad, who was straight, had no doubt (and this was still rare among heterosexuals) that it was "very wrong" to deny homosexuals their civil rights. He had even provided the sound system for a recent gay rally. Still, before he and Barbara thoroughly discussed the matter, Brad had also regarded "gayness as a kind of 'damage'" and gay relationships as substitutes for people unable to form satisfactory heterosexual relationships. He thought it obvious that genital differentiation between men and women represented the truism that nature's primary concern was procreation.

Barbara denied to Brad that the only purpose of sexuality was the production of babies. In her opinion, "our sexuality is given us so that we can commune with one another—and with our universe. It cracks our single selves." She further denied that "the biological inclination" was to be heterosexual; in her view, the biological inclination was "simply to be sexual." If society would stop insisting that everyone be heterosexual, "the power inequities that make most heterosexual relationships so distorting" would be greatly diminished. Like David McReynolds, Barbara felt that in a new, more natural world, "we would find ourselves . . . attracted to either sex. It would be a matter simply of which individual person awakened love in us." She did not add "or awakened lust in us"—as David probably would have.

Feminism had begun "erupting" in Barbara when she first read Kate Millett's *Sexual Politics* in 1970. During her year of recovery from the car accident, Barbara had focused her limited ability to read on the radical feminist literature that had recently been coming off the presses. The two books she ranked highest in importance were Shulamith Firestone's *The Dialectic of Sex*, published in 1970, and the philosopher/theologian Mary Daly's *The Church and the Second Sex* (soon followed by her still more influential *Beyond God the Father* in 1973). Firestone was only twenty-five when she published *Dialectic*—a daring, brilliant book that called for the abolition of the nuclear family, a postpatriarchal society, and the use of cybernetics to free women from pregnancy and child-rearing. Earlier, Firestone had helped to found New York Radical Women and then, in 1969, along with Ellen Willis, the radical feminist group Redstockings. Daly, more than fifteen years older and something of a disciple of the existentialist theologian Paul Tillich, was, especially with the publication of *Beyond God the Father*, a foundational figure in feminist theology.

The books had a profound impact on Barbara, and led to her personal friendships with Daly, the poet Adrienne Rich, the feminist leader Robin Morgan, and, somewhat later, Ti-Grace Atkinson, Karla Jay, and Andrea Dworkin. The initial contact was with Adrienne Rich, who'd read two of Barbara's recent articles, "Two Perspectives on Women's Struggles" and "On Anger," and had written to tell her that "your work has meant a great deal to me over years of my life."[15]

"Two Perspectives" opened with a brief rereading of various women writers whom Barbara, over the years, had found most meaningful to her; she wanted to see what they might have in common, though the authors and their books were very different one from the other. Her conclusion was that all the books shared at least one theme: "the danger in which the Self within stands if one is a woman—the danger that it will be blighted, because of the authority of men." From that point in the essay, Barbara proceeded to argue that it had for too long been assumed that the human race was "naturally" split between men and women, as epitomized by the popular saying, *"Vive la difference!"*

She begged to differ. Aside from the physical asymmetry in reproductive equipment, she believed that men and women shared a common humanity and that no task was more crucial at the current time than boldly to question the so-called differences between the genders. Every individual, Barbara argued, "is born *both* to assert herself or himself," an attribute previously considered primary in males, *"and* to act out a sympathy for others trying to find themselves," presumably the preserve of women.

She felt it urgent to reclaim both attributes, aggression and compassion, for both genders and, as Carolyn Heilbrun had recently argued in her seminal *Toward a Recognition of Androgyny*, to hold out androgyny (combining in every individual all the traits previously and artificially parceled out to men *or* women) as the ideal state. Barbara advocated that fathers also needed to become mothers and that motherhood needed to be redefined so that it no longer represented the female parent "giving one's very life for the father, then the son, to feed upon." Everyone had to learn that "we must give of ourselves, we are members one of another." Mutuality needed to replace sacrifice (the woman) and dominance (the man).

The genius of nonviolent action, Barbara added, was that it combined two impulses long treated as distinctly masculine *or* feminine: self-assertion and sympathy. Recombined, they restore "human community. One asserts one's rights as a human being, but asserts them with consideration for the other, asserts them, that is, precisely *as* rights belonging to any person." Barbara's further conviction was that there

existed between any two individuals ("if only they will allow themselves to be individuals") sufficient polarity "for desire to flourish."
Love, she concluded, did not mean the woman "cleaving to the man"
and the man "cherishing his so-called better self." There could be
"deep eroticism in comradeship." Indeed, Barbara suspected that one
significant reason why homosexuality was generally viewed as threatening was because "loving comradeship" *was* its ideal.

The second article, "On Anger," which deeply impressed Adrienne
Rich, remains one of Barbara's most influential essays. She started
from the proposition that many of the people who were struggling in
liberation movements—blacks, welfare mothers, women, gay men and
lesbians, vets, GIs, prisoners, etc.—were angry people. Yet the anger,
she was convinced, had to be expressed nonviolently "if we want to
make the changes that we need swiftly and surely . . . and if we want to
see the fewest possible people hurt in the struggle." In regard to the
women's movement, Barbara felt that men were so accustomed to the
present state of things that they were almost bound to panic at the very
idea of women's liberation. It was important, she felt, for women "to
reassure men continually," as their deeply entrenched privileges were
removed, that the pleasures of relating to others as equals were greater
than those of treating them as subordinates or appendages.

Barbara felt that one kind of anger was healthy: "It is the concentration of one's whole being in the determination: this must change."
Such a state does involve agitation and confrontation, but is not in itself violent because it respects oneself *and* the other. Barbara recognized that it was difficult for pacifists to acknowledge anger, "to have
to discover in ourselves murderers." Yet it was precisely when repressed
anger surfaces that a movement for change begins to show signs of
life. But what one does with the anger is all-important. If one disci-
plines it—takes the murder out of it—and uses it to join with others
comparably oppressed, the anger is transmuted into a determination
not to destroy the oppressor but to change one's subservient status
through conscious solidarity with those who are similarly situated or at
least sympathetic to one's plight—often because they recognize some
tyrannized portion of their own lives.

Barbara and Adrienne Rich began to correspond a little, met once,
and then soon after spent an evening together with Mary Daly ("whom
I would name a genius") and Robin Morgan, neither of whom Barbara

had previously known. She was especially impressed with Daly's "wonderfully bold mind," just as she had already been excited by Daly's articles ("did not read your essays but ate them, and they are now part of my flesh and bone"). Daly and Barbara agreed that "a genuine psychic revolution" had begun, with androgyny as its goal and with what Daly had called "the sisterhood of man" central to that evolution.

Having now met one another, a lively correspondence followed among the four women. To Mary Daly, Barbara confided her fears about shifts she'd been noticing in the nonviolent movement. Over the years, it had already experienced a variety of ups and downs in personnel, factions, and vision, but what currently worried Barbara was that she'd begun to encounter one woman after another who'd once believed in nonviolence but now, having at last confronted her own oppression, had abandoned that belief. It wasn't their anger that frightened her— she shared it—but the possibility that they would murderously employ it against others, "denying being to others."[16]

To Robin Morgan, Barbara emphasized her conviction that women, because of their ability to give birth, understood "that we are members one of another, that nobody, nothing is strictly *other*." But it's not that men can't learn about connectedness; "it seems to me that we have to insist they can." For Barbara, the truism that nobody is simply *other* lay at the very heart of the nonviolent struggle. Those aspects of oneself that we currently despise and cast out are the same ingredients central to an androgynous vision. Men cast out in fear, "all that is 'womanish' in them, then long of course for that missing part of their natures, so seek to possess it by possessing us." Critical to the potential revolution in consciousness was the need to embrace those very elements we previously chose to disown—which would mean destroying maleness and femaleness as we currently know them. But if women claim that their powers are unique, "we defeat ourselves. . . . *Won't we* always be men's prey until they come to acknowledge that in each one of *them* is what Adrienne beautifully calls a 'ghostly woman' . . . ?"

Barbara sent Adrienne a copy of her letter to Robin and also parts of the manuscript—essays, poems, letters, and memorials—that would be published in 1974 with the title *We Cannot Live Without Our Lives* (taken from Emily Brontë's *Wuthering Heights*). Adrienne's thoughtful set of reactions ran the gamut. Though she fully agreed with much of what Barbara had written, Adrienne was merely polite about the poetry—with some few exceptions, not Barbara's strong suit—and also questioned a few of the positions she'd taken in the essays.

She worried in particular that Barbara might have set up a false division with Robin over nonviolence. In case Barbara remained in doubt, Adrienne reassured her that the sometimes violent images in Robin's writings came out of "a need to distinguish revolutionary love in women from that old altruistic 'compassionate' love we have always been told was our only acceptable emotion." Too many people, in Adrienne's view—though not Barbara—viewed Robin as a "man hater," a "ballbreaker," and that false characterization caused Robin a lot of pain. She had courageously distinguished, according to Adrienne, between her love and compassion for her son and husband—who she demanded struggle with himself—from her anger with men as a class.

Adrienne found "nonviolence really difficult to think about." Part of the problem was her awareness that some of the greatest apostles of nonviolence—like Gandhi—"perpetuated psychic violence on women." Besides, "where women are concerned, we have only just begun to experience any collectivity, and most of us are still encapsulated in individual lives in which violence is being done to us and we are taught to be nonviolent. So much of our energy goes into repressing our anger . . . I cannot feel that I could say to a woman whose husband, ex-lover, or father tries to rape her (let alone a stranger) that she should not resist actively . . . if we understood more about the real connections between sexuality and violence, we might have a better chance of describing a kind of nonviolence which would be activist, creative and non-victimizing . . . most of the theories of non-violence have been derived from male thinking. . . ." Finally, Adrienne was "suspicious of the instant-androgyny solution. I do believe that real woman-power will be discovered & forged on that woman-chosen boundary . . . [otherwise] androgyny will be . . . simply an accumulation of 'feminine' qualities into the male mystique."

Barbara struggled to revise her formulations where she agreed with Adrienne's critique. In part to prepare for a weekend conference on "Women and Violence" in March 1974, Barbara wrote for herself a series of shorthand notes and observations:

- That term nonviolence . . . is negative, passive. The original Indian term—*satyagraha*—means "clinging to the truth." Much more affirmative, and much more precise.
- Patriarchy is based on an elaborate lie. The lie is: Women and men are basically different in their natures, and women belong to men . . . [but] nobody belongs to anybody else. . . . Here of course is our bond with the Left, with anti-imperialists . . . would still call self a leftist, I guess. Though would say until the left becomes feminist, it is flawed, can't make real revolution. . . .
- It's necessary, very necessary, to establish our *right* to violent self-defense. But if we don't manage to invent a way to affirm this without violence, I don't think we can win our full struggle.
- . . . one phrase of hers [Mary Daly's] seeming to me a wonderful definition of nonviolence (of clinging to the truth): Our liberation consists in refusing to be the Other, and asserting instead "I am"—without making another the Other . . . no-one is the Other.
- I recall when the black movement turned from nonviolence. My dismay. But can see now a little why.
- That we have been passive, the oppressed, is both in our favor and not. We haven't learned murder—except upon ourselves. Must unlearn it there, but not upon others.
- As child remember the masquerade where won the prize but felt oh that my younger brother should have had it. Remember when the home movie camera came out, trying to step out of the way of shots of him. . . . If small boys are in effect taught in their *homes* that there are some people—females—who are really born simply to make the lives of males easier, small wonder that they grow up to feel there are entire peoples born simply to do their will.

In writing that she'd still call herself a leftist then adding, "I guess," Barbara wasn't to any degree rethinking her commitment to the black struggle, pacifism, or the protest against U.S. intervention in Southeast Asia. (Laos and Cambodia had by now been added to the hawks' agenda as Nixon intensified the massive secret bombing campaign that had been conducted in both countries since 1965.) Rather, she was expressing her mixed feelings about the seeming indifference of male-dominated left-wing organizations and publications to the feminist revolution. She didn't yet feel able to disassociate from her male comrades: "The bond is still there," she wrote in a note to herself, but she wasn't sure that they could "any longer struggle side by side. . . . It is going to take non-cooperation with them to make them change." Her message to left-wing men wasn't intended to be moralistic—"you are bad, or you are good, etc."—but rather, "life is not possible this way. . . . The point is to make life possible for all."[17]

Though her message was phrased gently, most of the men she approached responded defensively. When she questioned the grounds on which the *Win* collective (a publication she often wrote for) had turned down articles by Andrea Dworkin and her partner John Stoltenberg (both gay), Barbara protested that "you take men more seriously than you take women—in spite of yourselves." But in her conciliatory way, she added, "I would *underline* 'in spite of yourselves.' I do think of you (of Maris at least [Maris Cakars, a leading figure in the *Win* collective]) as really struggling to treat us without difference. . . . I, for one, hope very much that Andrea will reconsider her decision never to submit anything to *Win* again. We are, so many of us, changing so fast these days that I think it a mistake to count any of us who *are* changing hopeless." In this regard, she singled out the historian/activist Marty Jezer and her "friend" David McReynolds, who'd recently visited Barbara and Jane in Monticello—"how very happy I was to see the changed way in which he wrote after his visit." But in a few years, she and David would again tangle.

However, the situation at *Win* was somewhat more complicated than Barbara seemed willing to acknowledge. The magazine's editorial board included several *women* who objected to the request by Barbara, Andrea, and the poet Leah Fritz for a page or section of their own. They didn't see why those three, a self-appointed group, should be given the right to speak for all women on the subject of feminism.

A similar situation developed at the War Resisters League, very nearly causing a split in the organization. This time it was a group of West Coast feminists who insisted that the struggle for women's rights had not been taken seriously enough. David was among those who held long personal talks with two of those women—neither of them lesbian—but he came away feeling that no minds were changed. He felt that he'd been genuinely eager to understand feminism better, but he remained puzzled about the degree to which the movement was concerned about left-wing political issues other than feminism.

Arthur Kinoy, the prominent and brilliant civil rights lawyer, was another man who responded positively to Barbara's feminist urging. Kinoy, late in 1973, was attempting to put together a mass People's Party, and he circulated a paper about it that stated "at the party's very core must be an understanding of the unique catalyst quality of the struggle for black freedom in this country." The paper contained no mention of feminism, either positive or negative. Barbara had lost none of her commitment to the black struggle, even while being disheartened at the current retreat from nonviolence, but since her terrible car accident, her energy wasn't what it had been and she was currently employing most of it in behalf of the women's movement.[18]

She wrote a long, eloquent response to Kinoy, arguing that if the People's Party was truly committed to its stated goal of "taking power away from the rulers on every level of life—political, economic, social and cultural," then it must take seriously the current agenda of radical women. She stressed that "until men, too, begin to desert patriarchal space, communication between us will be complicated." She understood that it would be foolish to expect some sudden transformation, and therefore asked only that the organization of the party be kept "very, very loose" until the time comes when men and women "are more ready to sit down together in common councils."

Kinoy, unlike most men on the Left, responded enthusiastically to Barbara's intervention, fully acknowledging the "glaring deficiency" in his own original statement. He wrote her that she'd illuminated for him "a fundamental truth with an explosive flash," and he now understood well that "the capitalist class . . . hides and camouflages the fact that women . . . are in reality an exploited laboring class in capitalist production . . . camouflaged by the ideology of the family and the myth of the 'woman's' role."

It now seemed to Kinoy that the feminist analysis "will have to become central to the building and growth of the concept of a mass party of the people." Without the active participation "and leadership" of women, no mass party would or should become possible. He smartly added that "male radicals particularly find it hard to 'see themselves as beginners.' This is part of the centuries of imprint upon all of us of the ideology of male supremacy . . . to justify the inequalities and exploitations flowing from the sexual division of labor within the family." Kinoy even signed his letter, "In the spirit of the struggle to build the 'sisterhood of man.'"

Kinoy and Barbara met in person, talked at length, and put down on paper the substance of their dialogue so that they could share it with others. Barbara wrote him to say that "your talk with me moves me very much. You enter territory that is strange to a man. It is hard, you admit, for male radicals to think of themselves as beginners. But you are willing to think of yourself in that way . . . you say you no longer believe that it is written in stone that a man can never feel what a woman feels—though he must struggle with himself for a long time before he can. I agree . . . the day may arrive when every one of us can freely feel neither as 'woman' or 'man' but as the complex individual person each really is—the very arbitrary sexual categories that now constrict us, and that now divide us from one another, at last shucked."

But the tide was against them. So-called "cultural" feminists were beginning to dominate the movement (some would argue that they still do), and they had no sympathy for the androgynous vision. Instead, they insisted on the "likeness" of all women (ignoring the special experience and perspective of nonwhite women) and their *essential* difference from men. The People's Party, in any case, never developed any significant strength and had a short life. Any basic challenge to the reigning categorical distinctions of maleness and femaleness awaited future claimants, many of whom would come from "queer" culture and theory.

In contrast to Kinoy, Jezer, and David McReynolds, Barbara's old comrade in CNVA actions Brad Lyttle practically erected a second Maginot Line in response to her feminism. He wrote Barbara that in her recent writings he missed any recognition of certain "biological realities." In fact Lyttle had touched on the one significant area where Barbara had found herself in disagreement with Shulamith Firestone's *Dialectic of Sex.* "Since pregnancy is barbaric," Firestone had written, "childbearing could be taken over by technology." But Barbara did *not* welcome the possibilities either of induced parthenogenesis or of cloning, the two major alternatives currently being discussed, for fear those procedures would produce "weak" children.[19]

But if she agreed with Brad that "male and female are required for the procreation of a strong species," she was quick to add that "heterosexuality is not required," thus prefiguring sperm donors, surrogacy, and the possibility of lesbians or gay men having children other than through female/male partnering. Like some other radical feminists of the time, Barbara offered as proof the claims that prehistoric lesbian Amazons and matriarchies existed, based on J.J. Bachofen's nineteenth-century *Mother Right* and Elizabeth Gould Davis's 1971 *The First Sex*—sources now largely discredited.

Barbara also agreed with Brad about the likelihood that certain "instinctive" elements (undefined by either) do affect human sexuality, but she did not agree that an instinct to reproduce need be included. Wilhelm Reich was one of Brad's two "Gods" (the other was Freud), but Barbara cleverly claimed Reich for her side of the argument: "Procreation . . . is a function of sexuality, and not vice versa, as heretofore assumed. . . . It is no longer possible to consider sexuality an unwelcome by-product of the preservation of the race." The primary biological reality was sexuality. Reproduction followed from it but did not give rise to it.

Barbara also intervened in what had become a major struggle within the women's movement over the personage of Jane Alpert. A member of the far left, Alpert had participated in planting bombs in eight separate buildings during 1969 to protest the war and the inequities of American life. Arrested with other members of her group, she'd jumped bail and gone underground for four and a half years. In 1973 she wrote (with assistance from Robin Morgan) a "Letter from the Underground—Mother Right, a New Feminist Theory," which both *Off Our Backs* and *Ms.* published. In it, Alpert saluted Shulamith Firestone as a "visionary" but took issue, among much else, with her notion that bearing and nurturing children was the "enemy" of the feminist revolution, rather than the source of women's unique consciousness and power. Alpert's emphasis on "unique consciousness"— on gender essentialism—marked her "Letter" as an important (if sometimes fuzzy) document in the growing commitment among many women to cultural feminism, with its emphasis on biological explanations of the presumably innate differences between women and men.[20]

Barbara agreed with some parts of Alpert's manifesto but not with all of it. Whereas Alpert insisted that the women's movement must center on affirmation "of the Mother," in Barbara's view (she was deeply involved with caring for Jane's two children), that should be revised to say "a potential imprinted in the genes of every woman," whether or not she ever gave birth. Barbara felt that Alpert should substitute sisterhood for motherhood as the more inclusive term, implying both "mothering others and mothering ourselves."

Barbara did strongly favor the diffusion of at least the child-*rearing* role and objected to Alpert's disregard of men. In Barbara's view, there had been men throughout history "who have been willing to accept the fullness of their natures [and] have had the power" Alpert spoke of as belonging exclusively to women and in particular to mothers. "And can't one say," she wrote Alpert, "that the very fact that every man before being born has lived within another's womb, and in some part of his being remembers that he has lived there . . . puts him, too, in touch with birth mysteries?—if he will only let himself be in touch?" To Robin Morgan, Barbara emphasized that at the heart of her qualified reaction to Alpert was her fear that women would make the fatal error "of guarding their powers as unique, instead of insisting that men, too, acquire them." But she could be somewhat inconsistent on this point; elsewhere she wrote that the ability to bear children did give women "a special consciousness."

When Barbara discussed Alpert with her newfound feminist allies, Mary Daly emphatically insisted that she was "concerned above all to give birth to *myself.*" And Adrienne Rich wrote Barbara to say that "much as I respond to a great deal in Jane Alpert's letter, I could not say that it represents where my head is now. . . . I would want to define much more precisely . . . how, if at all, mothers are a (rather than *the?*) 'cutting edge' . . . I think Alpert sees this too simply. . . . I would want to refine and redefine that in terms of the social burdens heaped on women who are mothers. . . . It may be that many women are prevented from being *any* kind of 'cutting edge' because they are completely swamped in maternal responsibilities."

Barbara's involvement with Jane Alpert continued. On November 17, 1974, Alpert surfaced from underground and turned herself in to the United States attorney in New York City. She was sentenced to twenty-seven months in prison for her role in the 1969 bombings and for having jumped bail. The FBI questioned Alpert at length about her years underground, and a number of feminists became convinced that in supplying the bureau with the locations where she'd hidden out, Alpert was jeopardizing the safety of a number of women still in hiding—especially Pat Swinton ("Shoshanna"), who had sometimes lived with Alpert when both were fugitives. Alpert claimed that she gave the FBI a fabricated account of her life underground, but when Swinton was arrested in mid-March 1975, those feminists already suspicious of Alpert—including Ti-Grace Atkinson and Flo Kennedy—became convinced of her betrayal. But Robin Morgan organized a support group for Alpert, which included Adrienne Rich, Gloria Steinem, and Barbara Deming. The feminist movement became thoroughly polarized on the issue.[21]

Barbara played a significant role in what followed. She and Jane Gapen spent an evening with Swinton and came away feeling sympathy for her as well as for Alpert—so typical of Barbara's philosophy that "no-one is Other." Following their meeting, Barbara wrote to Swinton. She began her letter in a uniquely Deming way: "I keep brooding about the fact that you are now persuaded that Jane Alpert risked your capture knowingly. You'll perhaps think I'm a fool, but I still cannot believe it of her. And I write to ask you gently, and very respectfully, but in spite of everything stubbornly: Are you sure, are you sure . . . ?"

She went on to remind Swinton that even the best-intentioned of friends can unconsciously distort events as they report them. And she raised the possibility that some feminists were branding Alpert a traitor in order to discredit other stands she'd taken, in particular the need for separatism. Barbara herself had come to believe "very deeply" in *temporary* separatism so that in consciousness-raising groups many browbeaten women would feel able to "to find their own personhoods." Yet she believed just as deeply that women and men were "essentially comrades" and that separatism should not be extended.

In subsequent talks and letters, Barbara raised other questions with Swinton. Since her lawyer had unwittingly revealed to the government that Alpert was still holding back a lot of information, the FBI had been pressuring Alpert—including threatening her with additional jail time—for more details about her years underground. Alpert had steadfastly refused, just as she would subsequently refuse to testify at Swinton's trial, thereby helping her win acquittal in September 1975. As a result, Alpert was cited for civil contempt and had another three months added to her jail sentence. Barbara put two rhetorical questions to Swinton: "How much would you have asked of her? . . . isn't she, in fact, now asking quite a lot of *herself*?"

Hearing of Barbara's attempt to befriend Pat Swinton, Alpert asked her to break off communication. Ever since word had been passed through a prisoners' liberation newsletter, *Midnight Special*, alerting women in Alpert's prison that they had "a traitor in their midst," Alpert had feared for her life. As she wrote Barbara, she didn't "think Pat herself wants me dead, at least consciously," but she'd become a tool of those who did, and Barbara's "sisterly overtures to her will be used against me." She understood that Barbara didn't want to exclude any woman from the movement, but she assured Barbara that what Pat needed now was to stay out of jail. "You cannot help her do that, Barbara, not with all your love and sisterly insights. *I can* . . . I pray that you will understand this."

Barbara did. She didn't want to do anything that might frighten Alpert and promised that she wouldn't see Swinton again and that if Swinton made the overture, Barbara would "make some plausible excuse for putting her off." But she did want Alpert to understand "what I think I have been doing." She'd hoped that by talking to Swinton, as Dave Dellinger and Grace Paley had also done, she'd "stop making some of the charges against you she was making"—and might even retract those she'd already made. She wanted Alpert to understand that she came "from the nonviolent tradition . . . where we always make a point of talking with the opposition—find it the strongest and the safest thing to do." She also wanted Alpert to know that there had never been "the remotest chance that I'd be seduced" into the anti-Alpert camp.

Curiously, given Barbara's passionate and ongoing commitment to the black struggle, she seems to have played no role in another important split within the ranks of radical feminists—that between white women and women of color. The latter, with considerable justice, became increasingly angry at the failure of radical white feminists to confront American racism and colonialism in any significant way or to acknowledge the very real cultural differences between their communities. Barbara did have some limited contact with Barbara Smith, the black writer and publisher, but never developed close relationships with prominent lesbians of color—Audre Lorde, say, or Pat Parker, Gloria Anzaldúa, or Cherrie Moraga—comparable to those she had formed with white feminists like Adrienne Rich. This is difficult to account for: all white Americans ingest a certain amount of racism with their Pablum, but Barbara seemed as free of it as is possible in our profoundly discriminatory society. Perhaps—to put the best face on it—it was in her case mostly a matter of the lack of common meeting places, automatic points of contact, in our separatist society.

Throughout this protracted interfeminist strife, Barbara's partner, Jane, was very much at her side. Also a committed feminist and Alpert supporter, she held nearly all the same political views as Barbara (unlike Mary Meigs, who as late as 1974 wrote Barbara that "the fact of my being lesbian is not the center of my life & never has been"). The one subject on which Jane and Barbara partially disagreed was the degree to which men could or would become allies. Barbara believed that most of the current distinctions made between the genders—differing reproductive equipment being the main exception—were socially not biologically mandated; she was *not* a "cultural" feminist. Barbara held out more hope than Jane that eventually men would come to embrace their "womanish" side and women to insist on the independent value of their own lives, that separatism would end and androgyny would come to characterize both genders.[22]

Jane was more cynical and angrier. She felt that men of the left, no less than their counterparts on the right, primarily wanted to replace the tiny male oligarchy now in control with "a larger group of masters." She believed that "those guys are all the same, still the same" and that "for a man to look at the truth of his sexist power and the threat of violence it contains is as hard as for a drunk to admit he is one." If Barbara was more optimistic about an ultimate transformation, she did feel disappointment with the lack of responsiveness to feminism among most of her male comrades, as well as the radical publications *Win* and *Liberation*.

The two women had many conversations about the new turn in female consciousness. The mother of two, having for many years fulfilled the traditional caretaker role, Jane had long had trouble emancipating her gifts as a writer and painter or even in believing in them. She may not have been *supremely* gifted (as Barbara thought her to be—"she is a gifted, gifted, inspired person") but did have talent and had long felt blocked in expressing and developing it.

Jane knew that she was often her own worst enemy, that her carelessness and lack of discipline reflected a certain amount of inner chaos that hindered her from achieving her goals ("it has got me over some sort of barrel") and also fed her resentment of Barbara's disciplined life. "You are master of your situation," she once wrote to Barbara. "I am not. No one would ever know that this was the case, being with us." Indeed, as one of Jane's friends wrote her, "the assumption I made from things you & Mimi [Jane's daughter] both said was that you were very content & had a very deep relationship. It all looked very idyllic to me." "But *I* know," Jane wrote Barbara, "the last thing I would ever want you to know is that I resent you . . . and that is partly because I love you."

It didn't help that Barbara was commonly showered with attention and admiration, while Jane was often ignored and shunted to the sidelines as if she were a person of no consequence. Understandably, the constant deference and respect paid to Barbara for her writing and her movement work did sometimes result in Jane's being treated as (or feeling like) a mere tag-along person, further undermining her uncertain self-esteem. None of which is to say that the criticisms she sometimes aimed at Barbara were without some substance: resentment can distort the content of one's accusations but doesn't automatically strip them of all validity.

Jane would accuse Barbara of *requiring* constant praise "and even arranging for it"—though in her diary Jane acknowledged that she was acting like "a rebellious child" and that Barbara was "too sensitive" and honorable to participate in such scheming. "One can always rely upon BD doing the decent thing!" Jane added. "I get so tired of it." At the heart of the matter was the sense of "rebuke and shame" Jane felt whenever she compared herself to Barbara: "*I knew* she was superior."

The accusation that Jane most often leveled at Barbara was that "it's a function of your character to dominate and control," which is probably best seen as a reflection of Jane's own conviction that she was unable "to keep up with what's expected of me," that she lacked a stable sense of worth. Consciously, she knew perfectly well that Barbara simply got back what she gave out: "an ambience of unconditional love for all her friends . . . all believed in a personal connection & all *had* it." Knowing that, Jane had "a very guilty conscience" about many of the charges she threw at Barbara (and which she expressed with still more fury in her diary).

It further contributed to Jane's unhappiness when Barbara would approach her sexually, or even affectionately. From the beginning of their relationship, their disparate appetites for sex (Barbara's high, Jane's low) had made Jane feel tense and guilty. "It's utterly baffling & grotesque that she doesn't hate or despise me." In her diary, Jane went so far as to accuse herself of an "inability to love . . . I couldn't surrender to my love for BD"—an incapacity (if true) that perhaps went back to Jane's loss of both her parents at age five. The unconscious equation became: to risk loving someone was to court the likelihood of being abruptly abandoned.

Jane's complaints—which she expressed with far more vehemence in her journal than directly to Barbara—did sometimes have a ring of truth, even if overstated. Central to Jane's grievances was the sense that "God has armed you, if not with muscle then with conviction beyond anyone I've known." Barbara's stubbornness in adhering to her principles was difficult for a constantly wavering Jane to match. "I am tired of feminism," she wrote in her journal as early as 1977. She understood and admired the fact that Barbara had forged her opinions through hard-won experience and tried to hold on to them despite some internal wavering of her own. The trouble came when Barbara acted—in her "intense, brooding" way—as if her truth was *the* truth. That could "distract" Jane from her own truth, as though she didn't care, for example, about the rumpled disorder of their household, as though being something of a slob was part of her temperament; she'd sometimes become (in her own words) full of "fury and frustration, as if being forced to succumb once more to Barbara's will."

And that could lead her to accuse Barbara of acting "just like her father," a charge that would make Barbara feel as if she were "losing the ground under my feet"—"to be accused by another woman of being a man when all your being and identity is dependent upon sisterhood." But if Barbara should then turn "pale, get sick and float away," Jane was likely to interpret her behavior as another "exercise of will on her part, since it prevented [Jane] . . . from speaking." When that happened, she had to remind herself that "as I've learned over the years, Barbara is a pushover if only the other person can explain or specify their needs and not just go off mad and beaten."

Even at the height of the adjustments and readjustments in their relationship, basically it remained secure. It helped that Jane, who'd been drinking too much, decided to go to AA and also became active working for the local Domestic Abuse Shelter—answering calls and finding volunteers and safe havens. The two women did love each other, and their periodic couple troubles, a nearly universal experience, never seriously threatened a breakup.

8

Personal Matters

For David, the early 1970s remained a period of political struggle—though harshly interrupted in 1973 by a serious personal crisis. His political activities were, as they'd long been, multiple and diverse. The ongoing opposition to the war in Vietnam continued to head his list of priorities and remained intense, but as the conflict slowly drew to a close in 1974–75, some of the outlets for expressing his disaffection and for articulating left-wing sentiments in general began to diminish.

A high-water mark in personal pleasure for David was reached in June 1972 when five men were arrested for breaking and entering Democratic National Committee headquarters at the Watergate complex. President Nixon's staff initially covered up the break-in, but when the Senate Watergate Committee discovered that Nixon had a tape recording system in his offices and the U.S. Supreme Court ruled that he had to turn over the tapes, the unraveling of his administration began.[1]

David couldn't help crowing to his father, who considered the Watergate break-in a minor matter typical of politics and had voted twice for Nixon. "I am stunned you take Watergate so mildly," David acidly wrote his father, ". . . for what did you fight in World War II? . . . Surely for some concept of the freedom we have known and . . . surely not for a society . . . where the official opposition party is bugged, raided, and disrupted?" He added that he was somewhat *more* stunned by his father's unwavering position on Vietnam, which he characterized as "well, as long as they will kill each other anyway, what does another B-52 raid matter—it will all come to the same thing in the end." "Did God send [Generals] Abrams and Westmoreland on a mission?" David rhetorically asked his father. "Did someone designate this country to help the Vietnamese kill one another? By what right did we ever intervene in that nation?" David's father remained unmoved— other than to remonstrate when David proceeded to characterize Rev. Billy Graham as the "chaplain for murderers" and made fun of Nixon's "prayer breakfasts" as reminding him "of the gentle Hitler who wept when his pet canary died."

David's father responded predictably: "I am distressed at your one-sidedness. . . . I find it odd . . . that in all that you have said and written over the years I find only criticism of your own country. . . ." Not surprisingly, David responded to the provocation with a four-page blast. Because he usually sent his parents offprints of his articles, his father had to be aware that David had been attacking the Soviet Union for many years, had taken part in a number of demonstrations at the Soviet Mission, and in the mid-1960s had organized a petition campaign to protest the jailing of dissident writers Yuli Daniel and Andrei Sinyavsky. His whole politics, David wrote his father, had been based on a "third camp" position that rejected both Washington and Moscow, and he'd several times said in print that the United States "was *not* the source of all evil."

Nor had he ever been a supporter of Mao and Chinese Communism, but he acknowledged feeling a "little humbled" by the fact that "we democratic socialists and you Christians between us could not end starvation and disease and illiteracy, and Mao did"—though he well knew that the cost in lives was high. As for Vietnam, he felt that if North and South ended up tearing each other to shreds, *we* were "the agents of their destruction and to ask me to be equal in my opposition to the two sides . . . is about as serious a suggestion as to urge that, when the Jews of Warsaw rose against the Nazis, I should take note that both sides had, in fact, used violence and I deplored the actions of both sides more or less equally." His father's response contained not even a remote hint of capitulation.

It in no way diminishes David's genuine outrage to point out that in his very next letter to his father, David intimated that something in addition to politics had fueled his rage: ". . . my personal angst transferred itself, doubtless, to my reply to your letter." The cryptic reference was almost certainly to David's escalating drinking and to the problems it had caused. As he later described it, "the bottle struck back, hit me in the head, made my hands tremble, made me . . . fearful of some storm gathering in a part of my mind." The fear carried him to some four or five AA meetings, but he'd concluded that they weren't for him—though it was nice that "there was a place for the poor folks who needed that kind of thing."

But then, in August 1973, he received two letters, both from old friends, that broke through his denial: they sharply dressed him down and cut off all future ties with him. The first was from his California friend Marsha Berman, with whom he'd recently stayed on a trip to the West Coast: "You are not welcome in my house ever again as long as you are drinking . . . I hope that you will be gone by the time I come home. . . ."[2]

The second was from Igal Roodenko, like David a gay man and long affiliated with WRL: "I am cutting off all social relationships with you until you stop bullshitting about your alcoholism and get some professional help. . . . I looked at you one evening as you were leaving the office. You looked like a bum. Your coat lining was torn and dragging behind you and your shoes were so worn at the heels that no one on the Bowery would have picked them up. Your shoulders drooped so that, for a moment, I couldn't believe that this was the person who writes and talks so well to the world. It was heartbreaking."

Both letters hurt terribly—*and* led David to take immediate action, with no time out for denial or self-pity. At first he was a bit baffled about where to turn, but within six weeks he'd found a psychiatrist. The sole condition David placed was that the therapist not try to "cure" his homosexuality, because he "didn't view it as an illness." The therapist agreed, and they settled on three sessions a week at reduced fees (from $75 a visit to $30) for one year. Thereafter David would, they hoped, find a clinic to take him on. He figured that by cutting out drinking—he was up to a pint of vodka a day—and by doing more writing, he could afford about one third of the cost.[3]

He already lived a marginal material life and was in debt to his parents for $500. David now wrote them the full truth: "There is absolutely no question that a problem with alcohol exists" and, at forty-three, that he could no longer dodge it. Asking whether his parents, now approaching old age, could lend him part of the money he needed for therapy, he honorably warned that "there is a risk in such a loan." He told them that he was also considering AA, which was free, but as "a supportive device," not as a replacement for therapy. In the end, his longtime friend—and supporter of WRL, along with many other progressive groups—modest, unassuming Carol Bernstein Ferry made sure that he could afford therapy.

As "a proud person," undergoing therapy was for David "a breaking thing," but he was determined to follow through. He felt fairly certain that his alcoholism "reflects other problems." He had, after all, had something like a nervous breakdown back in 1958, when he had no problem at all with drinking. The therapist initially put David on Valium but within weeks substituted the heavy-duty tranquilizer Thorazine, combined with Elavil. They left him feeling "a little disoriented," but he had an atypical reaction; instead of feeling drowsy and spacey, he felt as though he was on "a freakish Dexedrine pill." The therapy sessions were uptown at 8:30 A.M.—which for night owl David felt like the middle of the night—yet he made *nearly* all of them on time.

For the first few months, "the pain and depression and hurt of not drinking" proved a difficult struggle. He'd hit bottom, as he put it, "with a sonic boom only my nerves could feel." He "sweated buckets in dry weather . . . water poured out of me as the body worked to detoxify," and to compensate he drank huge amounts of tonic, along with grapefruit juice and sugar. Throughout he kept repeating the mantra "I cannot drink I cannot drink I cannot drink." It was a hellish period for him, but by the end of October, David was finally able to write again and to start planning protest demonstrations—against the military takeover in Chile, the war in the Middle East, the imprisonment of Soviet dissenters.

He felt somewhat guilty "in a world so desperate with pain and problems greater than my own" that he should be caught up in his own recovery. But he was wise enough to understand that the guilt might well represent "a kind of defense—an altruistic defense," against making therapeutic progress. Of course he did have a valid point. To whom can the poor turn when beset by medical and emotional issues? And didn't most therapists tend to enforce conformity to current norms in the name of "comfort," even when they were aware of how much the norm changes across time and culture?

David's therapist stuck to his promise not to try to "cure" David's homosexuality, even though he did encourage him to dredge up "repressed" elements of heterosexuality—which David knew perfectly well were there but felt were no more repressed in him than were homosexual attractions in "normal" people. But the analyst did, as David wrote to a friend, agree with him "that I'm a rather cold, forbidding, intellectual character, needing to seek help by helping." That may have been a disservice. David, who had a strong self-deprecating streak, had always been prone to equate his "distancing" tendency with the whole of his often warm personality and in the process falsely characterize—as conservatives often love to do—all acts of compassion as self-soothing. It was precisely the sort of equation—to provide a different reference point—that had led several generations of historians to disparage the actions of whites working to abolish slavery as "an unconscious acting-out of anger at their own reduction in status." Overall, though, David did believe that the therapy was helping, and he no longer mocked "the insights to which a good psychiatrist can lead one."

He also began to swim regularly and to experience "some return of energy, even of joyfulness, something I haven't felt in a very long time; there is a sense of hopefulness rather than despair." His old friend the ex-CP leader Dorothy Healey, who'd come East for a conference, stopped by to give him a pep talk: "And don't forget, David, I *am* a Jewish mother!" By mid-November he was again making a few speeches, including one in Philadelphia to a gay liberation group. But that gesture toward involvement, like the few that had preceded, didn't take. David wasn't sure what to say during the meeting, for he knew little about the movement "and disagreed with a large part of what I do know about it."

Unlike Barbara Deming, whose shift to feminist and lesbian politics was of profound importance to her, David would remain on the outskirts of gay politics. Yet in ways that he himself found difficult to explain, he felt that his "homosexuality is closely tied to my sense not only of self—of who and what I am—but, strange as it may seem, to my masculinity, my sense of manhood." But sex in general seemed to him far less necessary these days, and he became something of a celibate, having begun to feel that some of his old sexual outlets, like the subway johns, were "too impersonal and self-destructive."[4]

David was soon off all the drugs prescribed by the therapist to ease the transition to sobriety ("they leave me as less than myself") and felt very much better than he had before giving up drinking. His parents did come through with a loan, but money remained a problem, and restaurants were out of the question. Fortunately David was a good cook and tended to make enough at one time to last for a week. He did still drink sometimes socially, and on New Year's Eve 1973, following an AA meeting that let out at one A.M., he walked the thirty blocks home, weeping all the way, and found himself back at his old haunt, Phebe's on the Bowery at East Fourth Street, where he got drunk, kept stealing the bartender's champagne, broke up a fight, and stayed till four thirty A.M. He was not yet out of the woods.

For a while, David had less time for political activism than before—which is a bit like saying Fatty Arbuckle went on a diet and had only four meals a day. David did maintain his association with the small Debs Caucus, designed to loosely hold together those who'd resigned in 1971 from the SP over the Vietnam War, some of whose members were half in and half out of the party. David felt it was "like playing unimportant games with the long-since lost cause of the Socialist Party." He also got involved with a grassroots movement to impeach Nixon rather than allow him to resign. Beyond that, he remained on staff at the War Resisters League, mostly writing its publications and newsletters.

With the war in Vietnam drawing to a close, the league began turning more toward "positive programs" and away from protests. The new focus, according to David, was "to replace the present economic system so we can stop protesting the 'fallout' from it, such as Vietnam." But there was a dreamy quality to this new emphasis. After all, the Socialist Party and other left-wing groups had struggled for generations to replace capitalism, with little to show for the effort. The chimerical nature of WRL's shifting emphasis was heightened by the recent fall-off in membership and funding, typical of left-wing organizations in 1974–75 now that the war was ending and Nixon on his way out of office. He finally resigned from the presidency on August 9, 1974, leaving David feeling—along with outright hatred—a little bit sorry for him.

Early in 1974, the league took a lot of flak for giving its peace award (originally intended for Dave Dellinger) to, with Dellinger's approval, Dan Berrigan instead—not only to honor his courageous antiwar actions over the years, but also to bolster his spirits. Berrigan had made some remarks about Israel's wrongheaded treatment of the Palestinians and as a result had become the subject of a denunciatory assault on him as an anti-Semite. Unused to such treatment, he'd taken it hard. Barbara Deming, in private notes to herself, recorded her "further thought" about Dan Berrigan: "the jealousy of the sufferer . . . He in [a] sense jealous of the suffering Jew . . . is saying: I am the real Jew. I wrest that title from you. This kind of hubris."[5]

David had also taken Israel to task on several occasions, including an article in the *Village Voice* several years before, and been attacked for it. But the award to Berrigan stirred up an especially virulent reaction. Irving Howe, the editor of *Dissent*, wrote personally to David denouncing the Berrigan award as "insufferable . . . nothing less than a provocation toward those of us on the left who have strong feelings of sympathy with Israel. In fact, I think it a good deal worse than that." Howe demanded that his name never again be used in association with the WRL (he'd recently lent his name to honoring the league on its fiftieth anniversary).

David responded by sending Howe a copy of the league's full statement on Israel, of which he'd been the sole author. In it the WRL again declared the importance of Israel's survival and pointed out that even before World War II the league had denounced Hitler "and pleaded for the doors of this nation to be thrown open to Jewish refugees." But the statement then went on to say that the WRL increasingly believed that "Israel has become Sparta, not Athens. Increasingly she had turned from the prophets to the kings." Howe didn't reply.

During his comparative respite from politics, David developed a new hobby to add to his long-standing fascination with cooking and photography. It was an offbeat one—mixing perfumes. For a number of years he became absorbed with recipes that used a large number of essential oils and fixatives (and no synthetic chemicals). Within a short time, he succeeded in doing "a pretty fair job" of duplicating a number of distinctive basic perfumes, like Jasmine or Fougère Royale, and decided that mastering the process was much like the dynamics of cooking: "I had somewhat the same sense of triumph as when I found that by mixing this and that and cooking just so that I had a Chinese 'flavor' on my dish."[6]

At the end of a year of analysis, David did feel that it had "helped"—but AA "perhaps even more so." He stopped therapy but continued for several more years with AA. It didn't seem to him that he'd managed "any kind of integrated breakthrough on any front but one—the sexual question." Women had made a "tentative, hesitant (and generally non-erotic) appearance" in his dreams. That had at least confirmed his long held view "that all homosexuals have a repressed heterosexual drive" (and vice versa). If younger, he felt he might have tried to "activate" that drive, but the knowledge seemed to him "rather academic"; he had no wish to "change," or even to expand his sexual range.[7]

But though David felt that he'd now settled these questions within himself, sexuality and gender were becoming central cultural issues, the newest hot topics of the day. When Barbara Deming and Brad Lyttle began their epistolary debate on the role of biology, in October–November 1974, Brad wrote to David about the exchange, soliciting his reaction. In his letter, Brad misstated certain positions Barbara had taken and assumed as facts some propositions relating to biology that David quickly recognized as distorted. But he was wary about getting involved. Not long before, Brad had attacked him face-to-face with the accusation that David "had blocked his position in the movement and prevented him from playing an active leadership role." David wasn't aware of any truth to Brad's accusation but nonetheless decided to write him back and correct some of his distortions.

Brad had insisted that "All mammals . . . are heterosexual. All primates are heterosexual. It seems very likely, therefore, that human beings are at least biased toward heterosexuality." Not so, David replied; homosexual behavior among animals not only exists but is "very common." Where the human species diverges from other primates, David argued, is in being *more* heterosexual, in its uniquely negative taboos against homosexuality and in the way it has generated a group of *exclusive* homosexuals—again, all but unknown among other primates. David felt that humans were *like* other primates in the sense that we are "profoundly sexual" and when young and in "rut" will settle for any orifice. "*That* is biology, and the present laws and customs of our society totally ignore it."

At the time, David's views were highly unorthodox. Most biologists were classifying homosexuality in the animal kingdom as taking place only under "abnormal" conditions or existing as "pseudo-copulation," dominance behavior, and "practice" for performing the real thing. But thanks to an accumulation of evidence since the 1970s from primatology and other specialties, such views have now given way to the widespread acknowledgment among biologists of the very patterns David had earlier enunciated.[8]

David also wrote to Barbara—but on a different matter. She'd phoned him for support in the effort on the part of a number of feminists to ban showing the film *Snuff*, which depicted an actress apparently being murdered on a movie set. No evidence has ever surfaced that the murder was authentic, as opposed to being staged. But that wasn't known when *Snuff* first appeared early in 1976, and David's opposition to banning the film was for other reasons entirely. He told Barbara that he opposed censorship of any kind, that he was a First Amendment purist. He thought the NAACP had been "stupid" in trying to get the 1960 movie *The Adventures of Huckleberry Finn* banned because of the character Nigger Jim. And he was "furious" at the Anti-Defamation League for trying to remove Shakespeare's *Merchant of Venice* from high school curricula because of Shylock.[9]

He expressed his surprise to Barbara that "*radical* women would try to deal with so real a problem as violence in films through censorship; liberals, of course—but radicals?" He hadn't seen *Snuff* and didn't want to, but even so he felt sure that his objection would be to the killing of a human, not a woman. He'd long been concerned over the rise of sadomasochism ("violence, pain, suffering") but not exclusively to the violence widely employed against women. He felt sure that most women would object in general to the rampant brutalization depicted in many films and wished that the women protesting *Snuff* had made that clear. He advised them that if they were going to abandon the First Amendment, "it had best be done by taking somewhat the Catholic line that 'error has no rights' rather than by using the highly debatable logic that *Snuff* is crying fire in a crowded theater."

Barbara dismissed David's views on the First Amendment. She turned it on its head: pornography was properly labeled a form of terrorism, one that suppressed free speech—"and even free thought . . . the 1st Amendment (which we are accused of ignoring) has always made exceptions of certain forms of expression that are threatening. . . . Do you want to repeal the laws against blackmail, against libel, against threatening letters? If not, then you, too, are for censorship in certain instances."

But David had a plateful of additional complaints against Barbara and her cohorts. Near the top was their refusal to continue to publish in or support *Win*. Though Barbara's group of feminists didn't agree, David insisted that *Win* and the League had taken feminism far more seriously than had other groups on the left, "had been a real friend and ally of the women's struggle, and will continue to be." (He was on the *Win* board and faithfully attended its meetings.) David particularly protested as "inexcusable" Andrea Dworkin's recent letter to *Win* charging them with "bad faith, malice and manipulation," which he characterized as "unjust, inaccurate and oppressive." He suggested that Barbara write to *Win* disassociating herself from Andrea's position.

Barbara replied that she and Andrea had "different styles"; she would have used words "less stark—but *she* speaks in the way *she* thinks is most likely to be heard." And Barbara reminded David that the oppressed are very often worried that they may not be heard unless they "tell it rudely." Besides, she reiterated that *Win had* treated them badly, to her "surprise and dismay," and she included Maris Cakars, "the real power" at *Win*, in her indictment, even though she'd earlier believed that he was open to feminism. She thought Maris might actually fear a feminist "takeover" (as had happened years before at the countercultural *Rat*). In any case, Barbara felt that the gentle Maris had shown her a side of himself that she hadn't seen before—the patriarchal side. She doubted if David really knew the details of how *un*gently the feminists had been dealt with by *Win*. She believed that although she'd never treated Maris as an "enemy," he really had treated her that way, had "broken faith with her" and "manipulated" her.

She gave David some details about what had happened when a *Win* delegation had come to her and Jane's house back in November 1975. Maris had asked the two women, who'd specifically said that they spoke for no one but themselves, "What are your [the feminists'] demands?" In her version, Barbara had objected vigorously to the way Maris had put the question and had then responded that *her* dream (no one else's) was that *Win* would allow them to edit a number of special issues, thereby acknowledging that she no longer trusted the editorial board (which had never called itself feminist) to do it for them. It was comparable, Barbara suggested, to husbands saying to their wives (as they often did), "trust me to do what's best for both of us . . . women put that kind of trust in them at their peril." Besides, Barbara felt that *Win* hadn't trusted *them*, hadn't given feminists a significant voice in editorial matters. Maris had often said that he believed that the feminist revolution was of profound importance, but when it came down to it, Barbara claimed, he was willing "to display a certain number of articles by us . . . but doesn't want it to go any further than that."

David might well have dropped the discussion there—or even profitably backtracked, as he most humbly did years later—but he was on some sort of self-assertive (or was it defensive?) tear, perhaps a side effect of his current analysis or detoxification, and he plunged ahead. He compared what radical feminists were currently doing with what the advocates of Black Power had done before them—"when integration ideology gave way to separatism, friendships of many years standing were broken, and a new racism grew up to challenge the old." During that period, he "saw many whites guilt-tripped into extraordinary bows and scrapes," and he was proud to recall that he had not been; he'd gone on "defending blacks despite and not because of the guilt-rhetoric."

And in the same way, he added, whenever he heard "Sisterhood is powerful" these days, he expected "a bomb blast" to go off immediately afterward. Adding a bit more salt in the wound, David referred to the Jane Alpert case (on which he essentially agreed with Barbara) as demonstrating just how gentle and unified the sisterhood *wasn't*. At times he was tempted to say, "How much like men these radical women truly are, and how depressing!"

But he refused, he wrote Barbara, "to let the radical feminists discourage me from a basic concern with seeing how we can move toward new relationships—not, for God's sake, the re-establishment of the matriarchy" (hardly something that Barbara advocated), "which is not only impossible in practice but reactionary in theory." Less than two years earlier, curiously, David had been lecturing his religious parents that "in the beginning God was almost certainly a woman and it was a matter of some thousands of years before Woman was dethroned; God took up His seat in the sky and sent down phallic thunderbolts." Perhaps David thought different people needed to be taught different lessons.

Finally, David thought it necessary to let Barbara know that in his opinion the lesbian wing of the women's movement—this was at the height of both lesbian separatism and the rejection of lesbianism (led by Betty Friedan) among reformist feminists—was "desperately in need of a little humility about how and why other women *do* love men, *do* want to live with them despite the pains and confusions of those relationships, *do* want sons as well as daughters." He further suggested, with more than a hint of patronization, that Barbara and her friends, having "chosen silence" until radical men learned more about how to listen, may have made a "healthy" choice, just as the *women* would learn by listening that "the discussions and struggles" among radical men "will continue" without them.

Barbara felt as if David had punched her in the stomach. In responding, she denied most of his charges. She did "not look forward with excitement [to a time] when women could dispense with men"; she wanted a world filled with men and women. She herself had never wanted to be a wife, "never wanted to lose my freedom in that way," but she felt love for a lot of men and felt it "for a few men very deeply indeed." The women she knew who felt the most anger toward men were "women who have married them." She herself believed that the current "polarity" between the sexes was at "the very root of violence."

She frankly told David that his characterization of her was "painful," and she felt "slandered" by it. She felt sure that he hadn't intended slander and hadn't willfully misread her. But now that she was struggling against her own oppression, she did feel "deserted" by most of the left-wing men with whom she'd long been involved politically. She feared that they simply didn't understand that women felt oppressed "as women, not simply as human beings, have pains that are specifically women's pains, not simply those of the human condition"—and she had been "astounded" at that part of his indictment. As for David's contention, at one point, that patriarchy was "in a sense, already over," it left her "wordless." She asked him to please try to persuade her "that it is so. And I'm not being sarcastic. Please do."

David responded briefly and hurriedly. He was so busy, he said, "that I must let an answer wait." But he didn't later follow through. Barbara, nonetheless, wrote him again in an effort to put his earlier accusation in a broader context: "Why is it bizarre to feel that we should have a right to be defended against terror? . . . women do have less recourse to the law than men do. . . . Think, just for example, of battered wives. . . . It seems to me a tragedy that *Win* felt it had to ward us off. No, we are not the only feminist writers around, but we *are* the feminists who see feminism and nonviolence as indivisible." Though communication between them would remain open, David felt that Barbara "really never forgave me."

He personally felt far more antagonism toward Andrea Dworkin than to Barbara. He'd had what he characterized as "long talks" with Andrea and her spouse, John Stoltenberg, and they hadn't gone at all well. Nor did he ever change his mind about her. When, in 1992, David's friend Petra Kelly, one of the founders of the German Green Party, was killed by her lover, Gert Bastian, who then committed suicide, the deaths came as a terrible shock to their many friends in the States. A memorial service for the couple was put together in New York City. At its close, after all the speakers had paid their tributes, Andrea stood up in the audience and announced her outrage that no one had denounced what had in fact been a patriarchal murder. Her statement infuriated David. He had known Petra and Gert well and had admired both of them, whereas Andrea was a stranger to them. No one, he insisted, could be sure what had been going on in the Kelly-Bastian household, and he considered Andrea's remarks "absolutely inappropriate."

David wasn't alone in regarding Andrea as fanatically adversarial by nature. After the publication in 1974 of her first book, *Woman Hating*, she'd quickly become the subject of intense and divided feeling: some women and most straight men detested her passionate, inflammatory views, but many feminists regarded her as a brilliant, brave, iconic figure. Andrea had taken a leading role in organizing the picketing of *Snuff* and had joined other prominent feminists—Barbara, Adrienne Rich, Grace Paley, Gloria Steinem, and Robin Morgan—in activating the feminist antipornography movement, which in 1979 became Women Against Pornography.[10]

Barbara found *Woman Hating* of "immense interest," even though she did question some parts of the book—"sometimes not so much the ideas as the context or method by which they are presented." She objected in particular to the absence of any discussion of how the transition might take place between the current state of institutionalized misogyny and their shared vision of an androgynous future, a falling away of distinctive genders. Not that she believed anyone could actually answer such a question, but it disturbed her that Andrea had let it go unasked.

Still, Barbara and Andrea rather quickly became close friends. A few years earlier, Barbara had taken the $20,000 in insurance money she'd gotten as compensation for her car accident and set up a kind of mini-foundation, a Money for Women Fund. Even before all the legalities for the fund had been completed, she told Andrea, who was struggling financially, that she could count on a $500 grant—and if she was desperate, Barbara would at once advance her the money. Andrea let Barbara know that the money "has helped to keep me alive." In 1975, she even let Andrea know that after she and Jane died, her estate would be divided between Jane's daughter (Mimi) and Andrea. The Money for Women Fund, incidentally, had trouble finding angels to add to its initial capital.[11]

Adrienne Rich had also had mixed feelings, both appreciative and critical of *Woman Hating*, as well as some of Andrea's shorter writings. There was "little that is substantive in disagreement," Adrienne wrote Andrea, but she did feel that her description of the " 'phallic-masochistic polarity' has little new or original in it. . . . I kept waiting for you to get down into the question of masochism, which seems to me a crucial problem—how do we distinguish between masochism and the suffering which characterizes vital processes of change? How *do* we purge ourselves of masochism?" But the main problem, Adrienne felt, "is that you are stating the same problems over and over . . . you need to go deeper than you are going, beyond the broad critique and attack on patriarchy." Both Adrienne and Barbara felt the need for feminists to push each other hard, that sisterhood required it. And Andrea agreed with that: "all of us . . . have to be very hard-headed about it. . . ."

But theory and practice rarely match. In the winter of 1976, Andrea and John paid Barbara and Jane a long visit, and from the very start things went badly. According to the private, voluminous, and anguished notes Barbara wrote to herself over two and a half months, she and Jane had worked very hard to spruce up the cottage that Andrea and John were going to live in. They put in new screens, changed the rim around the tub top, dug out all the garden weeds, spent hours pruning the plum tree, swept the patio clean, and applied two coats of polyurethane to the new bathroom floor.[12]

But no sooner had the two guests arrived than Barbara read Andrea's sour expression as "You expect me to live *here*?!" The implied rebuke was severe—and Barbara being Barbara, she became immediately anxious that some way, somehow, she'd grievously let her friend down, that she hadn't fully understood or planned for Andrea's needs. That night, when everyone went to bed, Barbara was unable to sleep, her stomach in turmoil. The next day, and the days following, they talked—and talked. Barbara spoke of her "anguish at having hurt" Andrea and kept "groping for a way to speak" to her that wouldn't make her feel blamed. Andrea implied that Barbara, the daughter of privilege, treated her very poor friends by a double standard: "Would *you* live here?"

It so happened that at the time Barbara was in debt, and on top of that, the federal government had begun to hound her for having failed to pay taxes during the Vietnam conflict. But Barbara, as she wrote in shorthand in her notes, didn't "mind seeing self in wrong if can recognize the act as mine." She couldn't, struggle though she did to discover ways in which she or Jane could be "reproached as unconcerned" about their guests' comfort. They had both—as "labors of love"—given endless attention to making the cottage attractive and comfortable.

Barbara felt that their labors had been invisible to Andrea and she felt "unable to communicate" with her, "though we had been before in such very deep communion." Andrea's unrelentingly sullen mood deeply hurt Barbara—and then finally angered her. It wasn't just that Andrea seemed "traumatized" but that Barbara felt "blamed for that trauma." Her old love and still dear friend Mary Meigs had been reading Dworkin's writing and had seen her on TV. She stirred up "a veritable tempest of objections" in Mary—"I think we belong to different species!"—and she believed that Barbara's "patient and suffering goodness" had led her wrongly to conclude that she "can lead the most intractable & destructive souls into ways of gentleness."

Jane agreed with Mary. She finally became so enraged at Andrea (not at John) that she wrote "the Dworkins" a fierce letter—which she never mailed, perhaps because Barbara, less sassy and outspoken than Jane, restrained her. In the letter, Jane let loose with a ferocious barrage: Andrea was "a 2 year old . . . with murder in her heart . . . on a power trip with mama," was "the most absolute self-justifying piece of human equipment I have ever personally met," and was "probably seriously, clinically ill with some sort of paranoid personality. . . ."

But though Jane thereafter gave up on Andrea and hoped never to see her again, Barbara occasionally wrote to her, without ill will. Often it was in response to some new accusation—like Andrea's chiding Barbara for considering payment of her own taxes rather than paying Andrea's. Barbara patiently explained that that was the only way she could hope to carry out her new plan to build up the Women's Fund for feminist writers—she even invited John to apply for a tax-free grant from it. And she continued to express her love and admiration for Andrea, as well as her bewilderment at what had gone wrong between them: "I had always expected that we two could talk about anything together, and find our way out of any misunderstanding."

But Andrea responded coldly. She insisted that Barbara had offered her money from the Women's Fund as a gift, not as a grant that would be taxable as income. Because she and John couldn't afford additional indebtedness and Barbara had refused to pay the taxes, she flatly turned the grant down, closing her letter to Barbara "Sincerely," not "Love." Though discouraged, Barbara persisted in trying to restore the friendship. Occasionally she sent information to Andrea about some feminist interplay or action, including her progress in prosecuting the owner of the movie house that had shown *Snuff* (her suit ultimately failed).

But by 1979, Barbara wrote her, "I've made the guess—rightly or wrongly—that you're happier not hearing from me (since you made no response to my last communications about the *Snuff* struggle)." Yet Barbara continued to defend Andrea against various criticisms of her, as when Ellen Willis wrote a shrewd but negative review of one of her books in the *New York Times*: "In Andrea Dworkin's moral universe the battle of the sexes is a Manichaean clash between absolute power and absolute powerlessness, absolute villains and absolute victims." Barbara sent in a letter of protest: "Dworkin herself makes clear that she considers male sexual aggression not innate, but learned. . . . If misogyny is not all of reality, it *is* everywhere that we look."

To Andrea, Barbara wrote a gentle letter thanking her for the latest book but adding that she did "have one difference with you . . . I think that men are more divided in themselves than you allow—think that when boys . . . abandon their mothers, learn contempt for them, that a *part* of them regrets the choice, sees it as a lying act, and always will.

This regret [is] rarely conscious of course." She signed the letter, "Love." And Andrea did, over time, thaw somewhat. In 1979, after Barbara had unsuccessfully tried for three years to get her own book *Remembering Who We Are* published, Andrea put her in touch with the small house Frog in the Well (its editors accepted the manuscript for publication but later changed their minds). But the intense friendship she'd had with Andrea never truly revived, leaving Barbara feeling wounded and sad at its loss.

During the winter of 1976, Barbara fell ill again and again. She'd never fully recovered from the calamitous automobile accident in 1971, and her fragility—which she battled—now seemed permanent. As she wrote Mary Meigs, "Most of the last years that we lived only two hours away from theatres, galleries, etc. I never did actually get to them. A matter of life energies, I'm afraid. I tire so quickly. If I still could literally travel . . . I'd love to go to some of the huge women's musical events . . . I never have been. This I deeply regret."[13]

Barbara was about to turn sixty, and neither of Jane's children were any longer at home. Mim remained in frequent touch, but George "for a long time" treated both Barbara and Jane with "contempt" and had been difficult to live with. Barbara and Jane decided it was time to leave Monticello. Barbara couldn't take the northern winters any longer; her body told her that "if I didn't move to a [warm] climate I might die soon. And I didn't want to die." She and Jane began to talk about making a permanent relocation to Florida. Barbara acknowledged it was a "drastic step," but Jane had still more trouble adjusting to the idea. She felt both emotionally and financially dependent on Barbara (even though Barbara, in an effort to deal with Jane's discomfort, had set up a joint banking account), and resented moving "so far away from what had become familiar."

But she decided that their relationship, after all, was much like a marriage, with "a mutual dependency & loyalty thereof." And so the decision was finally made to buy a small house on Sugarloaf Key, about twenty miles north of Key West. They moved there in late spring, 1977, and Barbara, too, felt the decision "a great tearing away" from friends and family. Mim resented her mother's being so distant and characterized her move as "self-emancipation." No, Barbara told her, Jane "didn't experience the move as a liberation, but as a *sharp wrench*. . . .

She made the move because *I* felt I had to move to survive (and I, too, hated to have to). . . . I also felt that I couldn't financially afford to maintain two houses."

Initially both women did feel "isolated" at Sugarloaf—or, as Barbara put it, as if they were living "in a convent." Jane, at first, thought their new home "isn't different from any other" place—"it's the same old shit-pile-America"—but admitted that she was "too cussed, and had a lot of undifferentiated wrath." Before much time elapsed, they began to feel better about the move. The small house was on a canal, half a block from the water. It had separate, though tiny, guest quarters and opened out into a yard filled with coconut, banyan, and banana trees and a copious bounty of flowers. They began to make their adjustment. Their spirits further lifted when they found a shortcut road—only thirteen minutes from their house—to the beach, which they loved. And before long, they'd formed a new feminist C-R group and organized a local chapter of NOW with some twenty or thirty members. Barbara also took up tai chi. And as well, they housed local women in emergency situations—a woman eight months pregnant and alone, a woman who'd been raped. They would introduce them to the C-R group for support and help them find a nearby agency that could provide long-term assistance.

Barbara's companion Jane Gapen in an undated photo.

Barbara with Jane Gapen's children, Mimi and George, 1966.

David speaking at the War Resisters League 50th National conference in 1973.

From left, gay rights activists Sylvia Ray Rivera, Marsha P. Johnson, and Barbara Deming at a Demonstration at City Hall, New York City, in support of gay rights bill "intro 475," 1975.

David at the Armed Forces Day Parade, 1979.

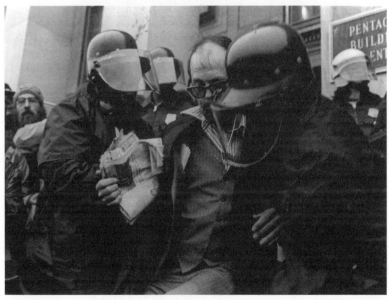

David being arrested during a protest at the Pentagon organized by the Coalition for a Non-Nuclear World, April 28, 1980.

Barbara with friends at Sugarloaf Key, Florida, Barbara and Jane's home, where they moved in 1977 (1980).

Mary Meigs in her later years seated in front of her painting of Barbara.

Barbara at the 1983 Seneca Women's Encampment for a Future of Peace and Justice (with Blue London to her left) to protest the planned deployment of NATO first-strike Cruise and Pershing II missiles to Europe from the Seneca Army Depot.

SENECA CO SHERIFF
ARREST NO   DATE
0022   07 30 83

A mug shot of Barbara, at age 66, following her arrest at the Seneca Women's Encampment.

Barbara a few months before she died of cancer in 1984 at the age of sixty-seven.

David (with Ralph DiGia, third from left, and Karl Bissinger, far right) at the War Resisters League, 1991.

David in Soho in the 1990s.

David protesting at the Smithsonian on the first day of the 1995 exhibit of the Enola Gay, the B-29 bomber that dropped the atomic bomb on Hiroshima.

David speaking at his eightieth birthday celebration, November 2009.

9

The War Resisters League, Socialism, and the Arms Race

It is true," David wrote, "that I am not a passive bystander—and that is what makes life exciting." With the war in Vietnam finally over, David, as a WRL staff member, shifted his energy to a number of projects that had necessarily been on the back burner during the war. Chief among them was the drive for unilateral disarmament, but considerable time also went into setting up links with black churches in the South and organizing protest rallies on behalf of Soviet dissidents. David sometimes worried during 1976 that he had too much on his plate and wasn't doing enough for any single issue—to say nothing of being unable to find time for writing. Still, he thought it something of a miracle that WRL was able to do so much with a small staff and little money. He felt, some days, "so delighted and happy to have such a full life that all other problems are nothing."[1]

The War Resisters League had quickly shrunk in size and resources after the war. Only a few regional offices remained open and the ten thousand people on the mailing list at its high point had rapidly declined to less than half that number. *Win* also soon closed its doors, along with many other radical publications and organizations. The Socialist Party, too, dwindled to a mere five hundred members, and David, who was no longer officially involved, was shocked when he got a call sounding him out about heading the party's presidential ticket.

He immediately said no and added his two cents that it was absurd for the party, given its low estate, to be running *any* candidates for office.

Historically, the membership of the WRL had always been white and middle-class, and that hadn't changed over the years. The league had many women in it, but the barest scattering of working-class people or people of color. At an earlier point, many members in its ranks had held dual membership in the Socialist Party, but that was no longer true. David defined the current guiding principle of the League as "the defense of the right of individuals to be different; we always respect differing values"—an emphasis that has the decided ring to it of philosophical anarchism rather than state socialism—which meant, among other things, that the League remained fiercely opposed to the totalitarian regime of the Soviet Union.

There were those in the League, David among them, who considered *some* of Karl Marx's insights profoundly true yet disagreed with other aspects of Marxism and were aware that the Soviet Union was far closer to a dictatorship than to a socialist state. David, for one, never thought of himself as a committed Marxist; he'd never read *Das Kapital* and wasn't at all sure that he understood the "labor theory of value." But he did accept certain basic Marxist concepts: that consciousness is shaped by the environment; that social structures change as the means of production change; and that the class struggle over the means of production and distribution was valid and essential. But he never regarded Marxism as a science, nor as a guide to when and why social revolutions begin. "A science can predict, and Marxism can't."

Though the staff and Executive Committee of the League had the usual share of internal disagreements, these tended to arise over issues like whether or not to adopt direct mail rather than which aspects of Marxist or socialist ideology to accept or reject. David, in retrospect, believed that a chief weakness of the League was its lack of discipline, not in regard to ideology but simply to office work. After the death of A.J. Muste, Ralph DiGia was regarded by many as the leading figure in the League, but he was reluctant to lead in regard to issues involving conflict. David had learned as far back as high school that in order to lead, "you have to sense where people are willing to go—and then push; but you can't push further than that." He felt that normally Ralph, despite his reluctance, "was able to lead the organization precisely by knowing where it was willing to go."[2]

Internationally, pacifist organizations did have more clearly defined structures. The War Resisters International, which David chaired at one point, met every three years, with representatives from a variety of countries (Great Britain had a particularly strong pacifist group). The WRL Council, which David served on for ten years, met for about a week every year, and the International Executive Committee, which was smaller, met more frequently and was mostly concerned with Western European matters.

The WRL chapter in New York City had long been the most active U.S. local, and over the years had seen several fierce internal debates, some due to personal antagonism, some to policy differences. David was involved in at least his share. At the height of the Vietnam War, he and Al Hassler, a prominent figure in the League, went at it hammer and tongs over the policy of unconditional withdrawal, Hassler fearing that a Communist victory would pose a threat to the Buddhists, with whom he'd become deeply involved. David and Ed Hedemann, also a leading member, could be reduced to shouting matches, especially over the 1976 Continental Walk for Disarmament and Social Justice: in David's view, he was interested in "what's the most effective thing we can do, [while] Ed wants to know how to arrange an arrest scenario." Arrests were perfectly fine with David, but only as the inescapable result of a strategy designed primarily for effectiveness.

In general, David felt that he sometimes became controversial because he was often asked "to do the difficult and unpleasant things," like getting WRL to adopt *Win* magazine "over the dead bodies of two or three people" or his failed effort at the international level to open up some kind of dialogue with the Communist peace front. Some of the occasional antagonism surrounding David was also due to his frequent lateness in submitting written policy statements, as well as his late arrival at the office nearly every day. He constantly berated himself for his inability to go to bed early and his tendency to stay in bed too late in the morning, but he was never able to change the pattern.

Despite these occasional resentments and flare-ups, the WRL staff generally got along well. Ralph DiGia was, in David's words, "everybody's favorite uncle and could do no harm. Ralph was a saint to everyone, to all of us. And Ralph was the one person you could rely on." WRL was not structured as a collective; different people were informally put in charge of one aspect of organizational work—David, for example, wrote the various policy statements. Yet Ralph was uniformly acknowledged as the person who "made that office function and work. He made us work hard because he worked harder than the rest of us. He ran that office—but not like a 'boss.'"

David was also very fond of another WRL mainstay, Karl Bissinger, an "aristocrat" who came into the movement and stayed until his death in 2008 but never tried to put himself forward. He was probably the WRL's staunchest defender of the feminist movement, but unlike David and Igal Roodenko, who were both openly gay—which seemed to be fine with everybody—Karl refused to discuss his private life. In fact, he had a long-standing relationship with a man but had also been heterosexually married and had a son and grandchildren. According to David, Karl "did not like to think of himself as gay"—and indeed may more accurately be called bisexual. In any case, David felt that Karl "came from a time and place where he wanted to be 'himself,' and not a category"—which was pretty close to the way David felt.[3]

An indication of the warmth and comradeship the WRL staff usually felt for one another came when David's camera was stolen from the office. The cost of replacing it was so high (David had become close to being a professional photographer) that he put it on his "eventually but possibly never" list, along with reading glasses or going to see a dentist. But a collection was taken up among the staff and volunteers, including those he'd often quarreled with over political issues, and Karl was able to surprise him with what David called a "monumental check" to buy a new camera. The gesture meant "a great deal more to me," David wrote the contributors, "than I can put into words—and normally I have an excellent command of words."[4]

In fact, the check arrived just three days before David was due to leave for Santa Barbara to spend Christmas with his family. "It was a joyous holiday"—and he was able to take pictures of all of it. But at the end of David's visit, his father came down with the flu. No sooner had David arrived back in New York on January 11, 1977, than he was told his father had been taken to the hospital. Learning that he wasn't expected to live, David flew back to California just in time to see him the night before he died.

David had many regrets about his father. As he wrote his brother, Martin, "Certainly his life has been, by his own testimony, more haunted than yours or mine." David felt that his father had artistic talent that he never explored; instead, he substituted a profound antipathy to dance, theater, and music. Though both his sons were gifted photographers, their father considered that pastime vaguely tainted—"feminine." And despite surface tolerance, he'd never been able to accept David's homosexuality as healthy or integral to his personality. He even distrusted heterosexuality as contaminated unless clearly confined to marriage and procreation, and deep in his being, he thought of himself, a highly sexed person, as dangerously close to sin and damnation.

On returning to New York, David's chief political engagement in the late 1970s became disarmament. The world was then more highly armed than when the United States first talked about "disarming from a position of strength" some twenty-five years earlier. Since then, in David's view, the U.S. had placed itself in rigid opposition "everywhere and without exception" to social justice movements and had thereby "driven people who did want change toward violent revolution and toward the Communist world"—Cuba being a case in point. He felt that American aggression from the 1950s to 1970s outstripped either Soviet or Chinese aggression.[5]

The Soviet Union, as David well understood, had its own deplorable record, but he felt that in the late 1960s the U.S. had outstripped the Soviets in barbaric behavior. It had been chiefly responsible for the killing of half a million alleged Communists in Indonesia (compared to some fifty people the Soviets killed in Czechoslovakia), more than a million in Vietnam and Cambodia each, and an unknown number during the secret war in Laos. David viewed the U.S. toppling of the left-wing Allende government in Chile and the many thousands of deaths and mutilations by torture that followed "worse than anything the Soviet Union has done in the past twenty years." He felt deeply that men like Henry Kissinger had almost as little regard for American lives as those of foreigners. The leadership of the U.S., the Soviet Union, and China had all proven unable to face reality—that we could all be killed in a nuclear war—unlike the pacifists, so often dismissed as dreamy visionaries.

David had for some time been trying, without significant success, to find a way to bind together those splintered fragments on the Left that shared some basic affinities. Michael Harrington was working along parallel lines, but he and David, due to their past antagonisms, never joined forces. By 1972 Harrington had finally moved into opposition to the war in Vietnam, declaring that "the historic party of Eugene Victor Debs and Norman Thomas is today doing the work of Richard Nixon." Shachtman died of a heart attack that same year, but his followers renamed the SP the Social Democrats USA (SDUSA). Also in that same year, the left wing of the old SP—strongest in Wisconsin, Pennsylvania, New York, and California—reorganized as the Socialist Party USA, which continues to the present day.[6]

Harrington, unlike so many of his liberal intellectual friends— Daniel Bell, Nathan Glazer, Irving Kristol, and Norman Podhoretz— did not move to the right and denounce the social welfare programs they had all once championed. To the contrary, Harrington continued to defend the Great Society and in 1973 helped put together what became the Democratic Socialists Organizing Committee (DSOC), later named the Democratic Socialists of America (DSA).

When DSOC was initially formed, David wasn't invited to join, and it's doubtful that this was an oversight. He was still considered too radical for a group that held out hopes of combining with left-wing unionists to strengthen the liberal wing of the Democratic Party, and besides, the relationship between David and Michael Harrington had long been problematic. David wasn't surprised at being passed over, though he did later join the DSA.

At roughly the same time, another organization, the New American Movement (NAM), came into being. Less interested in defending the programs of the Great Society, it focused on community organizing and the newer issues of feminism and gay rights. NAM would merge with DSA in 1983. It grew through the 1970s (up to about five thousand members) until it had at least some peripheral influence on policy; but perhaps more important, it provided something of a beacon in an increasingly bleak atmosphere, economic as well as political. Shards of the Left were piling up into a metaphoric junkyard. Certainly the New Left was no longer viable. Its once-powerful numbers had dribbled off into ever less effective, ideologically purer fragments, like Revolutionary Youth Movement I and II or the Weather Underground.

On behalf of the Socialist Party USA, David appealed to the secretary of the International for formal recognition. But as the secretary explained to him, the International had to recognize and give a "half vote" to the Shachtmanite SDUSA because it had the legal majority, and it had already given Harrington's group the other half vote because of the work he'd done with the Socialist International. Not wanting to recognize three separate groups, the secretary asked David not to press the matter. He agreed, not least because it wasn't at all clear that SPUSA could afford the International's dues or where they'd get enough money to send delegates to its annual convention.

Whether in the form of SPUSA, the Shachtmanite SDUSA, or Harrington's DSA, the vast majority of Americans were not about to embrace socialism in any of its manifestations. The association with totalitarian Stalinism had become too deeply ingrained. And besides, most Americans, even in the face of the grossest social and economic injustices, still continued to believe the country's foundational myths: that no institutionalized inequities stand in the way of our ability to pull ourselves up by our own bootstraps, and that if we don't, it's our own fault entirely, because we *do* live in an equal opportunity society. Hard work is the highway, entirely free of potholes, to success; lack of determination and effort, the low road to failure.

David and Harrington had similar reactions to feminism—initial defensiveness followed by vigorous efforts (incomplete in the eyes of some radical feminists) to understand and accept. As early as DSOC's founding convention in 1973, Harrington was waylaid by a group of intense, angry women incensed over the pitiful female representation and the lack of comprehension of feminism as an issue of importance. The confrontation left him (in his own words) "shocked and uncomprehending." He came gradually to understand that most of the men in DSOC had been "profoundly insensitive" to feminism and that they needed to change, to realize that the exploitation of women was as important to socialism as racism and class. By the 1986 congress of the Socialist International, Harrington, the principal author of a new Declaration of Principles, was able to include a strong feminist plank that was unanimously adopted by the representatives of the seventy-five nations in attendance—though the extent to which feminist insights and demands were actually implemented was and is the real sticking point.

David had followed a trajectory comparable to Harrington's. Initially resistant to certain aspects of feminism, as demonstrated in his earlier clashes with Barbara Deming, his sympathies gradually broadened. During the period of Barbara's resettlement in Florida, the two had taken a breather from their ongoing debate, yet another round of discord between them was waiting in the wings. But first Barbara needed time to attend to her health—the trip down to Florida had been "exhausting"—to get used to her new surroundings, and to finish the "endlessly distracting" work on their house. Early in 1977, she was already writing Adrienne Rich that "the Keys do very much agree with me." But she still tired early in the day, and the novel she'd begun to work on was proceeding at far too glacial a pace to please her. Barbara felt lucky if she could manage to eke out a few sentences a day.[7]

Yet she somehow managed to maintain at least intermittent political involvement. The C-R group that she and Jane had formed soon after arriving in Sugarloaf Key continued to thrive, and Barbara, whenever her "ration of energy" would permit, also worked for passage of the Equal Rights Amendment. In 1972 both houses of Congress did pass it, but it failed to be ratified by the necessary number of states. Working for ERA in Florida was tough going. It was an increasingly conservative state and had recently spawned the Anita Bryant crusade against gay rights. In 1977, Dade County (now Miami-Dade) passed an ordinance prohibiting discrimination on the basis of sexual orientation. Anita Bryant, a moderately well-known singer who'd been second runner-up at the 1958 Miss America pageant, immediately inaugurated a successful campaign, called Save Our Children, to repeal the protection. Only in 1998 did the county reauthorize an antidiscrimination law—by a 7–6 vote.

Even while working against Anita Bryant, Barbara typically ("No one is Other") managed at one point to express a bit of sympathy for her. It came while watching a Miami TV show called *To the Point*, on which Anita and her then husband Bob Green were the guests and the host a woman whom Barbara called "a cheery feminist." When discussion turned to the famous 1977 incident in which a gay activist threw a pie in Anita's face, the host told Anita that she'd been surprised her husband hadn't taken out his handkerchief and helped her wipe the guck off her face, instead of feeding her lines like "Say a prayer" and "Say 'I forgive you.'" Anita burst into delighted laughter and told the host "I like you!" then pummeled her husband playfully with her fists. In Barbara's view, the host had done "a beautiful thing—actually managed to reach Anita."[8]

For a time after she publicly "came out," Barbara kept casting about for the lesbian caucus at various women's conferences she attended. But she soon stopped bothering. She'd never been a separatist of any kind, and even at the height of the split between lesbians and heterosexual women, she was primarily interested in finding common ground between them—just as she was between men and women. She recognized, of course, that there were significant and culturally produced differences in both cases, and didn't gloss over them. In regard to women, she felt that class differences were the most important impediment to mutual understanding, and that C-R groups were a useful tool for bridging that gap. She also felt that Marxists, in defining class struggle, were describing only a partial reality—conflicts among *men*, the class affiliations of women automatically resulting from the status of the men they were associated with. The struggle of women against the oppression of men wasn't even a Marxist sidebar. Even Marxist-oriented women were often so reflexively attached to a traditional view of the "class struggle" that they considered the feminist movement of secondary importance at most.[9]

The tension in the feminist movement between lesbians and heterosexual women was epitomized in the relationship between Barbara and the journalist, poet, and radical feminist Leah Fritz. Leah had earlier interviewed Barbara, and the two women had gotten along well—except for the fact that Barbara, given her past experience with straight women, "couldn't quite believe" that Leah felt no fear or antagonism about Barbara's sexuality. She made the mistake of saying something like that to Leah, which upset her. She insisted that Barbara was quite wrong: "You assume too much when you say I am either fearful or ill at ease with lesbians qua lesbians. The truth is that I am only uncomfortable when I am preached at and forced to defend myself. This I experience as tyranny. In the women's movement I demand complete parity." She made the further point that as a *feminist*, the world at large already treated her as both a lesbian and a communist.[10]

A series of elaborate mea culpas on the part of both women quickly followed, and their friendship was restored—but not before another kind of disagreement between them had to be resolved. Jane had formed a separate friendship with Leah and had taken to occasionally confiding in her, especially about some of the difficulties she experienced in being Barbara's partner. She made it clear to Leah that she adored Barbara and marveled at her many qualities and gifts: she "is so sensitive, tries so hard, does so much better than most or anyone I know . . . her particular genius is a real capacity to empathize with the very soul of others."

But, Jane confided, Barbara had "a sense of conviction so deep that it sometimes bordered on certitude . . . there's an element of coercion in it . . . I don't ordinarily carry my own thoughts at variance to hers far enough." Leah reassured Jane that she was "a person with a real spine" and one able to vent her anger. That, she went on, was precisely Barbara's problem—"she doesn't express hers, and so to disagree with her is often like picking a fight with Jesus when he's bleeding on the cross. At the point he tells you he feels your pain, you have no recourse but to kneel down and shut up."

Jane, perhaps in the hope of unlocking those unshared feelings between herself and Barbara, passed on Leah's words. Barbara immediately wrote to Leah: "You say that the problem with relating to me is that I don't express my anger. Let me, then, express some anger." She reiterated the fact that she'd earlier misunderstood Leah's feelings about lesbians and still regretted having hurt her. But she added, "I am *not* just concerned with 'coming out on the right side of an argument' when a hurt to a friend is involved. . . . And I *don't* care more about my ability to empathize (which I know is *deficient*) . . . than about your feelings. I've been struggling to find a way to behave that would respect both your feelings and mine." She went on to defend herself against some of the criticisms Leah had made (partly to Jane) about a piece Barbara had written for a book Leah was editing, and then closed with "So—there's my anger. You're right that it's hard for me to speak it . . . here is also, as you must know, much love." All three women did reconstitute their relationships. Yet their discord again illustrates that all movements fall short of the harmony to which they aspire, just as the truest hearts must forever remain incompletely linked.

Barbara agreed with David McReynolds that nuclear war could (in her words) "destroy all life on this planet. It couldn't be more obvious than it is that to prepare for such war is wildly insane." But from a seemingly shared perspective, their views parted—again. David believed nuclear disarmament hinged on the acceptance of the nonviolent principles of the War Resisters League. Barbara believed that disarmament hinged on men surrendering their self-image as *"masters* of nature," owners of nature, their doubly insane view that the end of the world could somehow take place while their male selves remained intact, like "the Self of the man-god many of them worship." What women could do to help them wake up from their delusional state was repeatedly to "name ownership a lie" by refusing to be owned.[11]

And so the two were off and running, never losing their affection for each other, never losing the conviction that his or her view was the correct one. Their latest spat began over the comparatively small issue of the WRL's latest annual calendar and broadened out from there. Regarding the calendar itself, neither of them seems to have been definitively right. David insisted that the current calendar was affirmative about feminism, and he pointed Barbara back in time to calendars he himself had edited, in which Alice Paul and other early feminist leaders had been given special attention *before* the feminist movement had applied any distinct pressure. Barbara's view, quite simply, was that not *enough* attention was being paid, especially to *contemporary* feminists. To decide what "enough" meant would have required several Solomons.[12]

David made clear that he never laid claim to being "an orthodox [undefined] feminist" and insisted, probably accurately, that "very few groups have taken feminism as seriously as WRL and *Win*." Barbara remained unpersuaded: "I used to feel listened to, there at the League," she responded, "but the painful truth I'm trying to speak is that now that I'm a feminist, I *don't* feel listened to." She spelled that out more fully in a one-page piece she entitled "Should We Be Alarmed?" Although many whites, she wrote, "took part in the black struggle, and paid close attention to the words of black leaders, men on the left have paid no comparable attention to the words of feminists. They may speak up for the ERA," but—here she repeated an earlier charge—they don't read any of "the many extraordinary books feminists have written over the past few years."

Since Barbara had already recycled those charges several times (which didn't mean they weren't true) the repetition got David's dander up. He replied that, speaking only for himself, he had too little time to read more than a few books, "often mysteries written by women (but not by the right kind of women—I know)." Besides, David felt that at this point Barbara "was fighting old battles which had been won." WRL had shifted radically toward structural equality, declaring that henceforth both its Executive and National Committees had to be at least 50 percent staffed by women. But he then also repeated certain stale charges that Barbara had already answered. He again inaccurately accused her of "having chosen a separatist road" and again repeated an inflammatory indictment: "I don't have any obligation to sit down and read a book written by someone who won't attend planning meetings with men, someone who insists on separate demonstrations, separate book stores, separate bars—they can bloody well have a separate audience for their writing."

Barbara remained comparatively calm. But she did insist that David was making "assumptions about what it is that I believe which are inaccurate" (he'd also again accused her of wanting to restore "matriarchy" and of believing that men and women had essentially different natures). Since she'd earlier refuted those interpretations, she settled for citing some of her published essays that argued the opposite and concentrated instead on David's charge that she was a separatist. "I have never given myself that name," she wrote him. "Yes, I do feel strongly that *for a time* women must talk above all among ourselves, act above all together." But she assured him that she had *not* abandoned her old comrades: "Many of the actions I have taken and the actions WRL has taken have been the same actions. Do I repudiate my past? I do not. I will always be proud that we took those actions. And many actions indeed"—like protesting nuclear proliferation and demanding unilateral disarmament—that "we still take in unison."

David also tried to turn down the heat and to emphasize instead their commonalities. In a short, somewhat formal note that marked the end of their latest quarrel, he even directly acknowledged past omissions: "You were absolutely correct," he wrote Barbara, that although WRL had emphasized past contributions by women in its literature, "we could, as well, have found current actions taken by women." He promised "to do my best" in honoring "the women and the men, the brothers and sisters, past and present, who have stood on the front lines." Another round of recriminations had ended. The friendship held.

A different sort of retrospective—more congenial than incensed—took place between Barbara and Mary Meigs. Mary sent Barbara a copy of the manuscript for what would become her autobiographical book, *Lily Briscoe* (published in 1981). The manuscript revisited in detail the two women's relationship of sixteen years, and then the shorter period when Marie-Claire Blais had joined their household, ultimately leading to Barbara's departure. After carefully reading the material, she sent Mary a long, thoughtful critique that revealed much about Barbara's past and present states of mind.[13]

She thought the book "very wonderful—and a brave one, too," but she was forthright about certain sections of it having hurt her. This was especially true in regard to her political life; "I feel unseen by you," she wrote Mary, "or seen in distortion. . . . You make me heroic but simpleminded." In her own view, she was neither. Mary had written that "like all true revolutionaries," Barbara was "unaffected by the weight of evidence," a charge Barbara felt was quite untrue. Nor did she feel it accurate for Mary to describe her as having been made inflexible by her "wonderful fidelity to the ideal."

In rebuttal, Barbara offered her *fluctuating*, not "inflexible," attitude toward the Cuban revolution over the years. She stood by her initial impression that "many lives have changed for the better . . . in the old Cuba, most people were illiterate, diseased, seasonally unemployed, etc." Nor did she put any trust in the negative testimony of Cuban political exiles: "For they live now in a country hostile to their mother country, and the more charges they make, the more welcome they are here." But that didn't mean that she entirely dismissed the views of the exiles either. Through the years, she'd told herself over and over that she no longer had firsthand knowledge of what was going on in Cuba: "I don't *know* what the truth is." What she did still remain certain of was that the Cuban revolution "was a struggle for independence from the U.S.—just like the Vietnamese struggle." She insisted that she didn't "*idealize*" any of these regimes which have won independence. As a pacifist, how could I? They rely still on armed struggle. And as a feminist, how could I ? They remain patriarchal."

She felt offended that Mary had "completely misrepresented" her purported indifference to the news that Cuba had been sending homosexuals to "correctional" camps. To the contrary, Barbara had "heard that news with *horror*." She gathered that Cuban policy had changed since then and that homosexuals were (this was 1978) no longer interred, but that hardly made her feel "that it had all been simply 'a mistake.'" She also recognized that despite "some real gains against sexism," she continued to feel that the Cuban revolution was "at the core dangerously sexist still." She begged Mary to make the needed corrections about her attitude toward Cuba—and Mary did.

A more overarching complaint on Barbara's part was Mary's view of her as "rigid." Barbara protested "that there is a great deal more skepticism in my nature than you have noted." In support of that comment she cited the "delight" she had often felt in Mary's sometimes "inspired" counterarguments when they lived together. In the manuscript, Mary had contrasted her own stubborn pursuit of happiness with Barbara's equally stubborn adherence to conscience. Barbara offered a different, spirited view: "I didn't walk through the south, didn't go to Vietnam, out of some sense [as Mary had written] that it would be nice of me to help the downtrodden." No, Barbara argued, as she had earlier when Rita Mae Brown had made a similar assertion, "I walked because I am a nigger—and a gook—too. It always felt like my own struggle that I was waging." It was not her superego, her conscience, that had led her into various battles—"it was that part of us that can identify with other figures in dreams."

Mary had written that Barbara had urged her to become politically active too. But Barbara denied that: "It would have been hard to excuse you if you had made yourself do it, without really wanting to, and at the expense of your painting." She thought Mary was "belittling" herself in writing that she felt "humble" in relation to Barbara: "You didn't take the road I took, but you took *your own* road." But Barbara was perhaps forgetting or taking too lightly the charismatic power of her example and the implicit pressure it exerted on others to also "do good and be good." Like many conscience-driven people, Barbara focused on her own inadequacies, which obscured the fact—Mary described her as "a horse in blinders"—that others tended to see in her an exemplary model of "saintly" behavior.

In the increasingly conservative climate of the late 1970s, it became difficult for left-wing groups to find affordable housing in New York City. The A.J. Muste Institute had its own headquarters and owned (as of 1969, the high point of its financial security) a three-story, run-down little building at 339 Lafayette Street. The paint was peeling off the walls, the narrow staircases alarmingly rickety, the corridors piled high with old files, and mice constant companions. Still, the place had heat and water and, though barren of creature comforts, was serviceable.[14]

The League decided that it had an obligation to turn landlord and rent out space in the building at very low rates to other movement groups. Due to the enfeebled, marginal nature of many of the organizations, the turnover in tenants was frequent. In the spring of 1979, the nine occupants included SHAD (Sound and Hudson Against Nuclear Development), the Middle East Peace Project, the Turkish Students Association, the Anarchists Black Cross, and the Gay Activists Alliance. A number of the other tenants were antiwar groups, and 339 Lafayette got the nickname of the Peace Pentagon. The building's rental fees were so low that it ended up in the red every year.

David's own apartment on East Fourth Street was also small and crammed with boxes and books, which made 339 Lafayette seem a natural extension of his home life. He never complained about the League's cramped and run-down office, and rather got a kick out of the endless war he waged with the WRL's tenacious mouse population. Besides, he was often on the road. In the fall of 1979 alone, he went on a six-week speaking tour that took him to the West Coast, Colorado, New Mexico, and Texas. He was about to become far busier still.

The Socialist Party USA (the left wing of the old Socialist Party) nominated him to run for president in the 1980 election. This time around, David accepted—in part, as he was quick to admit, out of plain old egotism, but in part, too, because the campaign would enable him to reach and educate a variety of audiences, especially on the high-priority issue of disarmament. This had become all the more urgent when in March 1979 a nuclear power plant at Three Mile Island in

Pennsylvania had nearly melted down. Other outlets for left-wing protest had been drying up since the mid-1970s. *Liberation* was gone, the rambunctious *Ramparts* closed its doors in 1975, *New Times* in 1978, and *Win* in the early 1980s. That didn't mean the well had gone entirely dry. There was still the *Progressive*, the *Nation* and (until it became centrist), the *New Republic*. A few new publications—in particular *Rolling Stone* and *Mother Jones*—partly replaced the old ones and continue to the present day. And there was also a real surge of feminist and gay publications, though they tended in most cases to have limited circulation and short lives.[15]

David realized of course that the vote for him as a presidential candidate would be minuscule and that the actual contest would be between the two major parties. The Democrats had nominated Jimmy Carter for a second term and the Republicans had picked Ronald Reagan. Early in his first administration, Carter had managed to alienate the trade unions, already in decline, with his lukewarm support for a reform bill that would have strengthened labor's right to collective bargaining; the bill died in the Senate. With fifty-two U.S. embassy employees still being held hostage in Iran, the economy moving into recession, and Carter's domestic agenda too conservative to head it off, Reagan's election seemed likely.[16]

David had to ask himself why he was bothering to run: "Am I not simply condensing Harold Stassen's career into a nine month period?" Besides, the environmentalist Barry Commoner was already running on the Citizens' Party ticket and was backed by Harrington and the DSOC. But Commoner's platform, by David's standards, made only "limited demands," failing to call for social ownership of at least natural resources and energy or for "dismantling all 30,000 of our nuclear weapons—and not just the 75 power plants." By contrast, David ran on a platform centered on the struggle for economic democracy and democratic control of the major means of production and distribution. It also urged severe cuts in the military budget, "militant" support of the rights of women, as well as "groups of differing sexual orientations," passage of the ERA, and withdrawal of all troops of all nations behind their own national borders.

Though it was remarkable—this, after all, was 1980, when the gay movement was essentially still in its infancy—for SPUSA to have put an open homosexual at the head of its ticket. David made it clear in his policy statement that he was "not going to run as the candidate of gay liberation—I think the arms race, racism, and unemployment are much more urgent questions." He was being honest about his convictions and priorities, but that meant neither gay people nor radical feminists would be particularly drawn to his candidacy. Nonetheless, he gathered an impressive list of endorsers, including Allen Ginsberg, Dwight Macdonald, and Seymour Krim.

By early April 1980, David had already set up a campaign office, gotten volunteer staff to keep it open, begun fund-raising for full-time staff, and put a man on the road in the Midwest to help with getting on state ballots. He also began to campaign vigorously—a week in Vermont, another week in California. While in Vermont, David conferred with Bernie Sanders and thought for a while that he might gain his support and that of the state's Liberty Union Party, which had been started in 1970 with the purpose—much like that of the Liberal Party in New York State—of trying to force the two major parties to the left. Sanders would soon become mayor of Burlington, and from there he'd move on to run successfully for Congress as an independent, without denying that he was a socialist. David's campaign manager tried several times to get Sanders's endorsement, but he never responded to the appeals.

David ended up getting more votes (about ten thousand) than Barry Commoner, who was much better known—and despite the support of Michael Harrington and the DSOC for Commoner. By then, Harrington and McReynolds had become still further estranged, and in the year following the election David charged Mike with "obscuring his actual record during the Vietnam war" and portraying himself as having been "a leader within the anti-war movement." He thought a more truthful characterization of Harrington would be "the hollow man of the American Left, just as DSOC, with its effort to contain socialists within the Democratic Party, is a weak substitute for a serious and militant socialist movement."

With Reagan's victory over Carter, the country intensified its long stretch of conservative dominance. Reagan made a number of pro-corporate appointments to the National Labor Relations Board, further weakening a trade union movement already in decline; he greatly diluted measures to protect the environment; and he named William Rehnquist chief justice of the Supreme Court, thereby turning what had been a moderately liberal Court into a right-of-center one. David, like many progressives (as they are now known) started to rethink what might or might not be possible in a country increasingly run to protect the already privileged and less and less concerned with the plight of the poor.

David's commitment to socialism and to nonviolence remained rock-solid. But in the face of the changed social climate, how he defined the first and strategized the second required some tuning up. Most Americans have long equated socialism with Stalinism, a failed system—and no more need be said. But that widespread attitude is based on ignorance of the *pre*-Stalinist Bolshevik period in Russia when the goal of egalitarianism *was* at the revolution's core. It's also an attitude oblivious to the huge variations across time and national boundaries among "Marxist" movements and "socialist" regimes. Even the Nazis called themselves the National Socialist Party.[17]

David had never been ignorant of such distinctions, but even from the early days of his political life he sometimes declared his *partial* adherence to Marxism, though he *never* referred to himself as pro-Communist. Like Barbara Deming, David had never been an ideologue rigidly committed to one particular set of theoretical abstractions. His only sustained commitment was to the betterment of the quality of life for as many people as possible. That was his core definition of democratic socialism. The preferred means to that end—whether the rule of the proletariat, government ownership of the means of production or decentralized communal associations—was far less certain in David's mind than the goal of improving the lot of the many, so long as the means remained nonviolent.

In a number of western European countries during the 1970s, social-democratic parties had won control. But due primarily to the mounting economic crisis, by the 1980s most of these had given way to more conservative governments. In the United States, social-democratic forces had in the twentieth century sometimes made progress but never triumphed, and they were certainly not about to prosper under Reagan's ministrations. Central to his agenda was building up allocations for military defense and cutting social welfare programs that aided the poor. In parallel to this shift in domestic policy, Reagan pursued interventions abroad that ranged from sending the marines into Lebanon to invading the tiny island of Grenada to supporting violent right-wing elements in El Salvador and Nicaragua. *Liberalism* became a curse word and *socialism* an expletive. Despite these discouraging developments, David remained committed to continuing the struggle to define the future. He knew what he *hoped* it would look like, even though he fully realized that in the early 1980s those hopes appeared to friends elusive and to enemies delusional. But if history was any guide, an *eventual* shift in the political climate was inevitable. And when that shift came, even if thirty or forty years hence, he felt it important to be prepared with an agenda for change, or at least an outline for ensuring that the profit motive would no longer demand that the vast majority live in squalor and the small minority in often undeserved, always indefensible wealth.[18]

In looking toward future foreign policy, David thought good starting points would be to ban all further arms sales, to put an end to economic sanctions as a substitute for diplomacy, to immediately withdraw from all foreign bases (like Guantánamo, a sovereign territory belonging to Cuba), and to dissolve all military alliances, beginning with NATO. On the domestic front, he wanted to guarantee an income above the poverty level, and advocated a low-income housing program, a national health care system, the release of all prisoners being held for nonviolent crimes, the shift from a legal to a medical approach to addictive drugs (including alcohol and tobacco), care for the environment, and the full defense of *everyone's* civil liberties.

None of these goals, David insisted, was particularly radical, none of them specifically socialist. What *could* legitimately be called socialist was his additional emphasis on speaking out for the poor, whether working or unemployed. He argued that we heard many laments about the condition of the middle class—itself serious enough—but next to no concern for the plight of those below the poverty line. He also wanted put into place the classic socialist demand for ownership and democratic control of the basic means of production. He called for an ongoing struggle against the effort to privatize our roads, bridges, schools, hospitals, and prisons so as to run them for the profit of the few. Furthermore, he wanted defense spending severely cut or abolished: "We get into wars because we have a military, not because we don't have one."

Finally, David thought that although "capitalism does work better than we sometimes admit," the fact remained that even when functioning at its best, the economic structure exacted a terrible price: it turned human beings into commodities and turned us against one another—in the process destroying fellow feeling, empathy, and any sense of a shared community. The popular, unexamined American assumption "that capitalism is in the interests of the people" was quite simply a lie; it wasn't.

In his itemization of the country's ills and possible solutions for them, David particularly emphasized the long-standing and intractable issue of racism and racial divisions. He offered no quick solution, but he did insist that socialists should view the building of alliances with communities of color as a high priority. As far back as the mid-1970s, he'd shifted from seeking an integrated society to a recognition that the United States had never really been a "melting pot." Rather, it was a country whose people shared some features and values yet had for many generations loyally held to a distinctive set of subcultural traditions, whether class-based, ethnic, racial, or geographical. This tenacious diversity, he felt, should be honored and sustained, not belittled as some unfortunate vestige of backwardness.

David also felt that special attention needed to be given to the ongoing plight of black people, thanks to their unique history of slavery and degradation here. A long struggle was required, and Americans weren't good at sustained attention or commitment. After a spurt of interest during the 1960s in reducing discrimination and tension, white America had settled back into the consensus view that "we've now done all that we can for *those* people; the rest is up to them." David thought otherwise. He hadn't been sympathetic to the Black Power nationalists who'd arisen during the 1970s but was deeply so to the ongoing suffering of many black people.

Why, he asked, did so many young black men end up in prison? They weren't *biologically* predisposed to drugs and crime—they were driven to them by a society that had dropped the doctrine but not the practice of segregated education and housing, by the minimal opportunities for work—let alone creative, meaningful work—and by the frustration, in a society that placed priority on the accumulation of goods, at not being able to afford (in David's words) "the symbols of luxury that are just as important to poor people as to rich ones." The sense of hopelessness in the ghetto, combined with cuts in city services, had helped once more to create profound bitterness among many poor blacks. Nixon hadn't gone to jail, but *they* often did for selling a dime bag of pot.

In regard to the peace movement, David saw the early 1980s as a period of new dangers due to the shared blindness of the American and Soviet leaderships. After the Soviet Union left the Geneva disarmament talks, Reagan deployed the first Cruise and Pershing II weapons—capable of reaching Moscow in six minutes—to England, West Germany, and Italy. He thereby created, in David's view, "a Cuban Missile Crisis in the heart of Europe." Like earlier ones, the new administration apparently thought that a nuclear war could be fought and won.

Though David despised Reagan and the numbingly self-satisfied men who surrounded him—such as Bush, Haig, and Weinberger—he felt that the Soviet leadership was no better. He traveled to Europe, Cambodia, Hanoi, Saigon, and Japan in the early 1980s to meet with peace workers and found them, like him, as frightened by the Soviets' reckless policies—the deployment of SS-20 missiles, the placing of Soviet submarines in Swedish waters—as by Reagan's. Late in 1978, David had been one of seven disarmament demonstrators who unfurled a banner in Moscow's Red Square. It said, in Russian, "USA-USSR DISARM!" And although the Soviets had by now caught up with the United States in nuclear strength, they remained locked into patterns of oppression in Eastern Europe.

But the attitude of "an equal curse on both your sides" didn't quite come naturally to David, who deep down was both an optimist by temperament and a wakeful patriot. He reminded himself and others that "no matter how discouraged we become over America's actions, we must see the deep strength of democracy in this country, the willingness of Americans, when the goal is clear, to make great sacrifices for the common good. . . . If the Vietnam War was criminal, let us take pride in the mass resistance to it. If racial injustice is hideous, let us remember that Martin Luther King Jr. is also a part of this culture."

Yet as matters currently stood, David was pretty much convinced that neither of the two great blocs, Soviet and American, could be relied on to end their dangerous stalemate. He put his hopes in a neutral or nonaligned movement—"on the dissident and unofficial forces *within* the two blocs, or outside of them, on the cooperation of disarmament groups, the movements for national liberation and self-determination, the ecological movements, and those socialist and communist parties which have broken with both blocs."

He didn't offer much by way of specifics. Yet as the old saying has it, "God is in the details." Some particulars were needed. *How* could these disparate groups be brought together? In the past, any number of them had quarreled bitterly. Was it realistic to believe that their combined strength, even if achievable, would be sufficient to exert any real influence over the two giants locked in struggle. David acknowledged that his "new international"—meant to include, among others, the War Resisters International, the International Fellowship of Reconciliation, the trade unions, the Green Party, and the feminist movement—was "vague, lacked a center, lacked an agreed-upon political line," worked with little money, and mostly existed only in the imagination. Even if such groups could work together harmoniously, it surely taxed the imagination to place much faith in their ability to make demands of the two Great Powers.

All that David knew for certain was that "American foreign policy is terribly, basically wrong—and Soviet errors and crimes do not justify ours." He felt that we had the obligation to *try* "to shape events responsibly." The obligation was moral: "We must refuse, in every possible way, to act as beasts driven toward the cliffs. . . . We shall fight for the survival of this human race." Fight? Yes, but not with arms. With "ballots and civil disobedience."

10

Sugarloaf Key

It wasn't long before friends from various chapters in their lives began to visit Barbara and Jane in Sugarloaf Key. Most stayed for only a few weeks or, at most, during the cold northern winters, several months. The property consisted of more than two acres of land and had to some extent already been developed during the 1930s as a residential compound—four houses, two small guest cottages, and a large campground where temporary tents could be set up. The climate was subtropical, which made it pleasant during the winter but decidedly hot in summer. The land was wondrously fertile, filled with every sort of greenery, from wildflowers to large banyan trees; it was surrounded by crystal-clear water and filled with wildlife—deer, raccoons, iguanas, egrets, hummingbirds, terns, and ospreys, along with many species of migrating birds.[1]

Over time, a few women began to settle in for longer stays at Sugarloaf, and a small lesbian community gradually emerged. At its height, ten women were in residence, most of whom left after several years; at one point in the 1990s, only one woman was living there year-round. Mary Meigs—though not Marie-Claire—came several times for extended stays, and she gave Sugarloaf the gift of some property (which the women named Maryswoods) and helped in the purchase of a second lot across the street from the community.

Several women did settle permanently at Sugarloaf. Ruth Dreamdigger and Doris ("Blue") Lunden probably were the two who became most integral to Sugarloaf's daily life. Sugarloaf meant a great deal to Barbara, though as a writer she sometimes had to withdraw from "too much communal living." As someone who wrote painstakingly, she needed "to spend long, long stretches of time alone"—"starving" for solitude, she would periodically have to pull back from daily involvement.[2]

Blue Lunden became a particularly vital part of the Sugarloaf community. She'd grown up in a working-class household in New Orleans, constantly harassed by the police as a young woman for her drinking and for "wearing the clothing of the opposite sex" (in those days a standing charge, along with loitering, for arresting queers). Courageously insistent on being who she was, Blue left for New York City, taking her baby daughter with her. She lived there for twenty years, got sober, coped with being a single parent, and transformed her life through political activism. She probably met Barbara initially through their mutual involvement in the peace and nuclear disarmament movements. Blue first visited Sugarloaf in 1981 and lived there for the following eighteen years, until her death from lung cancer in 1999, at age sixty-two.

She and Barbara became close friends and worked together in local, as well as global politics. Locally, they joined in the unsuccessful fight to get the Equal Rights Amendment passed in Florida before the ratification deadline of June 1982. When a Key West paper printed a letter from a local pastor denouncing the ERA as "devil-inspired," Barbara responded with a lengthy rebuttal. "I assume," she began, "that as a Christian minister you try to teach the words of Jesus. But he taught— did he not?—that we should love our neighbors as ourselves . . . [but] look around and note how well we are protected under patriarchy. We are raped, battered, exploited by the millions. . . . If a wish to be independent of men is interpreted as hatred of men—that just proves how men confuse love with ownership."[3]

About nuclear disarmament, Barbara circulated a general statement she'd written. "Our politicians tell us that we have to be strong," she wrote, but "we had better ask ourselves what the word means. Are we strong if we show that we are capable of destroying all life on this earth?" A national debate was currently taking place about the role of women in the military; Barbara joined it by asking the unorthodox question, what was it that the military trained you to be? Her answer: They "train you not to ask why the war is being waged, why these particular people should be killed—just do as you're told, kill when you're told to. Mindlessly." If women were drafted, the common assumption was that they wouldn't be sent into combat. In Barbara's view that wasn't because "the powers-that-be feel women shouldn't be subjected to violence. If they felt this, they would give battered women and rape victims help they don't give. No, they want to assure the men they're ordering around that dealing-out violence is reserved for *them*—and somehow proves that they are more than women are."

David McReynolds had earlier argued with Barbara's "woman centered" analysis of war and disarmament. Nor did it prove congenial to many politically involved women (especially heterosexual ones) who wanted men in their lives and who felt that men, too, were often victims—forced by macho values, for example, to deny the range of their feelings and to accentuate only aggression and anger. One such woman was Norma Becker, a prominent, compassionate activist and a colleague and close friend of David's. She tended to disapprove of all "women only" groups and demonstrations. As Becker wrote in *WRL News*, "women know all too well the connection between militarism and the violence in our lives. The masculine ideal which the military perpetuates encourages force, dominance, power and violence . . . [But] women-only events are often experienced as a political and personal affront to men who are comrades in the struggle."[4]

But Barbara's whole point, as she'd emphasized earlier in her dispute with David, was that most men on the Left *weren't* "comrades" to women; they failed to employ feminist perspectives in their work or to hear the call for the equal entitlement of all women. A recent illustration was Barbara's antagonistic exchange with one of her old antiwar "comrades," Father Dan Berrigan. Barbara came across a statement he'd written about abortion that included the words: "war is also an abortion, and abortion is also a war"; he directly compared abortion clinics to the Pentagon. (David, too, once wrote—but not to Barbara—that he felt "deeply torn" on the subject of abortion, but unlike Berrigan, he felt "strongly that women, not men, should make the laws on this.") Barbara reacted to Berrigan's statement with shock and indignation. "I can't not cry out to you in dismay," she wrote Dan. She accused him of playing with words—"and playing with the deepest feelings of women. *Women do not have abortions in the spirit of war!!*"[5]

Barbara asked him "to imagine—deeply—the lives of those women who decide they simply cannot bear a child. Still another child, it often is. Plead with these women, if you must, to count their own lives as nothing, to give *up* their lives to the life that is not yet formed, is still just a promise . . . remember, it is the mother, not the father (though this shouldn't be so) who is servant to that child for years. If her serving the child is *involuntary* servitude—what could be more cruel, Dan, for both mother *and* child? . . . to insist that women bear children that they don't want to bear—Dan, isn't *this* making war on *women*?"

Dan was unpersuaded and unmoved. He wrote Barbara back that "women (you'll pardon me for insisting) make a great mistake in isolating abortion questions as women's questions. There is a man somewhere in every conception"—but he failed to add: a man not often sharing equally in the responsibility of *rearing* the child. "I believe," Dan went on, "that when abortion becomes a socially acceptable way of coping with the inhuman status of pregnant women, the society has won again"—though it hadn't been pregnancy that Barbara had denounced as "inhuman," but rather the sacrifice of an unwilling mother's own life to serving the needs of her progeny. "The women who agree with this state of things, or push it," Berrigan concluded—without defining what "this state of things" was meant to signify—those women "are the ones who are aiding and abetting the war-making society. . . . I do not want murder legalized, by generals, by doctors, by priests, by women, by any of us." The fuzziness of Dan's letter, his Catholic faith apparently substituting for coherent argument, led Barbara to forgo a reply.

The "male comrades" had also shown considerable nervous anxiety about gay rights tainting any cause with which they were associated—nuclear disarmament being a case in point. The issue went back a number of years, and was ongoing. The pioneering gay activist Allen Young had earlier been involved in a number of antinuke actions, and in his opinion, "we gays and lesbians remain essentially an embarrassment. . . . Our presence at an antinuclear demonstration makes the demonstration somehow kooky—and marginal."[6]

On May 6, 1979, when 125,000 people marched in the nation's capital to protest nuclear arms, a small group of gay men was physically attacked while their fellow marchers passively looked on. Yet radical gay men and lesbians were a small number in 1979 when compared to the broad social justice agendas of organizations like the Gay Liberation Front at the start of the decade; the gay movement was heading, like the rest of the country, toward the center. Yet some gay people continued to believe that if the Left was ever going to have a serious impact on public policy, oppressed groups needed to become aware of their interconnections and to form coalitions. Besides, as longtime activist Leslie Cagan put it, "We have to uncover the many layers of domination and control so that we can see more about our own issues."

The War Resisters League, non-Marxist and secular, was exceptional among organizations on the Left in making gay people in its ranks feel comfortable—even though, much earlier, A.J. Muste had briefly resigned from the Executive Committee in protest against hiring Bayard Rustin, fearing that his arrest for homosexual behavior could threaten the organization's existence. But as early as 1969, almost immediately after the Stonewall riots, WRL's magazine *Win* had put out a gay liberation issue. David, along with Paul Goodman and Allen Ginsberg, had written pieces for it, leading Bayard Rustin, with tongue in cheek, to tell Ralph DiGia: "You guys are going to have to fire David—he will destroy the organization." The league even had two gay men and one bisexual man on its small staff (there were no known lesbians), though neither David nor Igal Roodenko put the gay rights movement high on their political agendas.[7]

David had marched in some of the very first Gay Pride Parades ("because I felt they needed support"). But his own primary concern remained the traditional socialist one: class oppression—though he did insist that "when we talk about liberating the oppressed, gays and lesbians are right up there at the top of that agenda." The Marxist Left, however—following in the homophobic footsteps of Marx and Engels themselves—tended toward rigidly macho and conformist cultural norms. Citing the possible danger of blackmail, the Communist Party had expelled gay members, and the leading Trotskyist and Maoist groups viewed homosexuality as a disease of capitalism.

David claimed to have experienced little antigay bias within the Socialist Party; it had, after all, chosen him to head its ticket in 1980, making him the first openly gay candidate for president in history. Still, individuals who called themselves socialists could be decidedly homophobic. One prominent member of the party said to David, "I've heard some nasty things about you, Comrade McReynolds, but I don't believe them." And Dwight Macdonald once asked him, "You aren't one of *those*, are you?"

As for Marxist attitudes toward feminism, Barbara's friend the critic and playwright Eric Bentley—who would soon come out as gay himself—having recently read a piece by her, wrote: "I am not sure you need Marxism at all . . . I think you latched on to it because others are talking Marxism all the time. . . . You are writing of something [feminism] which is outside what Marx called the class struggle. Women are not what he called a class, just a group not united by economic interest." Bentley also pointed out that he disagreed with Barbara's argument that a working-class housewife and an upper-class woman are both second-class citizens; Bentley felt a Marxist would have correctly pointed out that from the more privileged group "the Mary Wollstonecrafts, George Eliots and Barbara Demings" could more easily emerge—"they had a room of their own."[8]

Though Eric Bentley admired Barbara's writing and claimed to have learned a great deal from it, she had lately been having a difficult time getting published. For three years she'd been fruitlessly sending around her "book of dialogues," *Remembering Who We Are*, both to women's presses and to mainstream ones. Deflated, Barbara and Jane decided to set up their own publishing house, Pagoda Publications (managed by a lesbian-feminist community in St. Augustine called the Pagoda), to publish Jane's novel/autobiography, *Something Not Yet Ended*. Jane's only book, it appeared in 1981. She had shopped it around, and Rita Mae Brown, who felt that the book was too often arch but also "ironic, humorous, searching and above all *authentic*," enthusiastically recommended it to the feminist publishing house Daughters, Inc., but not even Rita Mae could persuade them to accept it.[9]

With the help of a friend, Barbara typed *Remembering Who We Are* on an IBM typewriter she rented, another friend in New York added title headings, and it then went to the Iowa City Women's Press, which decided to print it. Naiad Press, the leading lesbian publishing house, agreed to distribute *Remembering*, and Jane's book as well. But Jane's fared badly. The few reviews were almost entirely negative; even a gay paper, the *Washington Blade*, trashed it, and the book pretty much sank without a trace. A friend of Jane's told her that she thought the book "a new form" and that few people could handle radical departures. That, along with Rita Mae Brown's good opinion, may have salved the wound, but in fact Jane never wrote anything of substance again and returned to drawing and painting.[10]

Although Naiad had distributed both books, the following year saw a prolonged dispute between Barbara and Naiad's publisher, Barbara Grier—a pioneering but controversial figure—over the publication of another of Barbara's manuscripts, "A Book of Travail," an engrossing autobiographical account of Barbara's European travels during the 1950s. After holding on to the manuscript for nearly a year, Grier told Barbara that it was too long for Naiad to handle, but then soon changed her mind, and she and Barbara signed a contract. Before long, Grier again decided that the book needed considerable cutting. Barbara was "more than willing," as she wrote Grier, "to make any cuts that I think would improve the book. But I am utterly unwilling to make cuts simply to shorten it."[11]

As much as Barbara currently needed an outlet for her writing, she remained averse to any tampering with the integrity of her work. Her friend Judith McDaniel offered to read through the manuscript and suggest cuts, help that Barbara was glad to have, but she emphasized to Grier: "I am willing to give it a try. . . . But—again—to be very clear: I won't give any editor a final say."

More disagreement followed. With Naiad in debt and struggling to survive, Grier postponed publication of Barbara's book from the fall of 1983 to the spring of 1984. The two women had a long talk on the phone, Grier getting so angry when Barbara asked if another title had been substituted for "Travail" on the fall list that she had to put down the phone. There was a long pause and then Grier's partner (in the press and in life), Donna McBride, came on. Barbara asked if Donna realized how many times she'd been told her book would soon be out, only to have it again postponed. Donna said that she was tired of the conflict and that the book would be published the following spring. She added that "it was a very good book," though it would have been better still if Barbara had agreed to cut it more. Barbara let that go by but did ask for reassurance that "Travail" *would* be published in spring 1984. Donna replied that if it didn't come out then, Barbara "can take it to another publisher"—not exactly reassuring.

The following day, Barbara wrote to the two women: "I don't like conflict either. But I have written a book into which I put my whole heart. And how can I not care about its fate?" She then detailed the many shifts and postponements since Naiad had gotten the manuscript in May 1981—"surely you understand my distress at each one of them." She understood that Naiad was having financial problems and added, "Your survival means a lot to *me*—though of course still more to you." At the same time, *she* had to worry "about the life of my book." She knew that Grier had been ambivalent about the manuscript from the start and asked, Did she want to "cancel our contract at this point?" If they no longer thought they could manage her book, she thought she might publish it herself. The manuscript was returned forthwith. In 1985 the Women's Press in London published it as *A Humming Under My Feet: A Book of Travail*. The last word of the title substituted for "Travel," an allusion to the book's contents *and* its history.

When Barbara and Jane moved to Sugarloaf Key, they initially feared being isolated. By the early 1980s, enough feminists were dropping by for visits or longer stays to rouse the opposite fear—lack of privacy. As Mary Meigs wrote Barbara in 1981: "I couldn't possibly breathe in that kind of concentrated atmosphere . . . Ye gods!" Unlike Mary, Barbara and Jane mostly welcomed visitors—"Wave after wave here of visiting women. Wonderful women." But they did sometimes need to retreat— Barbara more than Jane—to be alone to do their work. Some of the visiting women they already knew and very much enjoyed having around. The poet Minnie Bruce Pratt and the writer Mab Segrest were among those especially welcome. They came to Sugarloaf, along with the photographer Joan Biren (JEB), primarily to interview Barbara, but their talks together were wide-ranging and satisfying.[12]

Barbara wished she had more time to facilitate the coming together of feminism and nonviolence, which she felt had thus far been insufficiently linked. When second-wave feminism began, she'd taken it for granted that feminists "would see nonviolence as an obviously natural approach for them." Instead, she felt that "many women in the nonviolent movement, once they became feminists, began to disavow it." She'd been shocked at first, but then realized that more "modes" still had to be invented to allow women "sufficiently to speak our anger, our refusal to be the ones to suffer"—without surrendering the traditions of nonviolence. What was also involved in the early, separatist phase of feminism, she believed, was the difficulty of feeling any "bond with the oppressor," but that bond, she felt certain, was essential to a true understanding of nonviolence. Women were initially "too vulnerable to be able to deal with the fact of kinship with, and likeness to, men."

Barbara had also assumed that men who believed in nonviolence would become involved in the feminist movement, and the failure of that to happen in significant numbers had come as a second shock. In her opinion, most men still felt the "need to hold on to power over others, to treat others as owned." What most feminists and most men needed to understand, Barbara felt, was that it was a misconception of nonviolence to think of it as "an appeal to the bully to be nice, to take pity." That, plus the belief among many women in the unspoken, even unconscious, concept of "redemptive suffering: If we let ourselves be hit and hit and keep forgiving, he will mend his ways, be converted." But that belief, in Barbara's view, was a caricature, "a travesty" of any true commitment of nonviolence.

Still, by the early 1980s, Barbara saw more evidence that the two movements had begun to merge. It hadn't happened sooner because the nonviolent philosophy *did* need "to be further invented"; the traditional modes hadn't "sufficiently allowed us to speak our truth (the best definition to me of nonviolence: clinging to the truth)." Barbara had long since rejected Christianity, while holding on, exactly like David, to her awe of Christ's message—Christ the human being, not the "son of God." Her guess was that "by the road of spirituality . . . through rituals that helped us strengthen one another, heal," a return to faith in the power of nonviolent principles had begun. In the 1970s she had felt a "division between two sorts of women—those 'political' and those 'spiritual.'" That split had never seemed real to Barbara, and to her relief, it now seemed to be narrowing.

Barbara occasionally left Sugarloaf—once to attend the National Women's Studies Association meetings; once, for six weeks late in 1982, to fly north to attend to her mother, who at age ninety-one had fallen and broken her hip. But such trips became increasingly rare. Barbara's energy level was lower than ever, which puzzled and frustrated her; she turned sixty-six in 1983—not old enough, she felt, to account for her constant enervation. She made her last extended trip north in the summer of that same year to participate in the Seneca Women's

Encampment at Romulus, New York, fourteen miles from Seneca Falls, where the seminal Women's Rights Convention had been held in 1848. The goal was to stop the planned deployment that fall of NATO first-strike Cruise and Pershing II missiles to Europe from the nearby Seneca Army Depot.[13]

In the days preceding the planned demonstration on August 1, 1983, some two thousand women gathered by the depot and built a "peace camp" patterned on earlier European encampments, the best known being the one at Greenham Common in England. The missile deployments were spreading alarm among liberals and radicals over Reagan's policies. In the fall of 1982, in violation of the War Powers Act, he sent American marines into the midst of a civil war in Lebanon, with the result that two hundred of them were killed when a bomb went off at their barracks. Before his first term was over, Reagan had spent more than a trillion dollars for "defense" while making deep cuts in programs for the poor (even eliminating free school lunches), lowering taxes on the wealthy, and supporting right-wing extremists throughout Central America.

David McReynolds was as concerned about the arms buildup as Barbara and the women who'd gathered at the Seneca Encampment. In a memo to the WRL's National Committee, he listed the many issues—including feminism and gay and lesbian rights—that "at least some of us here" care about deeply. Yet despite the many problems calling out for attention, David urged the League to put disarmament at the head of the list, above mounting joblessness, heightened tension in the Middle East, and racism—"the media has turned off the spotlight, but the reality is worse now than ten years ago; racism is entrenched, not fading." But the other issues, he felt, had groups already organized and active in their behalf. The "nonaligned, unilateralist disarmament issue" alone, he argued, lacked a "serious and sustained constituency." Major antinuke groups, like SANE and the Freeze, did not qualify because they accepted "the preconditions of the arms race, which is that we must have a good and proper defense."[14]

In support of his position, David raised a number of pointed questions: "What greater force for freedom can one imagine for Eastern Europe than to take away from the Soviet leadership the image of a foreign threat which [it uses to] justify its internal repressions? What could we not do in terms of the Chicano, Black and Asian communities in terms of jobs and retraining if we shifted funds from the military into the civilian economy?" David also cited the informed opinions of others on the disarmament issue, especially John Swomley, author of *The Military Establishment.*

Swomley had argued against the notion that the arms buildup really did serve as a deterrent—because it assumed that nations would be necessarily intimidated by superior armed might. Besides, the implicit threat of mass murder (deterrence) was morally wrong, and it had to be given up, along with the argument that the Soviet Union's failure to come up with an "acceptable" (to the United States, that is) plan for mutual disarmament justified American inaction. The truth was that the *will* to disarm had never existed among the U.S. power elite. Just as Mikhail Gorbachev announced a five-month moratorium on Soviet nuclear tests, along with his willingness to continue it indefinitely if the United States joined it, Reagan invited the Soviets to send a team to Nevada to watch our next nuclear test. Perhaps he expected shock, awe, and humble capitulation—though it should be added, in fairness, that *some* recent scholarship has suggested that Reagan himself wasn't the out-and-out hawk that at the time David, Barbara, and many others presumed him to be.

The area surrounding the Seneca Encampment was deeply conservative, and counterprotests and harassment soon became commonplace. Word was spread by the local media that the women were everything from witches to lesbians to—the real threat—vegetarians! The local press gave full play to the negative reaction of the citizenry: summed up, those complaints amounted to "these outsiders are disgracing our community." Among the most strident slogans were "Nuke the Dykes!" (a significant number of lesbians did participate at Seneca) and "Lesbian-Communists go home!" Police from surrounding areas arrived to "maintain order," and in nearby Waterloo fifty-three women—including Barbara briefly—were jailed. Local hostility had little impact on the women's determination, but within the encampment some potentially volatile issues arose, reflecting current debates within the larger feminist movement, especially the questions of feminist separatism, sexual preference, and gender "essentialism." These were allowed, perhaps wisely, to simmer along the edges rather than moved center stage for outright debate and attempted resolution.

After the large and dramatic demonstration on August 1, many women remained at the peace site for several more months, and for a number of years Seneca lingered as a center of feminist activity. As for nuclear weapons, the original reason for the encampment, no progress had been made. Missile deployments continued unchecked, on an uninterrupted schedule.

Barbara, feeling frail and unwell throughout her stay, somehow managed to remain for three weeks. She felt "it was worth it" but returned home exhausted, her energies spent. At least some good news awaited her: New Society Publishers in Philadelphia, a small press run as a collective with the goal of providing "a bridge between feminism and nonviolence," had confirmed that it would publish a collection of her essays, stories, speeches, and poems spanning the years 1959 to 1981, entitled *We Are All Part of One Another*. It appeared in 1984. New Society also held out the hope—but, given its limited resources, could not promise—that it might be able to reissue several of Barbara's previous books that had gone out of print; she put *Prison Notes*, her best-known work, at the top of her list.[15]

Soon after returning to Sugarloaf, Barbara began to have a series of what she called "gripes"—meaning flulike symptoms. She and Jane decided to go to New York City to consult with her brother, a physician. He put her in the hospital for tests and treatment. In March 1984, the diagnosis came down: Barbara had cancer. It had started in the ovaries and spread. Chemotherapy was the treatment of choice, though some of her friends suggested various "natural" healing methods. When Ruth Dreamdigger, who no longer lived at Sugarloaf, arrived in the hospital to visit, she was convinced that Barbara "was not ready to die" and that her "determined and powerful spirit" would heal her body.[16]

On June 20, 1984, Barbara returned to Florida with Jane and entered the hospital at Naples. But after a few treatments there, the attending doctor told her that the cancer had progressed too rapidly to hope for a cure; her life could be prolonged, but there was no hope of maintaining its quality. At that point, Barbara decided to go home to Sugarloaf, "to give to her dying the same passion" with which she'd lived and loved. Ruth got an urgent call on July 25 that the end seemed near. Arriving at Sugarloaf, she found that Barbara had wasted away to skin and bone, though her mind remained clear. Jane was distraught: "I've always seen her snap back," she wrote in her diary. "Now I am scared that she won't . . . this time is it & I am in great distress . . . disabling distress, not helpful tears relieving emotional tension."

At the time, only six other women, including Blue Lunden, were living in the community, but they tended to her lovingly. Barbara had always wanted a breadfruit tree, rare in Florida, but the women succeeded in finding one and buying it. Weak though she was, they managed to get Barbara to the kitchen window to feast her eyes on the five-foot stick with flurries of leaves in the middle and top. She also found the strength to select parting gifts for each of the women from her belongings and to have lengthy telephone calls with friends and family unable to come to Florida.

She asked the Sugarloaf women one night if they'd sing some of her favorite songs to her, and especially one she'd heard on a freedom march: "Leaning on the Everlasting Arms." As they followed up with other songs, Barbara lifted her long body off the couch and "with enormous dignity and grace" danced to the gentle rhythms. Two days later, her pain rose to excruciating levels, and she started taking a higher level of morphine. That made her sleep a great deal; when awake she remained aware of her surroundings, though unable to leave her bed. The women held a silent meditation, "trying to send her our energy, if she wanted to move out of this life."

Barbara dictated a final note "To so many of you":

> I have loved my life so very much and I have loved you so very much and felt so blessed at the love you have given me. I love the work so many of us have been trying to do together . . . but I just feel no more strength in me now and I want to die. . . . I want you to know, too, that I die happily.

Soon after, Barbara went into a coma, and two days later, at age sixty-seven, she died. She'd treated death in the same determined and courageous way she'd lived her life.

A bereft Jane, trying to sum up Barbara's unique qualities, wrote in her journal about her "innate shyness" and "self-deprecation," her "physical/spiritual beauty," her "passionate, attentive quality. She paid attention. She listened. She answered."

11

At Eighty

In November 2009, David's eightieth birthday was celebrated at a sit-down dinner in a large basement hall in lower Manhattan. Several hundred people filled the hall to capacity, and speaker after speaker gave ardent testimony to the impact David's lifelong commitment to left-wing causes had had on their own political lives. Some emphasized his organizational work, others his talent as a writer and speaker. Still others spoke more generally about his personal integrity, his honesty and directness, his willingness to admit to character flaws or errors in judgment.

The older radicals who took to the podium tended to focus on the years of the Vietnam War, the high point of their own political involvement; the younger ones concentrated on David's more recent contributions. As was fitting on such an occasion, it was left to the habitually self-critical David, when he responded to all the praise, to speak of his own periodic stubbornness, his mistakes, and his occasional relish of a good fight—of his disagreements over the years with, say, Barbara Deming about the relative importance of feminism or the gay movement when compared to the suffering that emanated from class or racial oppression.

Much of the tribute paid to David that evening was well deserved, if predictable at a milestone event. But there were surprises, especially in the amount of attention paid, mostly by the younger radicals, to David's later years. Several of them spoke of the inspirational quality of his ongoing activity, even as he aged, on behalf of assorted left-wing causes. He had continued to raise the alarm—at the widening gap in this country between rich and poor, at entrenched institutional racism, and at the ongoing insistence by our country of its right and duty (not to mention its imperialist profit) to interfere in the internal affairs of other countries.

In the mid to late 1980s, David had had several inklings that with Mikhail Gorbachev's ascendancy—he was elected general secretary by the Politburo in 1985—the Soviet Union was about to dramatically change course. As chair of the War Resisters International (WRI) during that period, David traveled extensively and was present at various meetings when hints were dropped that major policy shifts were imminent. People from *Pravda* would sometimes come by the WRI office and drop offhand remarks that in exchange for ending the militarization of NATO and the further deployment of missiles toward the east, the Soviet bloc might undergo some significant internal changes. The summit meeting between Gorbachev and Reagan in Iceland late in 1986 was generally regarded as a failure, but it did produce *in principle* an agreement to remove intermediate-range nuclear missiles from Europe.[1]

David sent a memo to a dozen of his key contacts internationally about his growing conviction that a historic shift was in the winds, and as a courtesy he sent a copy of the memo to the Soviet World Peace Council's party-line publication. To his astonishment, they published the memo—the first time they'd ever allowed a piece critical of Leninist theory to appear. Coupled with unexpected visits in New York from East Germans, one of them from the consulate in the capital, who told him directly that large-scale policy shifts of considerable magnitude would soon take place in the Soviet bloc, David tried to get both the WRL and the WRI to relate in a more open way toward the World Peace Council, even though it was widely considered a front for Moscow.

But David's excited overtures were considered naive and pro-communist, despite the fact that he'd been staunchly anti-Soviet throughout his political life, and they would be a major factor in his failure to win reelection as chair of WRI, a failure that proved "very,

very painful" to him. Yet his predictions were soon proven accurate. In 1988 the Soviet Union withdrew from its bogged-down invasion of Afghanistan, and that same year Gorbachev announced that the Warsaw Pact nations previously under Soviet control would henceforth be allowed to determine their own internal affairs—freedom that in 1989 led to counter-revolutions throughout Eastern Europe.

David gave credit for the subsequent ending of the Cold War not to Western policies but to the risks and courage of Mikhail Gorbachev in introducing *perestroika* and *glasnost*. Indeed, president-elect George H. W. Bush's first major foreign policy initiative after Gorbachev's announced reforms was to invade Panama (the Pentagon named it Operation Just Sword); the pretense for the invasion was Manuel Noriega's drug dealing—though Noriega had long been an employee of the U.S. government. By 1995, the U.S. had a military budget several times larger than the combined military spending of all the nations the Pentagon currently listed as enemies. As David put it, "conservatives ask 'how shall we defend our freedom without the military' when the reality is they are wondering how capitalism can defend its holdings."

The end of the Cold War did not mean to David the demise of socialism. It meant instead a new opportunity to distinguish between Soviet totalitarianism and the inheritance of Marx and Debs, a difference few Americans had ever been able to grasp. David had never felt that capitalism was without merit: "Capitalism is a system of enormous energy," he once wrote. "It has a remarkable ability to mobilize productive forces and it is flexible and inventive." But at the same time, capitalism had always contained what Marx had called "internal contradictions"; as more and more capital became necessary to start a major enterprise like a steel mill or an airline, the "free market" became ever less free, the means of production became still more centralized, and property became increasingly concentrated in fewer hands.

Too many socialists, David felt, continued to believe that state ownership of the means of production was essential, but in his view the goal was *social* ownership, with workers and consumers running, or helping to run, local factories. In this and other respects, David had always seemed grounded somewhere in the middle between socialism and philosophical anarchism; perhaps what was once called anarcho-syndicalism may have been his true home. Socialism, David believed, should be concerned with finding democratic ways of organizing the production and distribution of goods. That meant that the market would continue to play *some* role—not the current one of providing what people have money for, but what they want or need, like low-cost housing. Capitalism had proved that it could not, on a sustained basis, provide a large portion of the citizenry with decent housing, jobs, education, or medical care.

David freely acknowledged that currently socialism wasn't even a distant possibility in the minds of most Americans. And even western Europe has backtracked in the twenty-first century from its earlier commitments. The Labour Party in England turned away from socialism even before Tony Blair became prime minister; and on the continent the number of publicly owned industries in France and Germany has significantly shrunk while many public services have been privatized. But there would be no chance of a better life for most, David still feels, "if we abandon the vision and surrender to a planet controlled by competing corporate structures." To sustain any hope that someday it might prove possible to substitute a system that diffused economic power for the current one that concentrated wealth into fewer and fewer hands—a "saving remnant" keeps that dream alive.

During the 1990s, the WRL was in crisis, organizationally and financially, much of the time. Both Ralph DiGia and Karl Bissinger proved willing to work without salary on a volunteer basis. David couldn't afford to make a similar offer but did propose that he work full-time at half pay—but on projects *he* would chose, eliminating chores like answering the mail or phone. His offer was accepted, but it proved a tight squeeze for him financially. On his mother's death in 1986, her estate was divided among her three children, with David's share coming to approximately $70,000; only about $50,000 still remained in 2010. When he reached the standard retirement age of sixty-five in the mid-1990s, David also received (along with Ralph DiGia and Karl Bissinger) a lump-sum pension from WRL of $50,000—entirely spent by 2010. Social Security provided him with about $9,000 a year. Putting all that together, David's income came to roughly $15,000 a year. Hardly a princely sum, though for David, who'd always lived fairly close to the bone, manageable—barely. What helped was that he lived in low-income housing and had Medicare. Even so, he had to continue to draw down over the years on his limited savings, could never take vacations or buy new clothes, and could rarely eat in a restaurant.[2]

By the 1990s, David had long since become something of a public symbol for the League, thanks to his frequent travels (which WRL or the host group paid for), his gifts as a speaker, and his lively and lucid prose. He wasn't at all sure that was a good thing, and he urged the League to start grooming new public leadership. He thought that his own role should shift to becoming a more generally radical spokesperson, because he almost uniquely incorporated both socialist and pacifist views. He unequivocally wanted to remain identified with WRL and to continue to travel for the organization, attend meetings, and speak on its behalf—especially about the issue of unilateral disarmament. He came into the office two to three days a week, but when working on an article, he needed to be alone, doing the intermittent time wasting—washing the dishes, rearranging his books—that is a lamentably intrinsic part of writing.

David was well aware that a few people in the office found him quick-tempered and abrasive, making it difficult for him to operate in consensus mode. Usually when there was a quarrel, he'd blame his own "character issues"—the fact that he could be "very stubborn," wasn't "at ease with people," and "didn't work well in a collective environment." But with one staff member, he had an especially "long, unhappy relationship" dating back to the pivotal role she'd played in David's losing bid for reelection as chair of the War Resisters International, a position he keenly wanted to retain even though he'd had a mixed reaction to his own performance. The woman in question would ultimately resign from the staff—*not* at David's instigation—blaming the WRL's "patriarchal structure" for forcing her out.

Another ongoing issue within WRL was the recognition that it still remained essentially a white, middle-class organization. There had been occasional staff members of color, but none had stayed very long. As David put it in a memo, "If WRL wants to be an 'affirmative action employer' it must recognize that very few African Americans (and not many Latinos or Asians) can enter a predominately white organization and leave their own issues behind." He felt that whites in the League, including him—perhaps somewhat less than whites elsewhere—were insufficiently aware that "people bring their cultures with them" and that the differences between communities can be profound. If WRL wanted more people of color involved in the organization, David suggested, then "our *program* has to make sense to them." On the other hand, David wanted to make clear, amid all the breast-beating, that the WRL had made its first black hire *long* before other left-wing groups and had employed Bayard Rustin in the early 1950s, when homosexuality was widely considered a symptom of pathology.

On another significant issue, David took a still more controversial position. When the Communist Party USA had a major split in its ranks in December 1992, it still had between three thousand and five thousand members. David, a longtime antagonist of Soviet-style Communism, urged some communication and possible cooperation with dissident members of the CP. He thought limited coalition work, with WRL retaining its commitment to nonviolence and democratic social change, was possible, especially around issues relating to economic justice—issues, David felt, that were "far more central than most people in WRL understand."[3]

He reminded his pacifist and socialist friends that the Communist Party in this country had played "a generous and courageous role in building the CIO," in fighting racism in the South as early as the 1930s, and in playing a principled role during the anti–Vietnam War years. Past battles with the CP, he felt, should not obscure the fact that many of its members had humane instincts and had suffered for them—relentless persecution from the red-baiters, trouble in securing jobs, and imprisonment. To this day, David remains one of the few among non-Communist leftists—or among historians—willing to acknowledge the CPUSA's contributions.

David also took issue with those on the Left who cynically dismissed as utopian the effort to revive the concept of complete and comprehensive disarmament. He reminded them that immediately following World War II, antiwar sentiment had been widespread: "it was *official government policy at virtually every level and by all governments*" that disarmament was a necessary and achievable goal. He had come to agree that putting the emphasis on a single category of weapons—nuclear ones—*was* utopian, for getting rid of one category of weapons of mass destruction would simply lead to its replacement with another: biological, chemical, conventional, air bombardment, or whatever. David summed up his position as "either war goes or we go."

He thought it a mistake for the peace movement to focus on weapons systems rather then on "the institutions which use them—militarism and war." He claimed never to have "understood why conservatives are so happy to pour money into military approaches to problems—including police and prisons—and so reluctant to put money into humane approaches." Doubtless some on the Left would respond that a certain kind of person becomes a conservative—one lacking in empathy for the plight of others, one who assumes that such a plight represents a moral failure of the individual afflicted: they are the ones—not "the system"—responsible for their condition.

David felt he knew what "radicals should learn by heart and liberals never seem to learn at all"—that "the existing State is *not our agency, but the instrument of the dominant economic class.*" Yet what seems unclear, and too all-inclusive in his position, is whether all states should be equated. Is there nothing of validity in the view that the social welfare systems inaugurated in, say, the Scandinavian countries, had changed the State, at least in part, into an instrument and servant of the people rather than the agent of a small segment of it?

Besides, wasn't it one of the classic Marxist-socialist goals to capture the State for the working class, and then for the State ultimately to "wither away"? Or had David come to believe, as Emma Goldman and all true anarchists did, that the last stage of Marxism (the "withering away" of the State and all concentrated power) should be the *first* priority, with local entities, those having minimal power, becoming the instruments of communal decision making? If he did, he never said so. David had participated in the electoral process, thereby implying that through peaceful means the State could be made to redefine its mission beyond that of being the instrument of the dominant economic class. Had he now, late in life, changed his mind? It wouldn't appear so, since he again ran for office in 2000 and 2004.

Of course such issues had been argued without resolution for at least several centuries, so it was perhaps forgivable that David hadn't unraveled competing doctrines about the role of the State, electoral politics, and local decentralization. When it came down to specific events or policies, rather than theory, David was more solidly grounded. In the mid-1990s, for example, he felt sure that no good could come from U.S. intervention in Bosnia. He blamed NATO—which he felt should have been dissolved with the collapse of the Soviet Union in

1991—for laying waste to both Serbia and Kosovo. And he blamed the media for helping to build a view of the Serbs as "totally evil: the man who took over Croatia—Tudjman—is every bit as dangerous a nationalist as [the Serbian leader] Milosevic."[4]

He doubted if the United States, "a nation which has yet to deal fully with its own record of ethnic cleansing of Native Americans," could so easily sort out right and wrong from the distance of thousands of miles. But David admitted that beyond WRL's abstract slogan "End the bombing; end the ethnic cleansing," he had no concrete alternate solutions to offer. As he wrote to several correspondents, "in this life there are not only no simple answers, I am not sure there is always only one correct solution. . . . I truly believe there are many times *when nothing can be done* . . . I do not think there is always an answer 'in the now' for issues that demanded attention much earlier. . . . There is always hope, but not—in my view—in military action."

Yet military action continued to be the policy of choice as administration followed administration. The end of the Cold War was supposed to have brought a much-heralded "peace dividend" for domestic programs, but this never materialized. Instead the money went to a variety of new war projects. In 1991 Operation Desert Storm forced Iraq out of Kuwait, though the ballyhooed "smart bombs" managed to miss their targets 40 percent of the time, often hitting marketplaces and civilians, including children. Most such incidents went unreported due to the Pentagon's refusal of access to reporters and to the knee-jerk "patriotism" of most TV commentators. David was part of a peace delegation that went to Baghdad that year. He'd all along deplored Saddam's rule as "a terrifying regime," but thought the real reason for our intervention in the Kuwait conflict was "to control oil supplies" in the region. He approved of sanctions against Iraq for the invasion, but he wondered why they were being continued *after* Iraqi troops had retreated to their own country. If anyone remained in doubt about our government's motives and morality, he underscored the point (since most Americans had already forgotten the fact, if they ever knew it) that the U.S. had helped provide poison gas to Iraq in its earlier struggle against Iran.

Bill Clinton's election to the presidency in 1992 saw no reduction in military expenses—some $250 billion a year, though with the collapse of the Soviet Union, the U.S. government was running out of demons to blame for its continuing arms buildup, and for supplying a third of the weapons sold elsewhere. On it went: In Somalia in 1993 (where, David felt, the basic problems of starvation and disease wouldn't be solved by sending in troops), the U.S. intervened in an internal conflict that was essentially between warlords—yet ignored the genocide in Rwanda and cut off economic aid to thirty-five mostly poor countries.

Protest against the mounting dominance of militarism and corporatism may have been largely absent from media reporting, but in the country at large it continued, mostly at a local level. For David's part, he worked on several fronts simultaneously. Back in the mid-1980s he'd had a hand in helping to form a political-cultural task force based on the West German Green Party, and by the mid-1990s he felt that the Greens represented the greatest opportunity to recharge the New York activist scene. In 2004 he'd run on their ticket for the U.S. Senate, campaigned all over the state—and got a respectable 37,000 votes.[5]

As a member of the Socialist Party USA, he also spent considerable time urging the various democratic socialist groups to coordinate and consult more—though not necessarily to merge, as separate organizations were serving quite different constituencies. For example, the religious pacifist group the Fellowship of Reconciliation opened every meeting with prayer—which would have been intolerable for secular socialists. Besides, even if all the alternative groups did unite, at most they'd have only the beginning of any serious challenge to the status quo.

David also belonged to the Committees of Correspondence (the name taken from a method of united action in the Revolutionary War period against British oppression). The Committees had maybe fifteen hundred members and seemed to be losing rather than gaining strength. Of those groups committed to democratic socialism, the largest by far was the Democratic Socialists of America with, on paper, about twelve thousand members. It had some union support and, in David's view, had "some very good members" but "almost no real leadership." In general, David wished all elements on the Left would stop talking about "revolutionary formations in a totally non-revolutionary time," especially because he had no faith that the current "underclass" would be politically available, let alone revolutionary.

His health remaining sound, David kept active throughout his late sixties and seventies. A fairly typical month included: a piece for French TV, a radio spot for NPR, a TV appearance on New York's Channel 9, a meeting at the Rustin Institute, a talk at the Village Independent Democrats, a debate at the Marxist School on the Middle East, a piece for the *Progressive*, a student conference in D.C., a teach-in at NYU, a trip to California, an article on the Middle East for *Fellowship*. And on, and on. He made two more forays into electoral politics. In 2000 he was drafted as the Socialist Party USA's presidential candidate. He ran as an openly gay man (and among many appearances was on Bill Maher's *Politically Incorrect* TV show). Ralph Nader was also running for president that year, on the Green Party ticket. But to David "they weren't really the labor party that many of us would have liked to have seen"; there was a case to be made for letting people see what a democratic socialist looked like and stood for.

David campaigned widely, mostly by car, and in general enjoyed himself. He managed to get on the ballot in seven states—an improvement by two over the party's showing in the 1996 election. He got about ten thousand *recorded* votes, but the tally was almost certainly higher; people reported that they'd voted for him but no such vote appeared in their precinct count. Typically, minor parties don't have their votes counted. Nor were the media helpful. At an earlier point, the *New York Times* would print one-column interviews with many of the candidates from small parties, but it discontinued the practice in 2004. Neither PBS on television nor NPR on radio picked up the slack. Public access to dissident views no longer seemed important.

David also became a bit more active in the gay world than earlier, but unlike Barbara Deming his interest never developed into anything like a full-scale political commitment. He attended a Pride at Work conference of gays and lesbians who were members of the AFL-CIO—and thought it "very good." He and the libertarian WRL favored the right of gay men and lesbians "to engage in all aspects of our public life." That included the two items rapidly rising to the top of the gay agenda: legal marriage and the right to serve openly in the military—though David was no fan of traditional marriage and dearly wished that *no one* would serve in the military. He even went to an occasional gay social gathering but felt as out of place as ever. For his first such event in a number of years, he dressed in what he assumed were "casual" clothes—black sneakers, pink shirt, khaki pants, navy blazer. But on arrival, it became immediately clear that styles had changed. Since the 1970s, the new standard uniform tended to be work boots, very clean Levi's, and cotton plaid shirts. As David put it, "The fashion was no fashion."[6]

He also became something of a friend to Quentin Crisp, the gay (or perhaps transgendered) English writer and performer, who'd become famous with his memoir *The Naked Civil Servant*. Crisp was not exactly popular among gay activists, thanks to having called homosexuality "a terrible disease" and having referred to AIDS as "a fad." David had often passed Crisp on the street, as they lived only a block apart, and finally decided to drop him a note. "It may well be," David charmingly wrote, "that you are besieged with friends, relentlessly forced to move from dinner party to cocktail party to art openings, etc." But perhaps, David went on, "you sometimes find yourself at home, with no one on the phone because everyone thinks someone else is talking to you." He then invited Crisp to dinner: "I'm a decent cook and can give you vegetables or meat, as your conscience or doctor dictates." Crisp came and apparently enjoyed himself. Thereafter the two would have a meal together or go to a movie, and at least at one point David gave Crisp some medical advice, the nature of which is implied in Crisp's reply: "At the moment, I'm in the non-washing phase but it is true that my skin is now so dry that it even flakes off the soles of my feet. If I had a bathroom of my own, I might embark upon a washing phase."[7]

David had no interest at all in retiring. In the late 1990s, he even went back to full-time work (and a full load of staff responsibilities) at WRL—not because he wanted to resume answering phones, fielding inquiries, or fund-raising, but because both he and the organization were feeling financially pinched. To make up the difference between the half-pay he'd been getting and his actual living expenses, David had had to draw on the money his mother had left him. He blamed himself for not pursuing speaking dates more forcefully. Actually, he still had a fairly hectic schedule, but the radical groups that tended to invite him could afford a lecture fee of only $100 to $300. He also blamed his own "abominable" work habits. He was a slow writer, and he'd typically take on too many assignments; when a "down" period hit, which happened every few months, the work would pile up.[8]

David wasn't happy being back at WRL full-time. He "desperately" wanted to "use my remaining years doing something more creative than taking the minutes at the National Committee meetings." He felt he'd spent too much of his life "as a bureaucrat"—whereas in fact he'd been the intellectual backbone (or, as Karl Bissinger put it, "the voice") of WRL for most of that time. To reduce his commitments to some extent, David in 1997 "eased out" of Socialist Party USA work. Part of that decision resulted from his disenchantment with some of the SPUSA's new young staff. He thought one of them "dangerously poisonous" and another—who'd announced that Norman Thomas had been "not much more than a front for the CIA"—as "stunningly sectarian." Several others seemed to him unaware or unconcerned with the fact that the organization remained almost entirely white. Still, David retained his membership and remained willing to continue to write and speak for the cause of socialism.

Some of the younger people in WRL found David too contentious. But it wasn't until 2003 that he finally decided to leave the organization to which he'd given some forty-five years of service. He was more angry than sad about the decision, writing an accusatory final memo: "An organization committed to nonviolence has backed away from that. An organization committed to disarmament has wasted much of the last two years diddling with weird 're-organizational' plans . . . while people died in Afghanistan and Iraq (and God knows, in our own ghettos and prisons)." The very next day, he apologized for his vehemence, calling his memo "ill-tempered" and declaring himself to have been "absolutely off base." Everyone apologized to everyone. David left WRL with cordiality reigning, and as of this writing he continues to drop by the office with some frequency.

Even before his departure, David had been giving the bulk of his time to writing a long, incisive series of online political articles—the so-called *Infinite Series*, mostly about the history of various "socialisms," from Marx to Mao (and also writing an occasional column on a wider range of topics, called *Edge Left*). Only occasionally in his online pieces will David refer to more personal matters ("I do not believe in God, but I consider myself a religious atheist"—much the same self-definition Barbara Deming might have used, though she may have preferred "*pantheist*").[9]

High on David's list of current concerns is the Middle East. Though sharply critical of Israel, he doesn't support "the hard-line Islamic positions of Hezbollah" and is critical, too, of Hamas's refusal to recognize Israel. At the same time, he denounces what he characterizes as "the long Israeli policy of 'targeted assassinations' which too often had high civilian casualties." By David's calculations, the death rate of those killed by terrorist attacks is "very much higher for the Palestinians," which in his view "the U.S. media seems never to get clear." Barbara had felt exactly the same way: she "deeply" believed that "Israel must exist," yet also felt that "Palestinian Arabs must be allowed to establish a homeland, too."

David also has no doubts about Israel's right to survive as a nation. Way back in 1948, as an undergraduate at UCLA, he'd co-chaired the Christians and Jews for Israel committee and, along with other young socialists, danced the hora, sang Zionist songs, knew people who'd spent time on a kibbutz, and believed that Israel "was essentially a democratic socialist experiment." But times, and Israeli policies, have changed. David felt that Israel had been terribly mistaken, while Yasser Arafat was still alive, in refusing any longer to treat him as a crucial figure in the peace process. He had been, after all, the elected leader of his people, and though he'd chosen to follow a violent path (as had the Israeli leader Ariel Sharon), David seemed to recall that Gandhi had pointed out that resistance is preferable to submission, even if the resistance is violent. He feels, too, that for too long Israel has flouted international law and countless UN resolutions as a result of its "unscrupulous art of war."

David believes that "there has been justice—and errors—on both sides" of the Israeli-Palestinian conflict, just as he believes there are "good people in Israel, as there are in the Arab world." Yet he holds to the position that, given Israel's "consistently brutish and cruel policies," no supporter of Israel has the right "to condemn suicide attacks against Israeli forces in the Occupied Territory unless they have been even more forceful in condemning the Israeli Occupation." He asserts this conviction even though politically he feels "much closer to the freedoms of Israel for women, for gays and lesbians and for open political dialogue," as well as for "its extremely lively democracy" (and "rather strong peace movement")—and even though he can offer no alternative strategies for coping with the Arab world's ongoing anti-Semitism and its refusal to recognize Israel's right to exist.

The two other main topics that David focuses on in his decade-long series of articles are the war in Iraq and the future of the Socialist Party USA. He remains furious down to the present day at the "foolish and arrogant" attitude of the U.S. government toward Iraq in first launching the war and then in insisting that we have to "stay the course." Putting aside for the moment the ghastly carnage involved, the conflict has helped to give new life to Islamic fundamentalism; as brutal as Saddam's regime had been, it did have *some* few positive features: he didn't stow away *all* the profits from oil money in Swiss banks to be used for personal indulgence, but put at least some portion of it toward building hospitals, roads, and universities; and he created a far freer atmosphere for women than exists, for example, in Saudi Arabia, the United States' closest ally in the Arab world.

That, of course, is the *most* one can claim for Saddam's regime. Unprovoked, he'd invaded Kuwait and Iran—the latter war backed by the United States, which itself has a long history of violent intervention in the internal affairs of other countries. Taking the long view, David suggests that when the president announced a "crisis" in Iraq, every citizen should have asked "Why should we believe him?" Hadn't the government recently told us that there was no such thing as "Gulf War syndrome"? Hadn't it led us, with repeated lies, into the ten-year bloodbath in Vietnam? Why believe that Iraq was developing weapons of mass destruction, just because the government said so?

Governments—and not just the U.S. government—always have "rational" explanations to offer for justifying irrational policies. But why, David asks, again sounding like a philosophical anarchist, should "we ever believe any government knows what it is doing, or is necessarily doing" what it tells us it is doing? There had never been sound reasons for going into Vietnam—any more than the Soviets had had for invading Afghanistan. As for the policy of "staying the course," when we've taken a wrong turn on the highway should we proceed all the way to the Arctic when our intention had been to visit Grandma in North Carolina? And wasn't withdrawal a better way of "supporting our troops" than Bush and Cheney's willingness to send them home in boxes? To those who say that "we are weakening American influence," why not respond, "Yes—we are helping to limit pointless wars of aggression." When men like Donald Rumsfeld continued to do business with Saddam after he'd used poison gas on the Kurds, aren't we entitled to question the integrity and morality of such men—and to deny that they have anything to teach the world?

When David ran for president on the Socialist Party USA ticket in 2000, he described himself as "a badly read Marxist and a Gandhian pacifist who never found the perfect formula to blend Marx and Gandhi." Like many others on the Left, he'd made do throughout his life with forming organizational ties that *together* represented, or came close to representing, the sum of his political views. The War Resisters League served as an outlet for his commitment to nonviolence (but not for his socialism) and the Socialist Party—at least at some points in its history—became the vehicle for his social justice work (but not for his pacifism).

After his various disagreements with Barbara Deming—during which David now believes he'd been mostly in the wrong—he's consistently voiced support for both feminism and the gay movement and occasionally made a gestural contribution to each. But while never denying the validity of both causes, David remains unconvinced that either ranks in importance with oppressions based on class and race. Those are the inequities that continued most intensely to call out his committed concern. Given that most privileged people—and David, though poor, is also white and male—ignore the misery of others, and given that people who do become active about social justice issues find that some resonate for them more than others, David can surely be excused for not embracing *all* movements for social change with equal fervor. Nobody can, or does.

It had been no different for Barbara Deming. She, too, made choices and over time shifted her political priorities. Initially focused on matters relating to racism, nonviolence, and disarmament, she began in the 1970s to put most of her decreasing energies toward ameliorating the many discriminations facing women and lesbians—without losing interest in the earlier issues that had absorbed her. The Sugarloaf Women's Village (as it is now known) to this day continues to stress the importance of nonviolence and to adhere to Barbara's "unshakable faith in every human being."[10]

Sugarloaf Village begins its Statement of Purposes by declaring that "Barbara Deming's life and work is the spirit and guide" to a commitment to "resist injustice and abuse of power, racial and sexual inequalities and the hegemony of the nuclear and military industrial complex." And the War Resisters League, to which Barbara and, to a greater extent, David both devoted themselves, continues to connect violence with a masculine ideal that the military, above all, perpetuates with its emphasis on force, aggression, dominance, and power.

Barbara once wrote that "the words 'clinging to the truth' are not quite adequate. They would seem to imply that we know the whole truth. So we have to try to speak the truth as we think we see it at each moment. And we have to keep listening to ourselves, not shutting out any voice that rises up in us, even if it seems to be contradicted by some other voice in us. . . ."

David McReynolds would agree.

Acknowledgments

My first acknowledgment goes to The New Press, which has again done a wonderful job with all aspects of producing this book. Special thanks go to Jyothi Natarajan for her always graceful response to my many repetitive, picky questions, and to Ellen Adler, publisher of The New Press and also my editor; her acute comments on the manuscript greatly helped to tighten it. I'm also grateful to Gary Stimeling who did a remarkably smart copy edit of the manuscript, and to Maury Botton who carefully managed all aspects of production.

Three other people agreed to read this book in manuscript. My partner Eli Zal gave me his usual incisive, perceptive reading. My friend and fellow historian Marcia Gallo—to whom this book is dedicated—caught some significant omissions and helped me to further contextualize the feminist and LGBT movements. One of the two subjects of this book, David McReynolds, saved me from several factual errors and, though we had a few interpretative disagreements, magnanimously refrained from urging me to change my version into his.

I'd also like to thank the remarkably cooperative and efficient staff members of the various archival libraries in which I've worked. A few of them went beyond the call of duty: Jason Baumann of the New York Public Library dug out relevant material that I didn't know existed. Peter Filardo at the Tamiment Library at NYU kept promptly responding to my several inquiries. Monique Ostiguy at the Canadian Archives in Montreal helped me resolve several complicated issues. Kristen J. Nyitray of Special Collections at SUNY Stony Brook located some semiburied material for me.

In regard to photographs, I owe a special debt to Bonnie Netherton of Sugarloaf Village, Anthony Giannini, Judith McDaniel, Diana Carey at the Schlesinger Library, Linda Thurston at the War Resisters League, Maxine Wolfe at the Lesbian Herstory Archives (who also located the Jane Gapen material for me), and David McReynolds for letting me invade his private hoard. I'm grateful above all to David's brother, Martin McReynolds, who spent a great deal of time looking through his large collection of family photos and appending captions to them. Thanks, too, to David Kennedy and especially to Cassandra ("Ryan") Colletti, who helped in researching material, respectively, at Boston University and the Swarthmore Peace Center. Finally, I'm grateful to Quinn Dilkes (Jane Gapen's executor) for important information and to John Stoltenberg for allowing me access to the closed Andrea Dworkin Papers at the Schlesinger Library.

Abbreviations

The abbreviations below are solely for the primary sources on which this book is largely based. (For the secondary sources consulted, see the endnotes themselves.) Two manuscript collections have been by far the most important: The Barbara Deming Papers at the Schlesinger Library at Harvard and the David McReynolds Papers at the Swarthmore College Peace Center. At the time I read the McReynolds Papers, a large number were also at the War Resisters League office in New York, and a small number were in McReynolds's apartment; both collections were due to be sent to Swarthmore. Also of value were my five taped interviews with McReynolds, some two dozen tapes of his personal appearances that he loaned me, and the letters and e-mails he sent me.

ADSL: Andrea Dworkin Papers, Schlesinger Library, Harvard
AGSB: Allen Ginsberg Papers, State University of New York, Stony Brook
BDBU: Barbara Deming Collection, Boston University
BDSL: Barbara Deming Papers, Schlesinger Library, Harvard
BLPLHA: Doris ("Blue") Lunden Papers, Lesbian Herstory Archives, Brooklyn
BLSPC: Bradford Lyttle Papers, Swarthmore Peace Center

DDTL: David Dellinger Papers, Tamiment Library, New York University

DMSC: David McReynolds Papers, Swarthmore Peace Center

JGLHA: Jane Gapen Diaries and Papers, Lesbian Herstory Archives, Brooklyn

JNKNYPL: Jonathan Ned Katz Papers, New York Public Library

KJNYPL: Karla Jay Papers, New York Public Library

MBAC: Marie-Claire Blais Papers, Bibliothèque et Archives, Montreal, Canada

MMBM: Mary Meigs Papers, Bryn Mawr College

MSTL: Max Shachtman Papers, Tamiment Library, New York University (housed with the Gil Green Papers and a portion of the David Dellinger Papers)

NTNYPL: Norman Thomas Papers, New York Public Library

SCLHA: Sugarloaf Community newsletters and correspondence (including Mary Meigs letters)

TMSC: Tracy Mygatt and Frances Witherspoon Papers, Swarthmore Peace Center

Notes

Preface

1. Given how numerous the quotes are in the following six pages and the fact that they're taken from some dozen separate letters, I think it's simplest to provide an overall citation. I found most of the Deming/McReynolds correspondence in the Barbara Deming Papers at the Schlesinger Library (BDSL) and the remainder in the David McReynolds Papers. The latter, when I read them, were divided between a small number in David's apartment, a fairly large collection at the office of the War Resisters League (WRL), and a still larger one at the Swarthmore College Peace Center (SPC). All are scheduled for eventual deposit at the Peace Center and may already be centralized; thus the citation for all three sites will henceforth be DMSC.

2. Though I've read widely in feminist and gay sources over the years, I see no point in attempting to cite the entire bibliography. But I do want to single out two books by Alice Echols—*Daring to Be Bad* (Univ. of Minn. Press, 1989) and *Shaky Ground* (Columbia Univ. Press, 2002)—as having been of particular value for me.

Chapter 1: Barbara's Youth

1. For this and the following seven paragraphs: BD to father, "late summer," 1940; BD's private "notes," a diary of sorts (Sept. 30–Oct. 1, n.y.); two notes, June 11 and 16, 1977; "Feminary," thoughts during an interview with Minnie Bruce Pratt and Mab Segrest, *Feminary*, Spring 1981; Barbara to Mary Meigs, Apr. 26, 1969; Mary Meigs to Barbara, Oct. 13, 1973; and Barbara to Michelle [Cliff], May 21, 1982—all in BDSL. Also: BD, *A Humming Under My Feet: A Book of Travail* (Women's Press, 1985; henceforth BD, *Humming*), 228–29. Though the Deming Papers become extensive and rich once Barbara became politically active, they're much less full about her earlier life and

contain only a scattering of comments on her parents. Among Barbara's ancestors, incidentally, was the nineteenth-century reformer Elihu Burritt, who'd been active in the temperance and antislavery movements. Harold Deming's mother had been a friend of the writer Mabel Loomis Todd.

2. For this and the following three paragraphs: BD, "notes," Dec. 13, 1981, and BD, "notes for possible film interview," May 9, 1979, both in BDSL; and Judith McDaniel's introduction to BD, *I Change, I Change: Poems by Barbara Deming*, edited by McDaniel (New Victoria, 1996; henceforth McDaniel, *Change*). The poems quoted are in *Change*, 7, 34.

3. For this and the following paragraph: McDaniel, *Change*, 9, 44.

4. For this and the following three paragraphs: Jane Gapen to Barbara, Jan. 9, 1967; Mary Meigs to Barbara, April 5, 1973; and Barbara to Katharine Taylor, n.d. (1940?)—all in BDSL. BD to Philip Rahv, Aug. 29, 1945; BD to Richard Hart, Sept. 22, 1945; and BD to U. T. Miller, Mar. 6, 1947—all in BDBU.

5. The extensive correspondence between Barbara and Vida is in BDSL and mostly runs through the early 1950s. Unfortunately, many of their letters are undated, making it impossible to give specific citations for every quote—though I've done so whenever a letter does have a date. Barbara's later love Mary Meigs got to know Vida but never—and this wasn't due to jealousy—liked her very much. After spending two days with Vida at one point, Mary described her as "not happy: her strained, exhausted face, her will to power (concealed), her obsession with her children." Mary was unusually shrewd about people, and although she thought Vida "kind, generous," she disliked in her "an immense need to dominate, the ever-lasting TEACHER. . . . No matter what the subject, Vida can instruct and advise & produce examples from her own experience. . . . There is something in V. that *hates* what we've all accomplished, that puts it down. . . . A fury—at herself." Meigs to "dearest friends," Oct. 30 (1972?).

6. For this and the following paragraph: BD's foreword to *Humming*, viii.

7. BD to mother, Apr. 21, 1937; BD to her parents, (1939?); BD to father, Feb. 14, 1940, and Feb. 25, 1941—all in BDSL.

8. BD to Vida, Mar. 17, 1951, and BD, "notes," n.d., BDSL; and BD, foreword, xii, *Running Away from Myself: A Dream Portrait of America Drawn from the Films of the Forties* (Grossman, 1969), henceforth cited as BD, *Running*. Even earlier, Barbara had considered writing the film book and had gotten Houghton Mifflin interested in it. BD to Curtis Dahl, Jan. 26 and Mar. 21, 1946; BD to U. T. Miller Summers, June 7 and Sept. 13, 1946, and Mar. 6, 1947—all in BDBU.

9. For this and the following paragraph: BD to parents (1951?); Capote to BD, Mar. 28, 1951; BD to Capote, Apr. 6 and 20, 1951; BD to Vida, Aug. 9, 1951—all in BDSL.

10. For this and the following two paragraphs: BD, "Notes for Possible Film Interview," May 9, 1979; BD, "Notes for Kalliope Interview," n.d.; Barbara to Adrienne Rich, June 20, 1979; Mary Meigs to Barbara and Jane, Oct. 30, 1972; Annie to Barbara, Apr. 2 (1951); and five letters from Barbara to Annie, all but one (Apr. 13, 1951) undated, though probably also from 1951, BDSL. Also: Marie-Claire Blais, *American Notebooks* (Talonbooks, 1996).

Bessie Breuer's first novel, *Memory of Love* (Simon & Schuster, 1934), was praised by Carson McCullers as "a little masterpiece" and by Clifton Fadiman as "a classic." It was made into the 1939 film *In Name Only*, starring Cary Grant and Carole Lombard. Breuer's only play, *Sundown Beach*, opened on Broadway in 1948, directed by Elia Kazan. Bessie then put it away until Barbara, in the 1960s, persistently encouraged her to revise it. It then had a production in New York in 1964, directed by Salem Ludwig. Bessie, who could be "both kind and violent, gentle and fierce," then conceded that Barbara had been right in insisting she revise the play.

Annie Poor's World War II paintings were exhibited at both the Metropolitan Museum of Art and the National Gallery of Art. In 1964, *Greece*, a series of her landscapes with a text by Henry Miller, was published in New York by Viking. Later in life, she had a critically praised New York solo show and became a member of the American Academy of Arts and Letters. Thirty years later, Barbara and Annie were still close friends. BD to Karla Jay, Jan. 19, 1978, KJNYPL.

11. BD's undated and lengthy "notes" and BD to mother, July 2, 1958, BDSL; BD, *Humming*, 18.

12. The quotes in this and the following seven paragraphs are from BD, *Humming*, 15–16, 49, 52, 67–79, 144, 153, 156, 163, 178–79, 183, 218, 250.

13. BD to Vida, Jan. 1, 1951; Meigs to BD, Apr. 30, 1954; BD's "Notes for Kalliope," n.d., and "Notes for Possible Film Interview," May 9, 1979—all in BDSL.

14. For this and the following seven paragraphs: BD, "Notes for Kalliope," n.d.; Mary to Barbara, Aug. 18, 1974; and "Notes, Oct. 13, 1981"—all in BDSL. In her later years, Mary Meigs wrote several books, including the impressive, remarkably plain-spoken, and self-aware autobiography, *Lily Briscoe: A Self-Portrait* (Talonbooks, 1981), 36, 39, 74, 39, 47, 86, from which many of the details of her upbringing, as well as her unsentimental view of BD and their relationship, are drawn. Barbara felt that her own "resurrection as a writer" was the direct offshoot of her political actions: BD to Mary, June 2, 1978, BDSL.

15. For this and the following four paragraphs: Meigs, *Lily*, 149–57; and Barbara to Elena Wilson, June 12, 1972, BDSL.

16. The quotations in this and the following three paragraphs are from Barbara to Meigs, June 2 and Sept. 16, 1978; Meigs, *Lily*, 13–15, 24–27, 39–40, 111. The material about Mary McCarthy and Edmund Wilson is drawn primarily from *Lily*, *passim*, and from Wilson's journals *The Fifties*, ed. Leon Edel (Farrar, Straus & Giroux, 1986), especially 518–19, 551–61, and *The Sixties*, ed. Lewis M. Dabney (Farrar, Straus & Giroux, 1993).

17. For this and the following three paragraphs: Leah Fritz interview with BD, *Ms.*, Nov. 1978; McReynolds to Michael Randle, Apr. 15, 1997; Meigs, *Lily*, 96–103; BD, "Notes for Kalliope, Apr. 2, n.y., BDSL. Barbara wrote an article about her experiences in Cuba, her first piece of journalism. Edmund Wilson told her that he'd recommend the piece to the *New Yorker* if she'd make it less personal. She made a stab at being more "objective," but the *New Yorker* rejected the article anyway. The *Nation*, however, accepted it—in the original, personal version.

Chapter 2: David's Early Activism, Bohemia, and Homosexuality

1. Much of the detail in these opening pages about David's youth and family background comes from my five lengthy interviews with him in 2008 and 2009. Some of the material is also from the David McReynolds Papers.

2. The quotes in this and the following nine paragraphs: McReynolds e-mail to me, May 11, 2010; David to Paul Royce, Dec. 1955; David to Neil [?], June 26, 1952; David to San [?], Dec. 3, 1950; David to Harvey [Berman], Aug. 2, 1952; Martin McReynolds e-mail to me, May 12, 2010; father to David, June 23, July 25, 29, 1962, Dec. 3, 1972, and Feb. 27, 1973; mother to David, July 7, 1962; David to parents, Dec. 29, 1966; David to Bruce Friedrich, Dec. 11, 1994; David to WCTU (Women's Christian Temperance Union), Feb. 23, 1997; and David to Bess Sacker, Oct. 28, 1997—all in DMSC. David did sleep twice with women "accidentally" but is clear that he's "not bisexual. Absolutely not" (Feb, 16, 2009, interview with McReynolds). After his father died in 1977, David and his brother, Martin, went over his papers and found correspondence with "some theological person" about "his not knowing how to deal with the sin" of David's homosexuality (McReynolds e-mail to me, May 11, 2010).

3. For this and the following two paragraphs: David to Paul, n.d. [1951], David to Gene [Sharp], Feb. 3, 1953, both in DMSC; and Feb. 16, Apr. 15, July 4, 1969 interviews with McReynolds.

4. Feb. 16 and Apr. 15, 2009, interviews with McReynolds. David to Vern [Davidson], Aug. 19, 1952, David to Paul, n.d. [1951], both in DMSC. Also on Ailey: David's e-mail to me, Oct. 14, 2009. For more on the internalized homophobia (including my own) of David's generation: Duberman, *Cures: A Gay Man's Odyssey* (Dutton, 1992).

5. For this and the following three paragraphs: David to Alvin, Oct. 17, 1955, DMSC; and my five interviews with McReynolds. Also: Doug Ireland, "Socialism and Gay Liberation," Thomas Harrison, "Socialism and Homosexuality," and McReynolds, "Queer Reflections"—all in *New Politics* 12, no. 1. Also see Terence Kissack, *Free Comrades: Anarchism and Homosexuality in the United States, 1895–1917* (AK Press, 2008); Dan Healey, *Homosexual Desire in Revolutionary Russia: The Regulation of Sexual and Gender Dissent* (Univ. of Chicago Press, 2001); and Sheila Rowbotham, *Edward Carpenter* (Verso, 2009).

6. For this and the following seven paragraphs: David to Norman Thomas, Oct. 2 to Nov. 8, 1956, NTNYPL; David had been writing to Thomas since 1954. Also: David to parents, July 7, 1961, DMSC; Doug Ireland, "Socialism and Homosex," *Gay City News*, Jan. 25, 2009; Mar. 15, 2000, tape of David's speech at Allegheny College, courtesy McReynolds. The discovery of this organized effort within the Socialist Party, unique in its day, followed on the historian Christopher Phelps accidentally coming upon a 1952 article, "Socialism and Sex," by H.L. Small (Harry Small, whom McReynolds knew), which was originally published in *Young Socialist*, the mimeographed bulletin of the youth section of the Socialist Party—the Young People's Socialist League, or YPSL, pronounced "Yipsel." Though this is pure speculation, it's possible that Small was inspired by *The Homosexual in America: A Subjective Approach* (Greenberg, 1951), by Donald Webster Cory, the pseudonym of Edward Sagarin, a professor of sociology at the City University of New York. See Duberman, "The 'Father' of the Homophile Movement" in Duberman, *Left Out* (Basic Books, 1999), 59–94. According to Doug Ireland, it was McReynolds's close friend Vern Davidson who tried to draft an appropriate plank to present at the party's national convention, but he eventually gave up, though he believed that Norman Thomas would have supported it. McReynolds has no memory of either the H.L. Small article or Davidson's plank, though given the "live and let live attitude of YPSL," he wasn't surprised to learn of it. (See http://mail.google.com/mail/?hl=en&

tab=wm.) On his hero Eugene Debs, David once wrote: "Debs' whole attitude toward the working class was nonviolent and essentially gentle . . . he was very close to being an American Gandhi . . ." David to Richard Gralewski, Nov. 19, 1965, DMSC.

7. For this and the following two paragraphs: David to Hank Maiden, Oct. 5, 1955, David to Vern [Davidson], Aug. 28, 1952, David to Gene [Sharp], Feb. 3, 1953, David to WRL staff, Aug. 25, 1994, David to Rabbi Bentley, Apr. 1, 2003—all in DMSC; WRL pamphlet, *History of the War Resisters League*, June 1980.

8. David to Ben, Oct. 9, 1953, DMSC.

9. For this and the following eight paragraphs: David to Paul Royce, May 24, 1956, David to father, May 18, 1956, David to Paul Bram, May 15, 1956, all in DMSC; *The Nonviolent Activist*, Feb. 1991; David to Norman Thomas, Aug. 6, 1956, Feb. 18, "May" 1957, both in NTNYPL.

10. For quotes in this and the following three paragraphs: David to Bill Briggs, Sept. 17, 1956; to Vern Davidson, Sept. 15, 26, Oct. 3, 15, 1956; to Herman Singer, Sept. 22, 1956; to his father, Oct. 15, 1956—all in DMSC. David to Norman Thomas, Nov. 8, 1955, May 1957, July 22, 1957, Sept. 15, 1958; Thomas to David, Oct. 22, 1959; David to A.J. Muste, July 1, 1967; McReynolds, "Memo Regarding the Communist Party," Aug. 2, 1956; and McReynolds, "Suggestions for an Institute on 'The Politics of Peace'"—all in NTNYPL.

11. For this and the following five paragraphs: David to parents, Nov. 6, 1956, David to "Lief" [Paul], Jan. 21, 1956, David to Shachtman, Aug. 2, 1956, all in DMSC; plus my five interviews with McReynolds.

12. David to Margaret [Phair], June 13, 1956; to [Leo] Huberman (cofounder of the *Monthly Review*), June 24, 1956; to Vern [Davidson], June 25, 1956; and to his father, Oct. 15, 1956—all in DMSC.

13. David to his brother, July 4, 27, 1956; David to his parents, July 5, 1956; David to Vern Davidson, Aug. 6, 1956; David to City Committee of the SP's New York local, Aug. 9, 1956; David to Charles Curtis, Aug. 13, 1956; David to Jinni Baird, Oct. 30, 1956—all in DMSC.

14. David to Paul, Dec. 23, 1956, Oct. 10, 1957, Aug. 4, 1958; David to Lou Bloom, Aug. 5, 1958—all in DMSC.

15. For this and the following paragraph: David to Martin, July 6, 1958; Martin to David, Jan. 17, 1959, David to parents, Dec. 10, 1958—all in DMSC.

16. The discussion of homosexuality in this and the following two paragraphs: David to his parents, Jan. 22, 1959, DMSC. There had been a previous exchange on the subject (David to Martin, Aug. 1, 1956; David to father, Sept. 15, 1956; father to David, Jan. 20, 1957—all in DMSC) during which David had accused his father of having an "unhealthy" attitude about sex, and his father, in turn, accused David of wasting his gifts by "burying yourself in lost causes," and added that his lifestyle "is something between you and God, not between you and me."

17. For this and the following two paragraphs: David to "Comrades," May 27, 1957; McReynolds, "Report on Contacts . . ." [Oct. 1957?]; McReynolds circular letter to some dozen people, Apr. 13, 1958; David to California State Convention, Apr. 10, 1958; David to Phair and Davidson, Apr. 13, 1958; David to Bill Briggs, May 28, 1957, Apr. 13, 1958; David to Norman Thomas, July 2, 1957, May 27, 1958, David to his parents, June 8, 1958—all in DMSC. McReynolds, "Statement for *Hammer and Tongs*," May 27, 1958, copy in NTNYPL. The ISL had formerly been known as the Workers Party, which had come into existence in 1940 as a result of a split within the

Trotskyist Socialist Workers Party (SWP). In the late 1950s, the ISL seemed to be moving steadily in the direction of democratic socialism; furthermore, its leader, Max Shachtman, seemed to agree at the time with David's view that "State ownership and nationalized property do not in themselves constitute socialism when the state is controlled by an authoritarian one party regime." The anti-ISL minority at the convention insisted on a national referendum on the decision to admit the ISL—but lost that vote too.

18. For the quotes regarding the 1958 campaign in this and the following three paragraphs: David to Paul, Aug. 4, 1958; McReynolds, ms. "No Radiation Without Representation," Aug. 10, 1958; David to parents, Aug. 4, 11, Sept. 15, 1958; Norman Thomas to "Dear friend," Aug. 20, 1958; David to M.E. Paxton, Dec. 11, 1958; *Chelsea Clinton News*, Aug. 7, 1958; *Village Voice*, Aug. 27 and Oct. 8, 1958; *Villager*, Oct. 30, 1958—all in DMSC.

19. David to brother, Oct. 27, Nov. 2, 1958, DMSC. David today ascribes his recovery to the "serendipitous" discovery of Otto Rank's *Beyond Psychology* (Dover, 1958). (David's e-mail to me, May 5, 2010.)

Chapter 3: Joining the Black Struggle

1. For quotes in this and the following three paragraphs: David to Wolfgang Zucht, Nov. 15, 1966, David to parents, Apr. 10, 20, 1959, July 26, 1960—all in DMSC. In 1959 David had been emboldened by joining a peace walk the week before, in the rain, from Paterson, NJ, to Times Square, a distance of fifteen miles. The walk lasted from 9:00 A.M. to 7:30 P.M., and he was one of only two people who managed to walk the whole distance without stopping. Then, in early May, David participated in another demonstration against civil defense—this one drawing a thousand people—but through no fault of his own, he wasn't one of those arrested (David to parents, Apr. 4, May 3, 1959, David to brother, Oct. 3, 1960, DMSC). He also wrote a powerful piece, "Brave Men Do Not Hide" (1961? DMSC; the article doesn't seem to have been published), lambasting the notion that shelters could provide any protection: "the air will simply be sucked out [of them] and the inhabitants die from lack of oxygen . . . the dishonesty of the present civil defense program is its repeated statement that if you remain indoors for two weeks, it will then be safe to come out. This is simply not true . . . most of the government-sponsored 'facts' on nuclear war cannot be trusted . . . this is a major public hoax. . . . Our real security rests in building a nonviolent alternative to the present military defense of our freedom."

2. David to parents, April 4, May 29, 1959, Jan. 29, 1962, DMSC. When David appeared on the popular *Barry Gray Show* (along with Victor Riesel, the labor columnist, and Alexander de Seversky, the airplane designer), he asked so many pointed political questions that Gray finally blew up and expressed regret that David had ever been invited on the show. David, for his part, "rather enjoyed it."

3. David to parents, May 3, July 26, Oct. 23, Nov. 22, 1960, Feb. 3, 1961; David to "Comrades," Feb. 27, 1960—all in DMSC.

4. The quotes in this and the following two paragraphs: David to parents, Apr. 20 and May 29, 1959, July 26, 1960, and Jan. 11, Feb. 3, May 10, July 7 and 21, and Dec. 6, 1961; David to brother, Mar. 3, 1960; and David to sister, Nov. 4, 1961—all in

DMSC; David's e-mail to me, May 5, 2010; David to Bill Morgan, Mar. 12, 1984; David to Peter Orlovsky, Dec. 12, 1978; Allen Ginsberg to David (postcard), July 21, 1973, and Dec. 30, 1977; David to Ginsberg, Apr. 28, 1977; McReynolds, "Saturday Night Encounter," n.d.; and copy of undated material from FBI files, received Jan. 13, 1978—all AGSB.

5. David to parents, June 25, July 16, 1960, David to brother, Mar., 3, 1960, DMSC.

6. For this and the following paragraph: McReynolds to IRS, Mar. 15, 1957, DMSC. For his twenty-five-day jail term: "Life in Jail," in his book, *We Have Been Invaded by the 21st Century* (Praeger, 1970; Grove, 1971), 29–37 (henceforth, McReynolds, *Invaded*). In a vast secondary literature on the peace movement, I've found Scott H. Bennett, *Radical Pacifism* (Syracuse Univ. Press, 2003), particularly useful. Also helpful were David Dellinger, *From Yale to Jail* (Pantheon, 1993), Andrew E. Hunt, *David Dellinger* (NYU Press, 2006), the documentary history *Nonviolence in America*, Staughton Lynd and Alice Lynd, eds. (Orbis, 1995), and James Tracy, *Direct Action* (Univ. of Chicago Press, 1996). For an international context, see David Cortright, *Peace: A History of Movements and Ideas* (Cambridge Univ. Press, 2008). The reader should be somewhat wary of Dellinger's autobiography, *From Yale to Jail*, for it omits significant parts of his own history—for example, his failed project to start a left-wing weekly, *Seven Days* (David's e-mail to me, Apr. 25, 2010).

7. For this and the following five paragraphs: BD, notes for "Women's Struggle," n.d., and "notes for Leah Fritz Interview," n.d., BDSL. For Deming as a major nonviolent theorist: Ira Chernus, *American Nonviolence* (Orbis, 2004), ch. 12; interview with McReynolds, Feb. 2, 2009, McReynolds memo to EC of WRL, Oct. 14, 1968, DMSC. David to Norman Thomas, May 1, 1962, which includes the May 10, 1962, call for antinuclear demonstrations; in reply, Thomas questioned the wisdom of the demonstrations and feared his sponsorship would "weaken any small effect I might have on the President . . ." (Thomas to David, May 2, 1962, NTNYPL).

8. The quotes in this and the following two paragraphs are from Deming, "The Peacemakers," *Nation*, Dec. 17, 1960 (repr. in Jane Meyerding, ed., *We Are All Part of One Another: A Barbara Deming Reader*, henceforth Meyerding, *BD Reader*, New Society, 1984), 77–89. Also: BD to Carey McWilliams, May 30, 1961, and BD to Muste, Nov. 14, 1961, BDBU.

When reports of civil rights abuses in Cuba began to filter into the United States, a split occurred in the ranks of radical pacifists. Roy Finch, a leading figure in several organizations, was the most vocal in denouncing the Castro regime, and in the spring of 1961 he resigned from the editorial board of *Liberation*. On the other side, prompted by the April 17, 1961, U.S. invasion at the Bay of Pigs, the even more prominent David Dellinger organized both the Fair Play for Cuba Committee and the Nonviolent Committee for Cuban Independence. Barbara Deming joined the latter, along with A. J. Muste, Ralph DiGia, Jim Peck, and Dorothy Day. For more details, see Andrew E. Hunt, *Dellinger*, 118–22, and Dellinger, *From Yale to Jail*, 149, 183–85.

9. Deming, "San Francisco–Moscow: Why They Walk," *Nation*, July 15, 1961, and her follow-up piece, "New Mission to Moscow," *Nation*, Dec. 23, 1961.

10. Deming, *Prisons That Could Not Hold*, henceforth *Prisons*, Sky Vanderlinde, ed. (Univ. of Georgia Press, 1995), 2–5.

11. The quotes in this and the following paragraph: Edmund Wilson, *The Sixties*, Lewis M. Dabney, ed. (Farrar Straus & Giroux, 1993), 66–70.

12. For this and the following three paragraphs: Muste and Willoughby to BD, Mar. 15, 1962, BDSL; Meigs, *Lily*, 84–103; interview with McReynolds, Feb. 2, 2009; David to Sid and Louise Peck, June 19, 2001, McReynolds memo on Cuba to the National Committee of the Socialist Party, Apr. 22, 1961—all in DMSC. David had been uneasy about the drumhead trials and executions that took place in the early days of the revolution, but Bayard Rustin had more or less persuaded him that without the trials, however unjust, there would have been revenge killings throughout Cuba, along with "the destruction of the honest non-Communist trade union leadership." Later, as rumors mounted that homosexuals were being rounded up and detained in camps, David became less supportive. David to Andy Gollans, Nov. 30, 1960, and David to Al and Eve Scott, May 28, 1963, DMSC.

13. For this and the following nine paragraphs: BD, "Southern Peace Walk: Two Issues or One?" *Liberation*, July–Aug. 1962, repr. in Meyerding, ed., *BD Reader*, 89–99. Interview with McReynolds, Apr. 15, 2009. BD to Dellinger, Apr. 26, 1963, and BD to Muste and Dellinger, Nov. 29, 1964, BDBU. For Barbara's simultaneous involvement with *Liberation* magazine, see BD to George Willoughby, Sept. 29, 1962, and Willoughby to BD, Oct. 3, 1962, BDBU.

14. For this and the following four paragraphs: David to parents, Jan. 11, July 16, 17, 23, Sept. 6, 19, Oct. 17, 30, Nov. 24, Dec. 19, 21, 1961; David to brother, July 17, 1961—all in DMSC.

15. Even David's unpredictable and often critical father called his writing brilliant, his "great forte," and urged him to devote himself full-time to thinking and writing—"if you can find some way to support yourself." His father had special praise for David's (somewhat prescient) 1961 essay "The Bomb in the Brooks Brothers Suit" (repr. in McReynolds, *Invaded*, 91–102) about how elements from the middle class (e.g., the SDS and anti-Vietnam protesters) would replace the conservative working class as the new engines of radical change. David to parents, Jan. 11, Sept. 29, 1961; father to David, Nov. 1, 1961, Apr. 1, 1962—all in DMSC.

16. The discussion of David's views on homosexuality that follows is derived from: Apr. 15 and July 4, 2009, interviews with McReynolds; David to his brother, Apr. 16, June 2, 1962, Dec. 12, 1966; David to his parents, May 28, June 12, July 9, Nov. 20, 26, 1962; David to father, July 9, 1962, father to David, June 10, 1962—all in DMSC. For more on Cory, see my "The Father of the Homophile Movement," *Left Out*, 59–94.

17. David to Dave Rhoads, July 31, 1962, David to Dan Thomas, June 19, 1963, McReynolds, "Memo on Proposed Protest to U.S. Test Resumption," Mar. 22, 1962—all in DMSC. Concern about nuclear weapons continues to rise and fall down to the present day. In 1995, for example, the Smithsonian's *Enola Gay* exhibition produced a resurgence of opposition, including a demonstration at the Smithsonian in which David took part. For more on the ebb and flow of public concern, see Rosemary B. Mariner and G. Kurt Piehler, eds., *The Atomic Bomb and American Society* (Univ. of Tennessee Press, 2009).

18. David to parents, Jan. 10, Apr. 5, Oct. 29, 1962. Nearly all of McReynolds's articles, some in draft form, are in DMSC. When Baldwin spoke at a WRL fundraising dinner, David was one of two members assigned to bring him to the packed hall (the dinner raised $1,000). He concluded from their time together that although

Baldwin "was almost effeminate in private," he was "terribly proud" in public, "extremely perceptive," and "terribly gentle at his center."

19. BD, "The Ordeal of SANE," *Nation*, Mar. 11, 1961; "International Peace Brigade," *Nation*, Apr. 7, 1962; "Letter to WISP" [Women Strike for Peace], *Liberation*, Apr. 1963. In A. J. Muste's Apr. 4, 1963, letter to Barbara (BDSL), commenting on her "Letter to WISP," he hints at the kind of sexism (it does "occur to one about whether the women [in the peace movement] are aware of what they are really after . . .") among some of the pacifist men that would later, after Barbara became a committed feminist, anger her and lead to confrontation and alienation. In 1963, the editorial board of *Liberation* consisted entirely of men.

20. For the quotes in this and the following four paragraphs: BD, "In the Birmingham Jail," *Nation*, May 25, 1963, and BD, "Notes After Birmingham," *Liberation*, Summer 1963—both reprinted in BD, *Revolution and Equilibrium* (Grossman, 1971). See also the fascinating and touching letter BD wrote to Dorothy Day (Aug. 12, 1963, BDSL) about another white female pro-black demonstrator whose family had her committed to an insane asylum.

21. The account that follows, including the quotes, is derived from BD to Meigs, Nov. 7, 1966, BDSL; BD, *Prison Notes* (Beacon, 1966), *passim*; McReynolds interview, July 4, 2009; BD to Pritchett, Feb. 7, 1964, BDSL; CNVA *Bulletin*, Mar. 20, 1964, copy in BLSPC; McReynolds e-mail to me, Apr. 21, 2010; and BD to Carey McWilliams, Sept. 30, 1962, BDBU. For more on the Albany SNCC events 1961–62, see Howard Zinn, *You Can't Be Neutral on a Moving Train* (Beacon, 1994), ch. 4; Harry G. Lefever, *Undaunted by the Fight: Spelman College and the Civil Rights Movement, 1957–1967* (Mercer University Press, 2005), ch. 13; Tom Hayden, *Reunion: A Memoir* (Random House, 1988); and Clayborne Carson, *In Struggle: SNCC and the Black Awakening of the 1960s* (Harvard Univ. Press, 1981).

Prison Notes is, in my own view, Barbara's best book, the most impassioned and vivid of her works. And the critics at that time agreed. Dwight Macdonald wrote that the book was "beautifully written, imaginative and realistic," it is "not one of the better such narratives, but by far the best one." *Prison Notes* is also Barbara's best-known book and the only one that continues to be widely known. The writer Rita Mae Brown, who read the book some six years after its publication, holds a far more negative opinion. As someone from a working-class background, she sent Barbara (Rita Mae Brown to BD, Dec. 1, 1972, BDSL)—the two women had by then become friends—a lengthy denunciation of the book. Famously outspoken, and prominent in the post-Stonewall gay movement, Rita Mae made no effort to soften her indictment. She wrote Barbara that *Prison Notes* could only have been written by someone from a white, middle-class background: "even in jail you have more than my people." Parts of the book so "outraged" Rita Mae that she wanted "to break your neck," especially when Barbara was building "a beautiful case for these human touches between antagonists" and losing sight of "the power struggle between oppressor and oppressed." Herself white, Rita Mae accused Barbara of playing Lady Bountiful of behalf of black people, and of "sidestepping her own oppression and that of other Lesbians."

22. Those interested in pursuing the subject of radical education should probably start with Neill's book *Summerhill* (1960; rev. ed., St. Martin's, 1995), as well as his *Neill! Neill! Orange Peel!* (Weidenfeld & Nicolson, 1972) and *Freedom—Not License!* (Pocket Books, 1978). Beyond that, the literature is large. Some of my own favorites

include: Paulo Freire, *The Pedagogy of the Oppressed* (Continuum, 2006); Jonathan Kozol, *Death at an Early Age* (1967; repr. Plume, 1985) and *Free Schools* (Houghton Mifflin, 1972); John Holt, *How Children Learn* and *How Children Fail* (both rev. ed., DaCapo, 1995); Matthew Appleton, *A Free Range Childhood* (Resource Center for Redesigning, 2000). For more on the recent widespread conclusions among biologists, anthropologists, primatologists, and others that "babies are innately sociable and helpful to others," a useful beginning summary is the *New York Times*, Dec. 1, 2009, followed by the book-length arguments in Jonathan Lear's *Open Minded* (Harvard Univ. Press, 1999), Oren Harman, *The Price of Altruism*, (Norton, 2010), Matt Ridley's *The Origins of Virtue* (Penguin, 1998), Robert M. Sapolsky's *The Trouble with Testosterone* (Simon & Schuster, 1998), and any of the primatologist Frans de Waal's many works.

23. The quotes from here to the end of the chapter: BD, *Prison Notes*. BD to Suzuki, May 8, July 8, Oct. 9, 1964; Suzuki to BD, June 2, Aug. 5, 1964—all in BDSL. Barbara to Andrea Dworkin, Jan. 3, 1975, ADSL. CNVA *Bulletin*, Mar. 20, 1964; Cheryl Robinson to Barbara, Dec. 29, 1974, Barbara to Dellinger, Jan. 3, 1975, Dellinger to Barbara, Jan. 28, 1975—all in DDTL. See also MMSC for various BD and MM letters too numerous to cite individually. Also: Lyttle to BD, Dec. 31, 1963, Jan. 2, 3, 8, 10, 12, 14, 1964; BD to Lyttle, Dec. 27, 1963; BD to Judge Durden, Jan. 4, 1964; Erica Enzer to Lyttle, Jan. 29, Feb. 6, 8 (?), 11, 1964; "Statement of Barbara Deming," Recorder's Court, Feb. 5, 1964; Edie Mae Snyder to six fellow prisoners, Feb. 11(?), 1964, Peter Gregonis Log, Feb. 6, 11, 1964—all in BLSC, which also contains, remarkably, some of the jailhouse correspondence written on toilet paper; several of the letters were to Barbara: "Barbara, well I think you lost a little weight"; "I'm glad to be away from typing stencils for a while, how does it feel to be away from your typewriter"; "Barbara, how fine to be in the same jail with you. I would've guess[ed] the Nashville Walk would've finished you from CNVA for good-"; "Barbara, written any good books lately?"

Chapter 4: The Personal and the Political—the Early 1960s

1. The quotes in this and the following two paragraphs are from David to parents, May 13 (two letters) and May 15, 1963, DMSC.

2. "Two Faces of Dixie" is reprinted in McReynolds, *Invaded*, 61–67.

3. McReynolds, "Neither Run nor Hide, "*Village Voice*, Apr. 1961. For the shift within WRL, see Scott H. Bennett, *Radical Pacifism* (Syracuse Univ. Press: 2003), henceforth Bennett, *Pacifism*, esp. ch. 8, 204–38.

4. For more detail on the march and Rustin's role in it, see John D'Emilio, *Lost Prophet* (Univ. of Chicago Press, 2003), and Charles Euchner, *Nobody Turn Me Around* (Beacon, 2010). David to parents, Aug. 21, Sept. 5, 1963, DMSC.

5. David to parents, Dec. 2, 1963, DMSC.

6. For this and the following three paragraphs: David to his parents, Jan. 19, 1963, David to niece and nephews, Dec. 14, 1963, McReynolds memo, May 22, 1964— DMSC. David to Shachtman, Dec. 1, 27, 1966, Shachtman to George [?], Dec. 19, 1966, MSTL. For the 1962 SP convention's foreign policy positions: David to Norman Thomas, Feb. 20, June 14, July 27, 1962, the last with an enclosed "Foreign Policy Resolution"—NTNYPL.

7. For this and the following paragraph: Interviews with McReynolds, Feb. 2, Apr. 15, July 4, 2009. David to parents, Jan. 19, July 18, 1963; Joyce Brown to Saul Mendelson, May 10, David to Brown, May 25, David to Norman Thomas, May 18, David to Mendelson, May 26, David to E. Friend, May 26, David to E. Kettler, June, Norman Thomas to David, Oct. 7, and David to Sam Farber, Oct 20 (all 1964); David to Betty Elkin, Mar. 17, 1965, and David to Vern Davidson, March 26, 1965—all in DMSC.

8. Five interviews with McReynolds, esp. Feb. 2, 2009. In the huge literature on the war in Vietnam, I've been especially informed by and reliant on Marilyn B. Young, *The Vietnam Wars 1945–1990* (HarperCollins, 1991), and Mark Philip Bradley and Marilyn B. Young, eds., *Making Sense of the Vietnam Wars* (Oxford University Press, 2008).

9. For Peter Stafford and the background of his relationship with David: Interview with McReynolds, July 4, 2009. David to Pete, July 1, 6, 20, 27, 28; David to parents, July 2, Aug. 10, 28, Sept. 11, Dec. 12; David to mother, Sept 22; David to Oppenheimer, Oct. 29; David to father, Nov. 11, David to brother, n.d., Aug. 13, Oct. 20, 23, Dec. 16; and David to Vern Davidson, Dec. 29—all 1964, all in DMSC. After Pete left New York, David saw him only two or three times. Pete married, had a son, held low-paying, occasional jobs, and like his father before him became alcoholic; he died in 2007 from a fall induced by either a heart attack or alcohol (McReynolds e-mail to me, Mar. 16, 2010).

10. For this and the following fourteen paragraphs: David to parents, n.d., David to brother, Oct. 20, 23, 1964. Pete's book was published as *LSD: The Problem-Solving Psychedelic*, with Bonnie H. Golightly (Alarm, 1967).

11. For this and the following five paragraphs: *Liberation*, Oct. 1964; Bennett, *Pacifism*, 239–41; Young, *Vietnam*, esp. chs. 6–7. David to brother, Aug. 13, 1964; David to parents, Nov. 5, 1964; David to father, Nov. 11, 1964; and "David McReynolds, P.S. to San Francisco," n.d.—all in DMSC. See also Noam Chomsky, "The Responsibility of Intellectuals," *New York Review of Books*, Feb. 23, 1967.

12. David to parents, May 3, Aug. 26, Sept. 27, 1965, Mar. 9, June 28, Nov. 15, 29, Dec. 30, 1966—DMSC. The discussion of his relationship with Pete that follows is from: David to Pete, Feb. 10, Oct. 20, 1965, Nov. 21, 1966; David to parents, May 3; David to brother, Mar. 31, June 18, Sept. 7, Dec. 10, 1965, Dec. 20, 1966, July 12, 1968 David to sister, Dec. 1, 1966, David to Vern, March 25, 1965—all in DMSC; interview with McReynolds, Feb. 16, 2009.

13. My account in the following pages of the relationships among Barbara, Mary, and Marie-Claire derives from six sources: BDSL; Edmund Wilson, *The Sixties*; Mary Meigs, *Lily Briscoe*; Marie-Claire Blais, *American Notebooks, A Writer's Journey*, tr. Linda Gaboriau, dedicated to Elena Wilson (Talonbooks, 1996); Mary Meigs Papers, Bryn Mawr College (henceforth MMBM); Marie-Claire Blais Papers, Bibliothèque et Archives, Montreal, Canada (henceforth MBAC).

Chapter 5: David and the New Left

1. For the background history in this and the following two paragraphs, I'm especially indebted to: McReynolds, *Invaded by the 21st Century*; David Dellinger, *From Yale to Jail*; Andrew Hunt, *David Dellinger*; Nat Hentoff, *Peace Agitator: The*

Story of A.J. Muste (Macmillan, 1963); Maurice Isserman, *The Other American: The Life of Michael Harrington* (PublicAffairs, 2000): and above all John D'Emilio's rich biography, *Lost Prophet: The Life and Times of Bayard Rustin* (Univ. of Chicago Press, 2003).

2. David to John O'Brien, Sept. 29, 1998; David to Charlie [?], Jan. 4, 1998; and David to Walter Naegle, Jan. 11, 1998—all in DMSC. For more details on the Rustin-Muste relationship, see D'Emilio's *Lost Prophet*, especially ch. 9 and 10; and for more on SDS, see Paul Berman, *A Tale of Two Utopias* (W.W. Norton, 1996).

3. Dellinger, "The March on Washington and Its Critics," *Liberation*, May 1965; Lynd, "Coalition Politics or Nonviolent Revolution?" *Liberation*, June 1965.

4. Interviews with McReynolds, Feb. 2, Apr. 15, 2009; McReynolds, "Transition: Personal and Political Notes," *Liberation*, Aug. 1965; and "Pacifists in Battle," *New Politics*, summer 1965; McReynolds e-mail to me, April 25, 2010.

5. For this and the following eight paragraphs: Interview with McReynolds, Feb. 2, 1969; David to brother, Feb. 1, 1965; David to Betty Elkin, Nov. 6, 1964; David to Norman Thomas, Nov. 10, 1965; David to parents, May 12, 1965; David to Mulford Sibley, Nov. 22, Dec. 2, 1965; David to Gerald Rubin, Dec. 3, 1965; and David to Larry Gara, Dec. 12, 1996—all in DMSC. "Closed" Dellinger Papers, Tamiment Library, NYU.

6. McReynolds to "Comrades," Sept. 30, 1966; McReynolds, "Appeal to the British Labour Party, n.d. [1966?], *Tribune*, England; David to Paul Feldman, Feb. 9, 1967; David to William Allen, Dec. 13, 1966; McReynolds, "memo to *Liberation* editorial board," Dec. 23, 1966; McReynolds, "memo on compromise," Dec. 27, 1966, and "Memo to a Non-Existent Caucus" [1966]—all in DMSC. David to Shachtman, Dec. 1, 27, 1966; and Shachtman to George Noywod [?], Dec. 19, 1966, MSTL.

7. For this and the following six paragraphs: McReynolds, "The Pacifist Approach to Anti–Vietnam War Protest" [1990], DMSC. Interview with McReynolds, Feb. 2, 2009. David to Hyman Weber, Nov. 19, 1965, and David to Jim Peck, Jan. 30, 1966. For David's mixed feelings about Jim Peck, see David to parents, Aug. 24, 1972, and David to Charles Peck, July 13, 1993, BDSL. David to parents, Feb. 2 and 7, Aug. 30, and Dec. 29; David to Bruce Williams, Feb. 4; David to Myrtle Solomon, Feb. 11; David to Patricia Mills, Feb. 11; David to Robert Mitchell, Feb. 25; David to Donald Kaye, Dec. 1; David to Peggy Duff, Dec. 22—all 1966, all in DMSC. David to John Swomley, Nov. 16, 1988, DMSC. Raymond F. Gregory, *Norman Thomas: The Great Dissenter* (Algora, 2008), ch. 21; Michael S. Foley, *Confronting the War Machine: Draft Resistance During the Vietnam War* (Univ. of North Carolina Press, 2003). Thomas to David, Oct. 7, 1965, copy of David to Irving Howe, Dec. 6, 1965—NTNYPL.

8. For this and the following three paragraphs: Paul Booth to David, Mar. 24, David to Paul Booth, Apr. 3, David to WRL Exec. Comm. & NAC, Apr. 12, David to parents, July 1, David to Terrence Sullivan, July 8—all 1966, all in DMSC. *The Nonviolent Activist*, Feb. 1991. David to Dear Friend, June 30, 1966, along with memo "12th Triennial Conference of the War Resisters International, Rome, Apr. 7–12, copy in NTNYPL. David to Thomas, Sept. 8, 1966, and Aug. 2, 1967, with statement on being detained; David to "Dear Comrades," Aug. 9, 1966, plus "Statement Being Circulated to the Key List of the Socialist Party"—all in NTNYPL.

9. For this and the following four paragraphs: McReynolds, "Memo on Tentative Thoughts on the Impeachment of Johnson," Sept. 19, 1966, McReynolds, "Statement on W.R.L. Principles" [1966], and David to Peter Standish, Jan. 31, 1967—DMSC.

Thomas to David, Sept. 28, 1966, copy of David's "Dear Friends" memo, April 25, 1967—NTNYPL.

10. For this and the following paragraph: McReynolds, "Confidential Memo," Sept. 1, 1967, DMSC.

11. For this and the following five paragraphs: Interviews with McReynolds, Feb. 2, July 4, 2009; McReynolds, "Memo," Dec. 29, 1965, and "Reply to Brad Lyttle," n.d., DMSC. BD's talk at Muste's memorial service, repr., in BD, *We Cannot Live Without Our Lives* (Grossman, 1974, henceforth *We Cannot Live*), 183–85. As early as 1962, A.J.Muste had asked Barbara if *Liberation* could list her as an associate editor and had even suggested that she think about becoming the publication's editor (A.J. Muste to BD, Sept. 13, 1962, BDBU). There were three Muste memorials. David feels it's more likely that he spoke at the second one, the Quaker Memorial, rather than at the first, at the Community Church, where Barbara spoke, but given the contradictions in the evidence I've left the original description intact. David e-mail to me, May 5, 2010.

12. For this and the following two paragraphs: Hunt, *Dellinger*. Dellinger, "Tribute to A.J. Muste, *Liberation*, Jan. 1967 (though the issue is dated "January," it actually came out after Muste's death in February). David to parents, Feb. 21, Dec. 28, 1967—DMSC.

13. For this and the following three paragraphs: Interviews with McReynolds, Feb. 16 and July 4, 2009. David to Pete, Mar. 14, May 8, July 19, 1967; David to parents, Sept. 27, 1965, Jan. 9, 1967—DMSC.

14. For this and the following six paragraphs: Interview with McReynolds, Feb. 16, 2009. David to parents, Mar. 26, 1963; David to mother, Sept. 22, 1964; David to father, Nov. 11, 1964; David to Wenche Blomberg; Dec. 22, 1966; David to parents, Jan. 9, 1967—all in DMSC.

15. Michael Harrington, *Fragments of the Century* (Simon & Schuster, 1972), 219; Isserman, *Harrington*, esp. ch. 9; and Peter Drucker, *Max Shachtman and His Left* (Humanity Books, 1994).

16. For this and the following three paragraphs: McReynolds, "A Letter to the Men of My Generation," *Village Voice*, Nov. 30, 1967; Harrington, "A Question of Philosophy, a Question of Tactics," *Voice*, Dec. 7, 1967; McReynolds, "Philosophy and Tactics: Answering an Answer," *Voice*, Dec. 21, 1967.

Chapter 6: Protesting the War in Vietnam

1. Dellinger, *From Yale to Jail*; Hunt, *Dellinger*; Deming, "The Temptations of Power—Report on a Visit to North Vietnam," repr. in BD, *Revolution and Equilibrium* (Grossman, 1971).

2. For this and the following five paragraphs: BD, "The Temptations of Power," in Meyerding, ed., *We Are All Part of One Another*; and BD, "Shalom," *Catholic Worker*, Oct. 1968. Dworkin to BD, Jan. 10, 1966; BD to C.H. Ward, Feb. 9, 1967; and BD to "Mrs. Taylor," Feb. 9, 1967—BDBU.

3. The quotes in this and the following two paragraphs: BD's speech on receiving the WRL's Annual Peace Award in 1967, *Liberation* May–June, 1967. BD to Tracy [Mygatt], July 21, 1965, and Apr. 8 [1969], TMSC.

4. For this and the following three paragraphs: BD to Meigs, Nov. 7, 1966, BDSL; David to parents, Oct. 19, 1967, DMSC; Hunt, *Dellinger*, 172–82; interview

with McReynolds, July 4, 2009; *Cape Cod Standard-Times*, Oct. 23, 1967; Blais to Jeanne Lapointe, 3 July, n.y., MBAC; and McReynolds e-mail to me, May 10, 1010. See also: MMSC.

5. For this and the following three paragraphs: BD, "Mud City," *Liberation*, Sept. 1968.

6. For the quotes in this and the following eight paragraphs: BD, "On Revolution and Equilibrium," *Liberation*, Feb. 1968, repr. in BD, *Liberation* (Grossman, 1971), 194–221. Kay Boyle called *Liberation* "one of the first great books of the new America." BD to Picano, Nov. 1, 1983, copy in Andrea Dworkin Papers—ADSL. Blais to Lapointe, Apr. 11, n.y.; Nov. 6, 1966; and Jan. 24, 1969—MBAC.

7. For this and the following six paragraphs: Meigs to BD, Sept. 7, 1975; M-C to BD, n.d., 1966; BD "Notes," Oct. 8, 1976, and Jan. 3, 1982; BD to Meigs, Apr. 7, 1977, June 2, 1978, May 25, 1983; BD to M-C, n.d. [1971?]—all in BDSL. Meigs, *Lily Briscoe*. Blais, *American Notes* (in which not even a hint of anything negative about Barbara appears). Wilson, *The Sixties*, ed. Dabney, 407–8, 455–56, 664, 825, 872, and 888. Wilson, *O Canada: An American's Notes on Canadian Culture* (Farrar, Straus & Giroux, 1965), 153–57. BD to Jane Gapen, Apr. 17, [1969?] and Apr. 23, 1969, BDSL. Blais to Lapointe, Apr., [1966?], 24; postcard Oct. 22, 1967; and Jan. 24, 1969—MBAC. When Mary received what Marie-Claire described as an "enormous inheritance," she made generous gifts both to Barbara and to M-C, who wrote a friend that they both "have every intention of distributing our money to our friends. She has her pacifist friends . . . and I have the siblings from my family." Then, as a curious non sequitur, she added, "I hate these false feelings of generosity"—though whether she meant to refer to her own or Mary's feelings isn't clear. Blais to Lapointe, n.d., MBAC.

8. For this and the following eight paragraphs: Jane to BD, Jan. 9 and Feb. 25, 1967; BD to Jane, Jan. 19, 1967, Mar. 20, 26, 27, Apr. 15, 23, 29, 1969; BD to Paul [?], Mar. 28, 1969; Barbara to mother, Apr. 30, 1969—all in BDSL. BD to Mygatt, Dec. 26 [1969], TMSC. The matter of Jane's surname is complicated. Gapen was her mother's maiden name; Watrous was her father's name. According to Bonnie Netherington, who currently resides at Sugarloaf and knew both women, Verlaine—which Jane sometimes used—may have been the name of the aunt who had raised her after she was orphaned at age five. (Netherington to me, Apr. 20, 2010.) More likely, because both of her children use that surname, Verlaine was the surname of her husband, Oscar. Her legal papers are in the name of Jane W. Verlaine, but when publishing her only book, Jane used the name Gapen, and therefore I have as well.

9. David to brother, Feb. 8, July 12, Dec. 8, 1968; David to parents, Mar. 1, June 11, July 25, Aug. 1, Sept. 20, 30, Oct. 4, Nov. 11–12—all 1968, all in DMSC. *New York Daily News*, Oct. 13, 1968. McReynolds, "Memo to WRL's EC and NAC," Oct. 14, 1968, DMSC.

10. For this and the following twelve paragraphs: McReynolds, "New York Letter," ms. [1968?], DMSC. McReynolds, *Invaded*, 49–56, 144–46, 194–205, 213–21. David to parents, Aug. 30, 1967, June 11, 12, Aug. 1, Sept. 30, and Nov. 12, 1968; David to Gralewski, Mar. 20, Apr. 8, 1969—all in DMSC. Isserman, *Harrington*, 275–82; *Sunday News*, Oct. 13, 1968; *Village Voice*, Oct. 13, 1968.

11. For this and the following two paragraphs: McReynolds, "Prague: Viewing a Disaster," *Invaded*, 49–56; McReynolds e-mail to me, May 10, 2010.

Chapter 7: The Late 1960s—Militancy and the Emergence of Feminism and Gay Liberation

1. For this and the following two paragraphs: Hunt, *Dellinger*, esp. ch. 9–10; James Tracy, *Direct Action*; McReynolds, "Pacifists in Battle," *New Politics*, summer 1965. David to Charlie [?], Jan. 4, 1997; David to parents, Apr. 29, 1969; McReynolds, memo, Dec. 17, 1969, to Exec. Comm. WRL; and David to father, Jan. 13, 1972— DMSC.

2. For this and the following four paragraphs: Isserman, *Harrington*, esp. ch. 9. David to parents [1970]; David to brother, Oct. 2, 1970; David to Sam Friedman, June 17, 29, 1970—DMSC. For an excellent discussion of Fred Hampton's murder, see Jeffrey Hass, "Fred Hampton's Legacy," *Nation*, Dec. 14, 2009.

3. David to parents, May 6, 10, 1971, DMSC; David e-mail to me, March 24, 2010.

4. For this and the following three paragraphs: BD to Irma Brandeis, May 11, 1971, BDSL; BD to Mygatt, May 12, 1971, TMSL; and BD, "The Mayday Tribe," *We Cannot Live*, 17–35.

5. For this and the following two paragraphs: BD to Mary [1969]; Barbara to Mary, Dec. 2, 1969; Jane to Barbara [1971?]—BDSL.

6. Mary to Barbara, Sept. 27, 1971, BDSL. See also: MMSC—too many items to cite individually.

7. For the impact of antiwar protest, see Melvin Small, *Johnson, Nixon, and the Doves* (Rutgers Univ. Press, 1988). For Vietnam in 2010, see Bill Hayton, *Vietnam: Rising Dragon* (Yale Univ. Press, 2010).

8. For this and the following three paragraphs: Mary to Barbara, Aug. 21, Sept. 22, Oct. 4, 16, Nov. 2, 18, Dec. 17, 1971, and Jan. 6, 1972; BD to Madame Phan-Thi-An, June 7, 1972; BD, "Notes for Possible Film Interview," May 9, 1979—all in BDSL. David to parents, June 25, 1971, Sept. 5, 1972, DMSC. Dellinger, *From Yale to Jail*, 405–8. McReynolds interviews Feb.2 and Apr. 15, 2009. McReynolds tape, "Vietnam War Retrospective," Nov. 25, 1993, courtesy McReynolds. BD to Dellinger, [1972], BDBU.

9. For this and the following paragraph: BD to Denise Levertov, Aug. 12, Meigs to BD, "Nov./Dec.," BD to Dellinger, Dec. 25, BD to Madame Phan-Thi-An, Dec. 29—all 1972, all in BDSL; Hunt, *Dellinger*, 240–43.

10. David to parents, Oct. 3, 10, 26, 1972, and David to Hoopes et. al., DMSC; Isserman, *Harrington*, 299.

11. For this and the following three paragraphs: David to parents, Aug. 24, 1970, Nov. 17, 1972; David to Peter, Aug. 27, Oct. 15, 1970; and David to brother, Oct. 2, 1970—all in DMSC. Goodman's introduction to David's *Invaded* pulled no punches. He gave David ample praise ("his acute intelligence, his broad experience, and his stature as a human being") but also criticized him on several grounds: "He has no feeling for the fundamental unworkability of present world-wide urbanization. Talking to him about education, I found, to my surprise, that he had never questioned the premises of mass schooling." Goodman called him "an extreme oddball who respects the conventional, and that is the oddest thing about him." David appended an Author's Note to Goodman's introduction that read in part: "I suspect Paul has caught me as I am, limitations and all. I feel like the student I was in college, always receiving a 'C' at the end of the term. The final grade, in this case, will have to be given by

the reader." *Invaded* sold badly, despite getting some excellent reviews. David to parents, Oct. 1, 1971, David to Ralph Suter, June 21, 1972, DMSC.

12. For this and the following five paragraphs: David to parents, Feb. 27, Oct. 5, 1973, David to Don Frese, Sept. 28, 1972, DMSC. *Village Voice*, Mar. 25, 1959. Katz to David, Oct. 18, 1973; David to Katz, Oct. 19, 1973; David to Deevy Greitzer, Sept. 18, 1974—JNKNYPL.

13. David to father, Nov. 29, 1972, DMSC. It should be noted that David's father also expressed his love for his son and complimented him often, e.g., father to David, Jan. 20, 1969: ". . . you are truly a gifted and remarkable person. You have a rare intellect and a rare gift of understanding."

14. For this and the following four paragraphs: BD memo, "Try to recall phone conversation Mother July 15, 1974"; BD to mother, July 17, 1974; and mother to BD, July 20, 1974—BDSL. In the memo, BD jotted down this added exchange: "She said something at some point about nobody oppressing homosexuals. I replied that some would lose jobs if it was known, some would be thrown out of housing. She: I don't believe it. But, Mother, it's so. Nonsense."

15. For this and the following seven paragraphs: Adrienne Rich to BD, June 16, 1973; BD to Adrienne, June 25, 1977; BD to Mary Meigs, Aug. 30, 1973; and BD to Joan [Baez], May 1, 1973 (congratulating her on her coming out)—all in BDSL. BD to Andrea Dworkin, Feb. 6, 1976, ADSL. "Two Perspectives on Women's Struggle" was initially given as a talk at the Catholic Worker on Mar. 30, 1973, then published in *Liberation*, June 1973. "On Anger" was written as the talk Barbara had intended to deliver at the September 1971 War Resisters Conference, the one she'd never arrived at due to her car accident. A friend read it at the conference, and the essay was published in *Liberation*, Nov. 1971. Both essays are reprinted in Meyerding, ed., *We Are All Part of One Another*, 207–31. Since Barbara's day much hogwash has been written (and believed) about the hard-wired, essential, and ineradicable differences between the genders. Most claims have been based on sloppy or overinterpreted data from the neurosciences. For a thorough, accessible, and persuasive refutation of such claims, see Cordelia Fine, *Delusions of Gender* (Norton, 2010).

16. BD to Daly, Sept. 13; BD to Robin Morgan [fall 1973], Adrienne Rich to BD, Oct. 10, 22, and Nov. 7—all 1973, all in BDSL. Adrienne to BD and Jane, Jan. 19, 1974, BDSL.

17. For this and the following three paragraphs: BD, notes and memos for Women and Violence conference Mar. 1974; and BD to "Maris, Susan, and all those in the [*Win*] collective," Dec. 31, 1974, BDSL.

18. For this and the following five paragraphs: BD's letter to Arthur Kinoy, in longer draft form, BDSL; an edited version, *Liberation*, Dec. 1973; in full, *We Cannot Live*, 153–68. Kinoy's response in full (n.d.), BSDL; edited version, in BD, *Remembering Who We Are* (Pagoda, 1981). Barbara's response to Kinoy, "Love Has Been Exploited Labor—a Dialogue with Arthur Kinoy," as the pamphlet *Women and Revolution: A Dialogue* (National Interim Committee for a Mass Party of the People, Apr. 1975), is somewhat marred by Barbara's reliance on the work of Bachofen. On cultural feminism, see Echols, *Daring to Be Bad*, and Verta Taylor and Leila J. Rupp, "Women's Culture and Lesbian Feminist Activism: A Reconsideration of Cultural Feminism," *Signs* 19, no. 1 (1993).

19. For this and the following two paragraphs: 16-page draft letter, BD to Lyttle, Nov. 12–15 [1974], BDSL. I refrain (mostly because I'm unqualified) from entering

into any discussion of the complex distinctions among the terms *matriarchal, matrifocal,* and *matrilinear.* The most recent set of arguments for prehistoric martriarchies that have gained even marginal respectability have been put forward by Marija Gimbutas in the 1990s. See also the important Craig Barnes letter in *New York Review of Books,* Oct. 22, 2009; without claiming that a matriarchy existed in Minoan culture, Barnes does itemize the many significant roles that women played in both the religious and political spheres.

20. For this and the following three paragraphs: BD's "Letter to Jane Alpert," repr. in BD, *We Cannot Live,* 169–74. The poet Denise Levertov, whom Barbara had known earlier, also expressed her dismay about Alpert, calling her statements "nasty & hysterical" and declaring that "I don't think that anyone in her position has a *right* to be 'ignorant' & give 'inadvertent' assistance to the police which may endanger others" (see discussion that follows in text about Pat Swinton). More generally, Levertov added, "Men are to my mind more vulnerable in some respects than women." (Levertov to Barbara, May 10, 1976, BD to Levertov, May 15, 1976, BDSL.) Barbara wrote back to defend Alpert: "I do not do not do *not* believe that she is an informer. It seems to me possible—though far from proven—that she has *unwittingly* said things that helped the government . . . [but] I am not convinced that she has even done *that*." In a letter to Susan Sherman (n.d., ADSL), an opponent of Alpert's, Barbara added, "The most radical work that we have to do is to create a working trust among all of us—whatever our differences." BD to Robin Morgan, [fall 1973]; Adrienne Rich to BD, Oct. 10, Nov. 7, 1973; BD to Adrienne, Nov. 8, 1973; and BD to Leah Fritz, Dec. 22, 1977—all in BDSL.

21. For this and the following six paragraphs: Echols, *Daring to Be Bad,* 256–65; Meigs to BD, Aug. 18, 1974; BD to Swinton, July 1, 15, 28, 1975; Jane Gapen, "About Jane Alpert," *Win,* July 5, 1975; Alpert to Barbara, Aug. 18, 1975; Barbara to Alpert, Aug. 23, 1975—all in BDSL. Barbara to Andrea, Feb. 4, 1976, ADSL. Grace Paley thought Adrienne Rich, in refusing to see Swinton, had made "a very great mistake," because their meeting might have defused those charges that had already gotten into print. When writing to Leah Fritz (Dec. 22, 1977, BDSL) Barbara revealed that she had sent Shoshana a message through Grace Paley that she'd no longer be seeing her. Grace reported over the phone that "Shoshana took it hard"; months later, Grace elaborated: "Shoshana had been furious." Dave Dellinger, who became somewhat involved in the Alpert/Shoshana dispute, credited Barbara's "careful and sensitive approach" to all those involved with having been "extremely helpful" (Dellinger to Alpert, Aug. 24, 1975, DDTL).

The division within feminism was further heightened over the case of Susan Saxe. Arrested in March 1975 (she'd been underground since October 1970) for participating in two bank robberies—one of which she admitted to; the other involved the death of a policeman. Saxe's "Letter to the Movement," *Liberation,* Dec. 1975, which she insisted hadn't been intended for publication, attacked Alpert, defended the male left, and insisted that "dialectical materialism" remained "a tool of liberation." Barbara knew Saxe, and the two discussed their differing positions by mail: BD to Saxe, Jan. 10, Feb. 1, Mar. 2, 1976 [plus "postscript" to *Liberation,* n.d.]; and Saxe to BD, Feb. 12, 1976—BDSL. Barbara defended Alpert, questioned Saxe's commitment to armed struggle, and denied her assertion that pro-Alpert feminists saw "no connection between the liberation of women as women and the elimination of capitalism, racism, and imperialism." But she did agree with Saxe that "the split between the left and feminists [is] a tragedy." Despite such differences, Barbara signed a circulating statement in support of Saxe—"not an uncomplicated act for me . . . she *is* a prisoner of war, and yes, she *should* be immediately released." (BD to Phil Zwerling, Mar. 2, 1976, BDSL; Echols *Daring to Be Bad*, 262–65.)

Barbara agreed not to publish anything relating to their differences until after Saxe's trial, lest her defense be somehow jeopardized. But later she did publish "Remembering Who We Are: An Open Letter to Susan Saxe," *Quest*, Summer 1977. In it, she rhetorically asked, "What is the revolution that we need?" and answered, "We need to dissolve the lie that some people have a right to think of other people as their property." In 1980 Saxe and Barbara Deming had a heated correspondence (especially on Saxe's part) over these and other issues. Saxe distinguished between women's liberation, devoted to "the struggle for equal rights within the existing social order," and feminism, of which she was an adherent, which "demands the overturning of the existing order." She again accused the women's liberation movement of ignoring the struggles against racism, colonialism, and class oppression. She insisted, too, that Jane Alpert had given "information to the state that hurt other women." Barbara responded that although it was "possible (though unproven) that [Alpert] has *unwittingly* given information useful to the government," she gave "no information she *thought* could be useful." She apologized to Saxe for having assumed that "you were less critical of men on the left than you in fact are," but she'd assumed from Saxe's fierce "attacks upon separatists" that she accepted the indifference of left-wing men. She added that she, too, had been attacked "for not being separatist enough" but had chosen not to cut herself off from her own past. The key letters are Saxe to BD, Jan. 20, and Feb. 17, 1980; BD to Saxe, Jan. 25, 1980; and Karla Jay to BD, Feb. 17, 1980—KJNYPL.

22. For this and the following ten paragraphs: Jane Gapen, three sets of undated notes, one possibly a letter [Apr. 1973?] sent to Barbara; Barbara to Mary Meigs [1973?], BDSL. BD to *Liberation*, Nov. 10, 1974, in which she asked that her name be removed from the masthead, ADSL. On the tensions between women of color and white feminists, see especially Marcia Gallo, *Different Daughters* (Carroll & Graf, 2006); Barbara Smith, ed., *Home Girls: A Black Feminist Anthology* (Kitchen Table Press, 1983), and Gloria Anzaldúa and Cherrie Moraga, eds., *This Bridge Called My Back* (Kitchen Table Press, 1981).

The voluminous collection of Jane's diaries and correspondence at the Lesbian Herstory Archives (JGLHA) cannot be cited with any specificity. Almost all of her papers are undated and unsorted. In addition, her handwriting is extremely difficult to decipher, and some of it remains illegible to me.

Chapter 8: Personal Matters

1. For this and the following four paragraphs: David to father, Oct. 3, Nov. 29, Dec. 7, 1972; father to David, Feb. 27, 1973; David to parents, May 1, 7, 1973; and David to Mayer Vishner, July 11, 1994—all in DMSC.

2. For this and the following paragraph: Marsha [Berman] to David, Aug. 1973; Roodenko to David, [Aug. 1973], DMSC.

3. For this and the following six paragraphs: David to Roget Lockard, Aug. 26, 1973; David to parents, Oct. 2, 12, Nov. 16, 1973; David to Susan Kinloch, Nov. 20, 1973; and David to Carol Bernstein Ferry, Oct. 17, 1995—all in DMSC.

4. For this and the following three paragraphs: David to parents, Nov. 16, 1973, Apr. 4, 1974; David to brother, Jan. 8, 1974; David to C. Cooper Jr., Jan. 25, 1974; David to Dorothy Healey, Mar. 8, 1974; and David to Mayer Vishner, July 11, 1994—all in DMSC.

5. For this and following two paragraphs: Howe to David, Mar. 17, 1974; David to Howe, Mar. 19, 1974; WRL Statement on Israel, Apr. 19, 1974; and David to parents, Mar. 24, 1975—all in DMSC. BD's notes, Jan. 28, 1974, BDSL.

6. David to parents, July 14, 1972, Sept. 11, 1975, DMSC; McReynolds e-mail to me, May 10, 2010.

7. For this and the following two paragraphs: David to Mark Morris, Feb. 18, 1975; David to Susan Kinloch, June 19, 1974; and David to Robert Cooney, Oct. 16, 1994, DMSC.

8. Lyttle to David, Oct. 17, 1974; David to Lyttle, Jan. 13, 1975, DMSC. For the recent turn in biology, see especially Bruce Bagemihl, *Biological Exuberance* (Stonewall Inn Editions, 2000), and Joan Roughgarden, *Evolution's Rainbow* (Univ. of California Press, 2009).

9. For this and the following thirteen paragraphs: Interviews with David McReynolds, 2008–9, esp. July 4, 2009. David to Barbara, Dec. 29, 1975; Feb. 26, Mar. 23, 1976; and Mar. 11, 1981; Barbara to David, Jan. 3, Mar. 2, 29, and July 7, 1976; and David to parents, Apr. 4, 1974—all in DMSC. Barbara's reply to the charge of censorship is in fact from a letter to *Win*, Oct. 11, 1979. Barbara and Jane attempted to get *Snuff* banned under the state obscenity statute but failed. BD to Beverly [?], Apr. 1, 1976, Barbara to Mary Meigs, Dec. 20, 1975, BDSL. According to David, Barbara was "furious" that the WRL wouldn't join the call to the DA to close down the theater where *Snuff* was showing (interview with McReynolds, Feb. 2, 2009). See John Lauritsen's pamphlet *Censorship & Feminism* for correspondence on the subject printed in *Win*, Jan. 19–July 13, 1978, BDSL.

When Barbara received the 1979 WRL Peace Calendar, she was "disturbed" that the cover note talked about Gandhi, King, and Chavez but made no mention of the Pankhursts, Alice Paul, and their co-workers. She protested the omission in a long letter to WRL, which began, "Isn't it time that the WRL acknowledged the womens suffrage struggle as a major nonviolent struggle?" (BD to Andrea Dworkin, Mar. 30, 1979, ADSL.)

Maris Cakars of *Win* may well have been a supporter of feminism, but despite his own bisexuality he tended to deprecate the gay movement. While visiting Berkeley, he disparaged the "large dyke cult scene here—cult because there is a uniform, a 'look'—generally masculine, & working-class at that—but I don't see the courage & *strength* in action . . . I still see a lot of non-self-acceptance, competition & jealousy" (Cakars to WRL [1970s?], DMSC).

At Dave Dellinger's request, Barbara critiqued the galley proofs for his book *More Power Than We Know: The People's Movement Toward Democracy* (Doubleday, 1975). Barbara to Dave [Jan. 1975] and Dave to Barbara, Jan. 9, 1975, BDSL. In the process of thanking her for "the perceptiveness of your observations," Dave noted that at one point she'd written "I also can't help feeling that your resistance (in spite of yourself) to feminist insights is what blurs things." He responded that he affirmed "all the time" the view that "the spiritual condition of our lives cannot be changed without changing the relation of the sexes—without overthrowing patriarchy." He also wanted her to know that he'd "been reading quite a bit of feminist literature"—and listed a considerable number of titles. Yet his wife, Elizabeth Peterson, felt she had to leave him in 1972 (they later reconciled), resume her maiden name, and try to form a separate identity ("to find myself"). Their painful reconciliation only began in 1976, soon after Dave had been itemizing his feminist credentials for Barbara (Dellinger to BD, Jan. 9, 1975, DDTL). If his acceptance of feminism was partly rhetorical, Dellinger did make an effort to incorporate its insights into his own life. But his difficulty represents the obstacles radical feminists faced in trying to get radical men *really* to accept their message—and Dellinger was one of the few well-intentioned ones. But Barbara refused ever to "give up" on men in any absolute way (BD to Andrea Dworkin, July 11, 1983, ADSL; Dellinger to BD, Nov. 13, n.y., DDTL).

10. Interviews with McReynolds, esp. Feb. 16, 2009. David to Barbara, Dec. 29, 1975; Barbara to David, Jan. 3, 1976; Barbara to Karen Durbin, Dec. 1, 1975 (copy to David), BDSL. Andrea to Barbara and Jane, July 5, 1976, ADSL.

11. For this and the following paragraph: Barbara to Andrea, Jan. 20, 1974; BD's notes of talk with Andrea, Jan. 28, 1974; Adrienne to Andrea, Dec. 31, 1975; Andrea to Barbara [1975?]—all in BDSL. BD to Andrea, Nov. 12, 1974, July 17 and Dec. 10, 1975; Barbara to Kirsten Grimstad, June 23, 1979, Andrea to Barbara, Dec. 18, 1975—all in ADSL. In a comparably tough way, Barbara responded to Ti-Grace Atkinson's *Amazon Odyssey*, also published in 1974. Although she'd read it "with deep excitement," she wrote Ti-Grace, "learning much from it," she couldn't at all agree with her that "consciousness-raising is a virulent expression of running scared. . . . It has seemed to me that it is in C-R sessions above all that women learn to confront . . . truths" (Barbara to Ti-Grace, Sept. 15, 1974) BDSL. After Barbara's death, the Money for Women Fund became the Barbara Deming Memorial Fund, Inc. (Gapen Papers, LHA.)

12. For this and the following eight paragraphs: BD's extensive notes, written Oct. 8–Dec. 25, 1976; Jane to "Dworkins," n.d.; BD to Andrea and John, Mar. 19, 1977; BD to Andrea, Mar. 30, 1979 and July 22, 1981; BD to *New York Times Book Review*, July 20, 1981; Meigs to Barbara, Oct. 1 [1976?], Apr. 7, 1977; and Barbara to Mary, Apr. 7, 1977—all in BDSL. Ellen Willis review, *New York Times Book Review*, July 12, 1981. On the *Snuff* suit: *Middletown* (NY) *Times Herald-Record*, Oct. 4, 1977, copy in ADSL. Greenwald to Moran, Aug. 3, 1978; copies of 4 draft statements for Richard Dames to sign; Barbara to Andrea, Aug. 18, Oct. 3, 1978; and Andrea to Barbara, July 25, 1983—all in ADSL.

When Adrienne Rich criticized certain parts of Andrea's writing, Barbara leaped to Andrea's defense, writing to her that Adrienne "is blindly compelled (I do think blindly) to establish with you her *Authority*. . . . She is the way Bessie Breuer always was with me—wanting to give (and Bessie in many many ways [was] truly giving), but also unable in spite of herself not to have to try and keep one in one's lesser place. Yet Bessie really valued me—as Adrienne clearly values you." BD to *Liberation*, Mar. 12, 1975; BD to Andrea and John, June 15, 1976, and Feb. 18, 1977; BD to Andrea, July 26, 1976, Jan. 29, 1977, Mar. 31, Apr. 10, 1979, Apr. 24 and May 27, 1980; Andrea to Barbara, June 17, 1977; Andrea and John to Barbara, Mar. 14, 1977; and Andrea to June Dengel, Mar. 14, 1977—all in ADSL.

13. For this and following three paragraphs: Barbara to Denise Levertov, May 15, 1976; Barbara to Mim, Feb. 26 and Dec. 28, 1978; Jane to Leah Fritz, Mar. 5, 1978; Barbara to Mary Meigs, June 2, 1978; Barbara to Adrienne, June 20, 1979; and draft of Minnie Bruce Pratt and Mab Segrest interview with BD, "Conversations with

Barbara Deming"—all in BDSL. Barbara to Andrea and John, June 28, 1976, ADSL. BD to Karla Jay, Feb. 17, 1979, KJNYPL.

Chapter 9: The War Resisters League, Socialism, and the Arms Race

1. For this and the following three paragraphs: David to parents, Sept. 4, 1975 and Mar. 31, 1976, DMSC; interviews with McReynolds, Feb. 2, 16, 2009; Michael Harrington, *The Long-Distance Runner* (Holt, 1988), *passim*; Isserman, *Harrington*, esp. ch. 11.

2. For this and the following four paragraphs: David to parents, Feb. 27, 1976, DMSC; and multiple interviews with, as well as letters and e-mails from, McReynolds, especially, for this section, the interviews of Feb. 16 and Apr. 15, 2009, and the e-mail of May 10, 2010.

3. McReynolds e-mail to me, Nov. 25, 2008.

4. For this and the following two paragraphs: David to "the beloved community," Feb. 4, 1977, and David to brother, May 14, 1976, DMSC.

5. For this and the following paragraph: David to Mina DeHetre, July 15, 1976, DMSC.

6. Harrington's statement as quoted in Isserman, *Harrington*, 299; see also, Harrington, *Long-Distance Runner, passim*. The rest of the section that follows derives primarily from the dozens of online short articles by McReynolds with the collective title *Infinite Series* or from a smaller batch of online columns he called *Edge Left*, both written 2001–8 but containing many backward glances. These constitute too many items, some of which are fragments or untitled, to cite in detail.

7. For this and the following paragraph: Barbara to Adrienne, Jan. 9, 1977, June 20, 1979, Barbara to Mary Meigs, March 30, 1978, Barbara to Phyllis Chesler, June 23, 1976, BDSL.

8. Barbara to Leah Fritz, Dec. 15, 1977, BDSL.

9. Norma [Becker?] to Barbara, Jan. 15, 1977, Norma to Barbara and Jane, Mar. 26, 1978, Barbara to Norma, Mar. 7, 1977, and Oct. 6, 1978—BDSL.

10. For this and the following three paragraphs: Barbara to Leah Fritz, Feb. 4, Mar. 7, May 8, 1978; Leah to Barbara and Jane, Apr. 11, 1978; and Jane to Leah, Mar. 5, 1978—BDSL.

11. Untitled and undated 2-page essay by BD, BDSL.

12. For this and the following four paragraphs: David to Barbara, Mar. 11, 1981, Sept. 6, 1983, one letter n.d.; Barbara to David, Mar. 13, 1981, Oct. 20, 1983; and BD, "Should We Be Alarmed?"—all in BDSL.

13. For this and the following six paragraphs: Barbara to Mary, June 2, Aug. 16, and Nov. 22, 1978, BDSL.

14. For this and the following two paragraphs: Interviews with McReynolds, esp. Feb. 16, 2009; Jeremy Karpatkin, "Radical Real Estate," *New York Villager*, May 1979; David to Arctander, Nov. 19, 1979, DSML.

15. Peter Richardson, *A Bomb in Every Issue* (The New Press, 2009), 195–99.

16. For this and the following five paragraphs: Isserman, *The Other American*, 332–37; and Harrington, *The Long-Distance Runner*, 199–200. McReynolds circular letters, Apr. 8 and July 23, 1980; *Socialist Tribune* ("Voice of the Socialist Party-USA"), Apr.

1980; McReynolds, "A Brief History of the Liberty Union Party," 1980, and "The Socialist International: The Case for Affiliation," 1981—all in DMSC.

17. The literature on the assorted national and temporal varieties of "socialism" is vast. No one, I suspect, can cite (or read) that literature in its entirety. The best I can do is to record three fairly recent books that for me have proved especially useful: Donald Sassoon, *One Hundred Years of Socialism* (The New Press, 1996), Max Elbaum, *Revolution in the Air* (Verso, 2002), and Doug Rossinow, *Visions of Progress* (Univ. of Pennsylvania Press, 2008).

18. From here to the end of the chapter: David to Alice [?], Feb. 1975 and David to mother, July 25, 1977; McReynolds, "1976 plus 25 equals 2001," draft comments to WRL National Committee, 1976; McReynolds, "The Socialist International: The Case for Affiliation," ms. [1981?]; McReynolds, "What a Socialist Movement Can Be Doing," online *Infinity Series*; McReynolds, "Acceptance Speech at the SPUSA National Convention," from C-SPAN's coverage of speech; McReynolds, *Closer to Midnight or Toward a New Dawn?*, leaflet, 6 pp. (WRL, 1983)—all in DMSC.

Chapter 10: Sugarloaf Key

1. The Sugarloaf Women's Village, as it is now called, periodically issues newsletters; a collection of them, 1999–2008, are in the Lesbian Herstory Archives (LHA) in Park Slope, Brooklyn. Also at LHA are the Doris ("Blue") Lunden Papers (BLP), and a 35-minute documentary film, *Some Ground to Stand On*, about her life; the film was shot mostly at Sugarloaf and provides a good sense of the physical surroundings.

2. Barbara to Jane Rule, Sept. 4, 1975, BDSL.

3. For this and the following paragraph: *Woman Time* (a Key West feminist newsletter), Winter 1981–82; *Key West Citizen*, Aug. 18, 1985, plus BD's two letters to the editor, n.d. and June 4, 1978; Barbara to Mim, May 17, 1978; Barbara to Pastor Morris Wright [1982]; Barbara to Norma Becker, Mar. 30, 1977; and May 1980 disarmament statement—all in BDSL.

4. Norma Becker, "The Role of Women's Actions," *WRL News*, May–June, 1984; *Disarm and Survive*, a WRL pamphlet, n.d., WRL Archives; Lauri Lowell, "No Nukes Movement Rises Up in Washington," *Win*, May 24, 1979; and Chris Guilfoy, "A Matter of Survival: Dykes and Faggots Resist Nukes," *Gay Community News*, June 7, 1980.

5. For this and the following two paragraphs: Barbara to Dan Berrigan, Apr. 27, 1978; Berrigan to Barbara, n.d.; Barbara to Julie L., July 4, 1981—BDSL. Jane Meyerding, who would subsequently edit *We Are All Part of One Another: A Barbara Deming Reader* (New Society, 1984), had her own run-in with Dan Berrigan several years later. A poem of his, "The Woman," had appeared in a 1982 issue of *Year One*; to Meyerding and other women, it seemed, as she wrote him, "to echo so many of this culture's woman-hating attitudes" (Meyerding to Berrigan, Apr. 6, 1982), BDSL.

6. For this and the following paragraph: Guilfoy, "A Matter of Survival," *Gay Community News*, June 7, 1980. On the general issue of the relationship, historical and present-day, between socialism and homosexuality, see Dan Healey, *Homosexual Desire in Revolutionary Russia* (Univ. of Chicago Press, 2001); essays in the two-part 2008–9 series in *New Politics*; and Sherry Wolf, *Sexuality and Socialism* (Haymarket, 2009).

7. For this and the following two paragraphs: McReynolds, "Queer Reflections," *New Politics*, Sept. 15, 2008.

8. Bentley to Barbara, Dec. 22, 1978, and Jan. 20, 1979, BDSL.

9. Barbara to Adrienne Rich, June 20, 1979; Barbara to Brad Lyttle, May 11, 1981; Rita Mae Brown to Jane and Barbara, Jan. 10, 1978; Brown to June & Patty (the publishers of Daughters, Inc.), Jan. 10, 1978; and Barbara to Brown, Jan. 13, 1978—BDSL.

10. Jane Gapen to *Washington Blade*, Aug. 12, 1981, BDSL.

11. For this and the following three paragraphs: Barbara to Meigs, Feb. 8, 1981; Barbara to Grier, Oct. 26, 1982, Nov. 16, 1982, and Apr. 13, 1983; Barbara to Grier and McBride, Apr. 16, 1983; Barbara to McDaniel, Nov. 3, 1982; BD notes on call from B. Grier, Apr. 15, 1983; Adrienne to Barbara, June 21, 1981—all in BDSL. BD to Karla Jay, Sept. 29, 1982, and BD to Picano, Nov. 1, 1983—KJNYPL. The controversy over Grier centered on the pioneering lesbian publication the *Ladder*. When it seemed in danger of folding in 1970 Grier, then its editor, got Rita LaPorte, the last president of the lesbian group Daughters of Bilitis, to take the magazine's mailing list and other materials to Reno, where LaPorte lived. A number of women accused Grier of "absconding" with the *Ladder*. See Manuela Soares, "The Purloined *Ladder*," *Journal of Homosexuality* 34, no. 3–4 (1998), and Marcia M. Gallo, *Different Daughters* (Carroll & Graf, 2006). Adrienne Rich and Michelle Cliff, co-editors of *Sinister Wisdom*, published a section of *Travail* in the Jan. 1982 issue.

12. For this and the following three paragraphs: Meigs to Barbara, Aug. 31, 1981; Pratt to Barbara, Oct. 6, 1981; and BD, Notes, Jan. 21, 1982—BDSL; Jane Gapen diaries, n.d., LHA.

13. For this and the following paragraph: Cynthia Costello and Amy Dru Stanley, "Report from Seneca," *Frontiers: A Journal of Women Studies* 8, no. 2 (1985); and "Online Archive of the Seneca Women's Encampment," Jan. 3, 2008, http://peacecampherstory .blogspot.com.

14. For this and the following four paragraphs: McReynolds, "The Soviet Moratorium on Nuclear Tests," Sept. 1985; McReynolds "Memo to the National Committee," Aug. 20, 1986; and David to "Dear friend," Oct. 8, 1986—DMSC. For the recent scholarship that argues Reagan was seriously interested in eliminating nuclear weapons, see Paul Lettow, *Ronald Reagan and His Quest to Abolish Nuclear Weapons* (Random House, 2006), James Mann, *The Rebellion of Ronald Reagan: A History of the End of the Cold War* (Viking, 2009), and Martin Anderson and Annelise Anderson, *Reagan's Secret War: The Untold Story of His Fight to Save the World from Nuclear Disaster* (Crown, 2009).

15. Barbara to Ruthann [Robson], Oct. 4, 1983, Nina [at New Society Publishers] to Barbara, Dec. 28, 1982, and Barbara to Nina, Jan. 6, 1983, BDSL.

16. For this and the following five paragraphs: Ruth Dreamdigger's two-page summary of Barbara's illness, "August 1984," BDSL; BD "To so many of you," July 21, 1984, copy in ADSL; and Jane Gapen diary [1984], LHA.

Chapter 11: At Eighty

1. For this and the following six paragraphs: Interviews with McReynolds, esp. Feb. 16, 2009. McReynolds, "1995," ms. 3 pp.; and McReynolds, "An America Without Armies, a World Without War"; ms., 11 pp. [late 1980s?]—DMSC.

2. For this and the following three paragraphs: Interview with McReynolds, July 4, 2009. McReynolds to WRL personnel committee, Oct. 16, 1991, Feb. 8 and 10, 1995; memos from David, Mar. 28, 1990, Aug. 19, Nov. 18, 1991, and July 5, 1992; McReynolds, memos to WRL National Committee, Jan. 6, 1991, and Jan. 26, 1994—all in DMSC. David to Meurble Reagan, Mar. 4, 1992; David to Ping Ferry, Jan. 4, 1995; and David to Frida Berrigan, Sept. 16, 2003, DMSC. McReynolds e-mail to me, Mar. 15, 2010. David had long since acknowledged that he'd been "very, very slow to understand the rise of feminism" (David to Carrie Cooley, Mar. 23, 1995, DMSC), and in 1992, as if executing a legacy from Barbara Deming, he drafted an "Affirmative Action Policy" (June 25, 1992) that called for staff positions, WRL task forces, National and Executive Committees, and regional offices to include "a majority of women; at least 10% publicly-identified lesbians, bisexuals and gay men; [and] at least 30% people of color"—but those goals would continue to prove elusive; McReynolds e-mail to me, Mar. 15, 2010.

3. For this and the following five paragraphs: McReynolds memo to publications committee, Jan. 28, 1992, and David to Peter Drucker, Feb. 12, 1992—DMSC.

4. For this and the following three paragraphs: Interviews with McReynolds Feb. 16 and Apr. 15, 2009. Three McReynolds mss. or WRL printed pieces on Bosnia: "Bosnia: The Crisis, What Can Pacifists Say?" "No Intervention in Bosnia," and "Death, Bombs and Videotape"; McReynolds, "Somalia: Talking Points"; David to Si and Marilyn Meyer, Feb. 27, 1996; McReynolds on NATO, www.mytown.ca/mcreynolds, Sept. 13, 2008; and David to the editor of *Salt*, Jan. 17, 1995—all in DMSC. DM tape, "Teach-in on Iraq, 2000," which DM lent to me. See Howard Zinn, *A People's History of the United States* (Harper Perennial Classics, 2001), for a great deal more detail on U.S. militarism and corporatism and protests against them.

5. For this and the following four paragraphs: David to "Dear local Green organizer," Aug. 5, 1995; David to Clay Hodge, Feb. 27, 1996; and McReynolds, report from Jan. 25, 1996, meeting; *Capital Times*, Jan. 23, 2003—all in DMSC. Interviews with McReynolds, esp. Apr. 15, 2009. David has also provided me with some two dozen tapes recording various appearances, interviews, and debates. David's optimism about the continuation of protest on the local level in regard to a variety of issues has been vindicated by several important scholarly works, including Bruce Miroff, *The Liberals' Moment* (Univ. of Kansas Press, 2007), and Thomas J. Sugrue, *Sweet Land of Liberty* (Random House, 2008).

6. David to Kevin O'Connor, Oct. 4, 1995; David to Megal Powell, Oct. 29, 1995; and David to Barbara Webster, Sept. 28, 2003, DMSC. David was one of some dozen people Quentin left $5,000 each on his death (McReynolds e-mail to me, May 11, 2010).

7. David to Crisp, Oct. 15, 1991; Crisp to David, May 14, 1992; David to James Braun, Nov. 16, 1998—DMSC. David wrote twice about Crisp online: "Quentin Crisp: The Radical," www.crisperanto.org/memories/mcreynolds1.html, and "Notes on Knowing Quentin," www.crisperanto.org/memories/mcreynolds.html (both accessed Aug. 7, 2010, both also in DMSC).

8. For this and the following two paragraphs: McReynolds, memo to Oversight Committee, Dec. 2, 1994; "Report on Restructure . . ." 1995; memos of Sept. 8 and 9, 2003; David to Maggie Phair, etc., Jan. 20, 1997; David to Kari Fisher-Garcia, Aug. 12, 1997; and "Staff Review of David McReynolds," Apr. 14, 1998—all in DMSC.

9. In both series quoted from in this and the following eight paragraphs, there are many dozens of articles; see www.thesocialistparty.org/spo/archive/McR. The

Edge Left column is available on McReynolds's Web site: http:www.edgeleft.org. I'll cite here only the articles from which I've quoted: "Marx and the Class War," n.d.; "Current Political Issues in the Socialist Party," July 29, 2007; "The Deepening Crisis," n.d. (*Edge Left*); "God's Chosen People?" Aug. 5, 2006; "The Death of Yasser Arafat," n.d.; "Israel's Air Strike on Syria," n.d.; "Open Letter to Senator Hillary Clinton," n.d.; "A Thousand Coffins at the U.N.," n.d.; "Doomed to Fail," n.d.; "Iraq: A Deepening Tragedy," Apr. 22, 2004; and "Iraq: A Dissenting View," Feb. 9, 1998. Also: Deming to Grier, Sept. 5, 1981, BDSL.

10. For this and the following three paragraphs: Various Sugarloaf newsletters and correspondence, including several important letters from Mary Meigs (who died in 2002 at the age of eighty-five), LHA.

Index

first loves and early relationships,
9–13, 14–18, 19–23, 25
grandmother, "Amama," 14, 16
in New York City, 11–12
political views, 16–17, 20, 23–25,
38, 54
theatre work, 11–12
at Western Reserve, 11–12
writing efforts, 9–11, 13–14, 16
Deming, Barbara [and civil rights
movement], 59–61, 66–72,
75–78, 130–31
Albany Movement, 68–72, 75–78
arrests/jailings, 66–67, 69, 70–72,
75–78, 260n23
CNVA's 1962 biracial walk for
peace, 59–61
hunger strikes/fasts, 70
and nonviolent pacifist movement,
59, 67, 131–32
Poor People's Campaign and
Resurrection City, 129–31
Deming, Barbara [and
homosexuality]
coming out to her mother, 9,
158
experiments with heterosexuality, 17
sexual appetites, 20, 58, 134, 149,
174
thoughts on homosexuality/
lesbian sexuality, 9, 15–16, 18,
158–60, 167–68, 184–85
Deming, Barbara [and peace
movement/nonviolence],
24–25, 53–61, 65–66, 125–33,
218–19, 225–28
anti-Vietnam war, 117, 125–33,
147–48, 152–54
arrests/jailings, 56–57, 129, 148
CNVA involvement, 24, 55–57,
59, 68, 99–100
direct-action nonviolent protest/
secular nonviolence, 54–55,
131–33

disarmament and antinuclear
demonstrations, 53–54, 55–57,
58–59, 205, 218–19, 225–28
guerrilla theater, 147–48
link to women's liberation/
feminist movement, 3–4, 24–25,
55, 160–64, 224–25
North Vietnam trips, 125–26
Saigon trip, 117, 127–28
theoretical positions on
nonviolence, 3–4, 24–25, 54–55,
59, 67, 72–75, 131–33,
160–64
women in the military, 218–19
Deming, Barbara [and women's
movement/feminism], 1–4,
159–72, 185–89, 202–9, 218–20,
224–25
abortion issue, 219–20
androgyny and nonviolence,
54–55, 160–61, 162
correspondence with Rich, Daly
and Morgan, 161–63
and David McReynolds, 1–4,
165–66, 185–89, 201–2, 205–7,
245, 274n2
debates on biology and sexuality,
158–60, 167–68, 184–85
and Andrea Dworkin, 165, 186,
189–93, 270n12
ERA work, 202, 206, 218
and Jane Alpert case, 168–71, 187,
267nn20–21
and matriarchies, 2, 168, 206,
266–67n19
and men of the Left, 1–4, 164–68,
172, 185–89, 205–6, 219–20,
225, 269–70n9
and motherhood/child-rearing,
160, 168–69
and nonviolence, 3–4, 24–25, 55,
160–64, 224–25
and pornography/the film Snuff, 1,
185–86, 189, 192, 269n9

women's liberation movement/
feminism, 2–5, 159–72
abortion issue, 219–20
androgyny and, 54–55, 160–61, 162
antipornography movement, 1,
185–86, 189, 192
Barbara and, 1–4, 159–72, 185–89,
202–9, 218–20, 224–25
biological natures/gender
essentialism and, 2–3, 160,
167–69, 227, 266n15
"cultural" (liberal) feminism, 4,
167, 168–69, 172
David and, 1–4, 165–66, 185–89,
201–2, 205–7, 245, 274n2
feminist C-R groups, 194, 202, 203
feminist presses/publishing
houses, 222–24
feminist theology, 159
ideological divisions, 2–5, 167–72,
203–5, 227, 267nn20–21
the Jane Alpert case, 168–71, 187,
267nn20–21
Jane Gapen and, 172–73
key writings/radical feminist
literature, 3–4, 159–64, 206
lesbian separatism, 2–5,
170, 187–88, 203–6, 224–25,
227
Marxism and, 203, 222
matriarchies, 2, 168, 187, 206,
266–67n19
men of the Left and, 1–4, 164–68,
172, 185–89, 201–2, 205–7,
219–20, 225, 269–70n9

motherhood/child-rearing and,
160, 168–69
nonviolence and, 3–4, 24–25, 55,
160–64, 224–25
nuclear disarmament/antinuclear
movement and, 218–19, 225–28
radical feminism, 3–4, 159–64,
168–72, 185–90
second-wave feminism and link to
nonviolence, 224–25
in the South/in the North (late
1960s), 137
Win magazine and, 165, 172,
186–87, 269n9
women in the military, 218–19
women of color, 171–72
WRL and, 165–66, 186, 198,
205–7, 269n9, 274n2
Women's Press (London), 224
Women Strike for Peace, 65–66
Workers Party, 255n17
World Peace Brigade for Nonviolent
Action, 66
World War I, 35–36, 38
World War II, 27, 36, 38, 50, 177, 183,
236
WRL. *See* War Resisters League
(WRL)
WRL News, 115, 219

Young, Allen, 220
Young People's Socialist League
(YPSL), 109, 254n6
Youth Council's Traveling
Temperance Talking Team, 28